ASSASSINS
AND
ASSASSINATIONS

HISTORY'S MOST
INFAMOUS PLOTS

ASSASSINS
AND
ASSASSINATIONS

HISTORY'S MOST INFAMOUS PLOTS

PAUL DONNELLEY

NEW
HOLLAND

First published in 2008 by New Holland Publishers (UK) Ltd
London • Cape Town • Sydney • Auckland

10 9 8 7 6 5 4 3 2 1

www.newhollandpublishers.com

Garfield House, 86–88 Edgware Road, London W2 2EA, UK
80 McKenzie Street, Cape Town 8001, South Africa
Unit 1, 66 Gibbes Street, Chatswood, NSW 2067, Australia
218 Lake Road, Northcote, Auckland, New Zealand

ISBN: 978 1 84537 940 7

Editorial Director: Jo Hemmings
Senior Editor: Kate Parker
Design and cover design: Alan Marshall, Heron Recreations
Production: Melanie Dowland

Reproduction by Pica Digital PTE Ltd, Singapore
Printed and bound in India by Replika Press Pvt. Ltd.

For Sid and Jeremy, two of the most influential men in my life – I wish you were both around to read this one.

Front cover (left–right): Julius Cæser, Che Guevara, Abraham Lincoln and Grigori Rasputin all fell victim to assassination.
Back cover (left–right): Adolf Hitler survived two assassination attempts; Lee Harvey Oswald in custody after murdering John F. Kennedy; and Franz Ferdinand, whose assassination was the spark that caused the First World War.
Page 3: John F. Kennedy's state funeral.
Page 7: Members of the plot to assassinate Franz Ferdinand were quickly apprehended and taken into custody following the fatal attack.

Thomas Becket leaves for England, though warned by Milo, chaplain to the Count of Boulogne, of treachery.

Contents

Introduction

For several thousand years mankind has attempted to solve political problems with assassination. To kill one's enemy was seen – and in some countries of the world is still seen – as an acceptable way of changing governments. Don't like the leader? Shoot him. Blow him up. Stab him. Poison him. The methods of murder are almost endless.

The original "assassins" were active in Persia and Syria from about the eighth to the fourteenth centuries.

They were members of the Nizaris, a group of Muslim fanatics who opposed the Abbasid caliphate with threats of sudden assassination by their secret agents. Not every Muslim supported the Nizaris. They were regarded by some as outcasts and were called "hassassin", a word originally meaning "hashish users", a general term of abuse. In fact, there is no reliable evidence that the Nizaris did smoke hash. Despite this there were numerous stories of murderous, drug-crazed hassassin, or assassins, doing the rounds in Europe. The Venetian explorer Marco Polo told how young assassins were given a potion and made to yearn for paradise – their reward for dying in action – by being given a life of pleasure. The word passed through French and Italian to emerge in English in the sixteenth century with its present meaning.

The assassinations covered here range from the ancient world to the modern day. The book looks at both concerted conspirators, who wanted to change the status quo by killing a political leader, to "lone nuts" with a perceived grudge against someone.

However, it is not just political figures that can fall prey to the assassin's bullet, knife or bomb. Organized crime figures are often assassinated by foot soldiers wanting to move up the crime family to become "made men" and authors have found themselves the victims of murder because they held the "wrong" views.

One of the earliest references to assassination is by the Chinese politician Chanakya (c. 350–283BC). He wrote at length on the subject in his work *Arthashastra*. His protege Chandragupta Maurya, the founder of the Maurya Empire, learned well from his master, arranging for many of his enemies to be assassinated.

The Roman Empire was no stranger to assassination – Julius Cæsar being one of the most famous victims – and since then numerous kings, queens, emperors and other rulers have fallen victim to people using assassination as a political tool.

In the twentieth century, the nature of assassination changed once again when some countries began to realise that state-sponsored terrorism – the financing and training of disgruntled patriots – could be used to achieve their political ends.

This begs a moral question. It is argued by many that such action can be for the public good – if President Clinton had succeeded in killing Osama bin-Laden, would the world now be facing a threat from Muslim terrorists? Is it morally right for a democratically elected leader to order the assassination of another nation's leader, whether that leader was elected or not? Finally, does assassination by terrorism work? The answer, sadly but almost certainly, is that in many cases it does, given time. In Britain, the IRA assassination squads led by Michael Collins killed many British agents, soldiers and civilians. Now, Collins's heirs, Gerry Adams and Martin McGuinness, sit in power in the Northern Ireland Assembly. Indeed, McGuinness is the deputy first minister. In South Africa, the first black head of state was Nelson Mandela, the former head of the terrorist organisation the ANC, which assassinated opponents by bomb or, in many cases, by putting tyres with burning petrol around their necks. The ANC was financially supported by the Soviet Union.

In short, awful as it may be to admit it, political assassination can sometimes work, and changes to a regime or ruler are made. As this book shows, the bomb and the bullet can be infinitely more powerful than the ballot box.

Gaius Julius Cæsar (100–44 BC)

The Victim

Gaius Julius Cæsar, the son of Gaius Julius Cæsar, a *praetor* (magistrate), and Aurelia Cotta, was born on 12 July, probably in 100 BC. (Some authorities list 102 BC. His most recent biographer, Adrian Goldsworthy, states that Cæsar was born on 13 July.) The family claimed descent from Iulus, the son of the Trojan prince Aeneas, himself the son of the goddess Venus.

Little is known of the boy's early years. The family, which included two sisters, both called Julia, lived in a modest house in Subura, a lower-class Roman neighbourhood. In 84 BC Gaius Julius Cæsar senior died suddenly while putting on his shoes one morning and, at 16, the teenage Julius found himself the head of the family.

At the time he was engaged to Cossutia, the daughter of a family of wealthy equestrians, to whom he had been betrothed since boyhood. However, in 83 BC, Julius was nominated for the position of *Flamen Dialis*, or "High Priest of Jupiter". The job required the holder to be a patrician (a member of the privileged class) and to also be married to a patrician, so Julius ended the relationship with Cossutia and instead married Cornelia, the daughter of Lucius Cornelius Cinna, an ally of his uncle, and a four-time *consul* (chief magistrate). Cæsar was made *Flamen Dialis* but after the Battle of the Colline Gate in November 82 BC, when Julius found himself on the losing side, he was stripped of his inheritance, his wife's dowry and his priesthood, and was ordered by Sulla, the dictator, to divorce Cornelia. Cæsar refused and was forced to go into hiding. After an intervention by his influential mother,

whose father and grandfather were both consuls, Cæsar joined the army and served under Marcus Minucius Thermus in Asia.

In 78 BC, Cæsar felt it safe to return to Rome. He began a public life in which he was celebrated for his oratory skills. Even Cicero, no mean orator himself, commented, "Does anyone have the ability to speak better than Cæsar?" Cæser was making a name for himself and in 69 BC he was elected *quaestor* (a treasury official). His wife Cornelia died during that same year. Two years later, he married Pompeia, the daughter of Quintus Pompeius and granddaughter of his enemy Sulla. At this time, Cæsar began to move against the officials of Sulla who still ran the government.

In 63 BC, Cæsar was elected *Pontifex Maximus*, Chief Priest of the Roman state religion, following the death of Cæcilius Metullus Pius. The following year, Cæsar divorced Pompeia after she became involved in a scandal, saying, "My wife ought not even to be under suspicion." In 59 BC, Cæsar stood against Lucius Lucceius and Marcus Calpurnius Bibulus in an election for the consulship. He and Bibulus were victorious. Cæsar formed an alliance with Pompey and Crassus, known as the First Triumvirate. In late April or early May, Pompey married Cæsar's 15-year-old daughter Julia and Cæsar also married again. His third wife was Calpurnia, the daughter of Lucius Calpurnius Piso Caesoninus.

In 58 BC, Cæsar began a campaign to conquer Gaul. It soon became clear that he was a military genius; during his nine years in Gaul, Cæsar lost only two battles in which he personally took part. He conquered all territory east to the Rhine River, drove the Germans out of Gaul and crossed the Rhine to show them the might of Rome. He also invaded Britain twice, in 55 and 54 BC. In 54 BC, Julia, Cæsar's daughter, died in childbirth, leaving Pompey and Cæsar heartbroken. The Triumvirate then broke down when Crassus was killed in 53 BC during his campaign in Parthia. In 52 BC, Cæsar defeated the Gauls led by Vercingetorix at the Battle of Alesia.

THE MAN WITH THREE NAMES

The fact that Cæsar had three names – *praenomen* (or first name), *nomen* (family name) and *cognomen* (identifying the family branch) – was indicative of his social standing. Mark Antony and Cnaeus Pompey had just two names.

Julius Cæsar was, according to Suetonius, "tall, fair and well-built, with a broad face and brown eyes". He also had a receding hairline, as seen here, which he had to cover with a laurel wreath.

In 50 BC, Pompey, at the head of the Senate, insisted that Cæsar disband his army and return to Rome. His term as *proconsul* (magistrate) had ended and the senate did not want him to stand for a second term as they feared he would become too powerful. Cæsar refused; he felt he would be politically compromised if he returned to Rome without the protection of being consul. Pompey was angered by what he saw as insubordination and accused Cæsar of treason. Cæsar crossed the Rubicon (the frontier boundary of Italy) on 10 January 49 BC, at the head of 5,000 soldiers. He is reported to have said, "Let us accept this is a sign from the gods, and follow where they beckon, in vengeance on our double-dealing enemies. The die is cast." Civil war was now inevitable.

On 9 August 48 BC, Cæsar defeated Pompey at Pharsalus in northern Greece, despite Pompey having twice as many troops. In Rome, Cæsar was appointed dictator but resigned after just nine days in office and was elected to a second term as consul. Pompey fled to Alexandria, where two former Roman officers serving King Ptolemy XIII stabbed Pompey to death, aged 58. His head was cut off and kept as a present for Cæsar. The corpse was left to decay until someone did the decent thing and buried him.

Cæsar sided with the Pharaoh Cleopatra VII in the Alexandrine civil war between Cleopatra and Ptolemy, who was not only her brother but also her husband and co-regent. Cæsar won and helped Cleopatra to become ruler. He is also thought to have fathered her son, Ptolemy XV Cæsar, known as Cæsarion. On 2 August 47 BC, Cæsar defeated Pharnaces II of Pontus in the Battle of Zela in what is now northwestern Turkey, stating "Veni, vidi, vici" ("I came, I saw, I conquered").

"Death of Julius Cæsar" by Alexander Zick (1845–1907), based on Shakespeare's *Julius Caesar*, Act III, Scene II.

Back in Rome in October 45 BC, Cæsar wrote his will naming his grandnephew Gaius Octavius (Octavian) as the heir to everything, including his title. Cæsar also wrote that if Octavian died before Cæsar did, Marcus Junius Brutus would be the next heir in succession. The Senate bestowed all manner of honours on Cæsar including the right to wear a purple robe and a laurel wreath (which he loved because it hid his balding head). Suetonius reports that Cæsar was:

Tall, fair and well-built, with a broad face and keen brown eyes. He has a tendency to nightmares … and twice had epileptic fits while on campaign. He [kept] his head carefully trimmed and shaved; and [w]as accused of having certain other parts of his body depilated with tweezers. His dress was unusual: he had added wrist-length sleeves with fringes to his purple-striped senatorial tunic and the belt he wore over it was never tightly fastened.

Cæsar became the first living man to appear on a Roman republican coin. The Senate elected him consul for life. The month of his birth, Quintilis, was renamed Julius (hence the English July) in his honour, and his birthday, 12 July, was proclaimed a national holiday. All of the pomp, circumstance and taxpayers' money being spent angered some members of the Roman Senate. One of these was Cæsar's closest friend, Marcus Junius Brutus.

Date and Place of Assassination
15 March 44 BC, Senate, Rome, Roman Republic.

The Event
The reason for Cæsar's assassination, according to the historian Cassius Dio, was that he offended a delegation sent from the senate to inform him of new honours bestowed on him. Rather than standing up to receive the group as they arrived at the Temple of Venus Genetrix,

Cæsar remained seated. This great offence was apparently enough to cause the senators to plan his demise. However, it seems more likely that the senators were worried that Caesar might create a powerbase for his own family and descendants, in effect changing the republic into an empire. Some of Cæsar's supporters excused his remaining seated by saying that he had been surprised by an attack of diarrhoea; his enemies did not accept this excuse, as he had managed to walk home from the meeting without help. Brutus began to conspire against Cæsar with his friend and brother-in-law Cassius and other men, calling themselves the Liberatores (Liberators). Nicolaus of Damascus recorded:

The conspirators never met openly, but they assembled a few at a time in each other's homes. There were many discussions and proposals, as might be expected, while they investigated how and where to execute their design. Some suggested that they should make the attempt as he was going along the Sacred Way, which was one of his favourite walks. Another idea was for it to be done at the elections during which he had to cross a bridge to appoint the magistrates in the Campus Martius; they should draw lots for some to push him from the bridge and for others to run up and kill him. A third plan was to wait for a coming gladiatorial show. The advantage of that would be that, because of the show, no suspicion would be aroused if arms were seen prepared for the attempt. But the majority opinion favoured killing him while he sat in the Senate, where he would be by himself since only Senators would be admitted, and where the many conspirators could hide their daggers beneath their togas. This plan won the day.

The conspirators knew that Cæsar planned to leave Rome on 18 March and would be absent for years. It is recorded that Spurinna the soothsayer warned Cæsar to

"beware the Ides of March" and Cæsar's third wife, Calpurnia, begged her husband not to visit the Senate that day, having had a nightmare on the night of 14 March. In spite of them, Cæsar hastened to the Senate and he met Spurinna on the way. "The Ides of March have come." "Aye, Cæsar, they have come," replied the sage, "but not yet past." Cæsar was asked to read a petition asking him to return power to the Senate but no such petition existed. Before Cæsar entered the Senate it was the custom for priests to make sacrifices to the gods. That day the portents were bad, but Cæsar was still encouraged to go inside. In the Senate, he was approached by Tillius Cimber whose brother Cæsar had banished from Rome. As they spoke, Tillius Cimber ripped open Cæsar's toga at the neck – the signal for the attack to begin. Casca lunged at Cæsar but only managed to graze his chest (some say face). Cassius stabbed Cæsar in the face but he fought back. Two senators went to aid Cæsar but were unable to break through the throng. Marcus Brutus and Rubrius were accidentally stabbed in the melee. It was only when Cæsar saw Brutus wielding a dagger and was stabbed in the groin that Cæsar accepted the inevitable. He is said to have uttered the Greek words, "Kai su teknon" ("You, too, my child") and fallen at the feet of Pompey's statue. He covered his head and legs and awaited his death. He was stabbed 23 times.

The Assassins

The number of conspirators is in dispute. Nicolaus of Damascus records that there were more than 80. Suetonius settles on 60, but if Plutarch is correct and each assassin stabbed Cæsar once, then the number would have been 23. However, even this is challenged as Nicolaus says that Cæsar was stabbed 35 times. The assassins included Tillius Cimber, Publius Servilius Casca Longus, Cassius and Marcus Brutus, whom many believed to be Cæsar's son.

The Aftermath

Very few of the assassins survived Cæsar by more than three years, some dying violent deaths and some by their own hand.

A state funeral was held on 18 March 44 BC, the day that Cæsar had intended to leave Rome. Mark Antony spoke at the funeral and read out Cæsar's will. The bloodstained robe Cæsar was wearing was out on display and a wax statue of Cæsar was erected in the forum displaying the stab wounds.

The assassination of Cæsar sparked a civil war in which Mark Antony, Octavian and others fought the Senate for both revenge and power. Cæsar's death also marked, ironically, the end of the Roman Republic, for which the assassins had struck him down. As sole heir to Cæsar's vast fortune, Gaius Octavian gained both the immensely powerful Cæsar name and control of one of the largest amounts of money in the republic. Octavian, Mark Antony and Cæsar's loyal cavalry commander Lepidus formed a Second Triumvirate. A second civil war broke out between the triumvirate and Brutus and Cassius, whom Antony and Octavian had defeated at Philippi. A third civil war then broke out between Octavian on the one hand and Antony and Cleopatra on the other. This final civil war, culminating in Antony and Cleopatra's defeat at Actium, resulted in the ascendancy of Octavian, who became the first Roman emperor, under the name Cæsar Augustus. In 42 BC, Cæsar was formally deified as the Divine Julius (Divus Iulius).

Thomas Becket (*c.* 1118–1170)

The Victim

Thomas Becket was born on 21 December 1118 at the family home in Cheapside in the City of London, the only surviving son (four daughters survived to adulthood) of wealthy merchant Gilbert of Thierceville, Normandy, and his wife Matilda. Gilbert Becket was, for a term, sheriff of the City of London.

The Norman baron, Richer de l'Aigle, took an interest in the young Becket and the boy spent time at his estates in Sussex. Despite attending the best schools, Thomas Becket was not an intellectual and even his admirers admit that his Latin was only average. Instead, his charm, good memory, ambition and friendliness assured him of success. It was expected that he would follow his father into the City, but when Gilbert Becket lost his money after his properties were destroyed by fire, Thomas joined the church.

In 1145, he began working in the household of Archbishop of Canterbury Theobald, who had been appointed in 1139. His household was one of learning: four archbishops and six bishops were apprenticed to him. Impressed with Becket, Theobald sent him on several important missions to the Papal Curia in Rome. In 1154, Becket became the Archdeacon of Canterbury. It was not long before he came to the notice of King Henry II, who appointed Becket Lord Chancellor in January 1155. The two men became firm friends. However, Henry assumed that his friend would be of the same mind as him when it came to unifying the laws of church and state. It was to prove to be a very misplaced assumption.

On 18 April 1161, Theobald died, leaving the archbishopric of Canterbury vacant. On 23 May 1162, Becket became the new Archbishop of Canterbury. On 2 June, Becket was ordained priest in Canterbury Cathedral by Bishop Walter of Rochester and consecrated the next day. At that time Becket was archbishop, archdeacon, chancellor and the holder of a large number of ecclesiastical benefices and royal custodies – he was rich and powerful. Henry, perhaps sensing that too much power

was vested in one man (himself aside), forced Becket to resign as archdeacon in January 1163. On 23 July of that year, Becket and the king clashed over Henry's determination to divert a land tax from the sheriffs to the royal purse. Henry dropped the matter, but privately seethed that his friend and the man he had promoted was now using that power against him.

At a council at Clarendon Palace on 30 January 1164, Henry sought to lessen the independence of the clergy and weaken the links with Rome. Becket expressed his willingness to agree to the suggestions, known as the Constitutions of Clarendon, but when it came to signing the document, he refused. He realised that this was the end of the line where his friendship with Henry was concerned. He suspended himself from priestly duties, imposed penance on himself and sent a report to Pope Alexander III. Becket, who was accused of fraud by Henry, began to negotiate asylum with the king of France.

On Whit Sunday 1166, Henry and his followers were excommunicated. Now fearing for his life, Becket fled England in disguise on 2 November and landed in Dunkirk. Henry confiscated all his money so Becket was dependent totally on Louis VII of France. In November 1166, Becket and his entourage moved to the ancient Benedictine abbey of St Columba outside the north wall of the royal and archiepiscopal city of Sens. It was to be their home for the next four years. Becket celebrated Mass each day. His diet consisted of the finest wine (diluted with water), ginger and cloves. His bed was covered in fine white linen but during the day Becket wore a shirt and trousers made of the roughest goat's hair. At least three times a day, his chaplain whipped him on his bare back until he bled.

DATE AND PLACE OF BIRTH

Some sources state that Thomas Beckett was born in 1120 and that his place of birth was Rouen.

St Thomas landing in England on his return from exile, as depicted in
an early 13th-century French verse life of Becket.

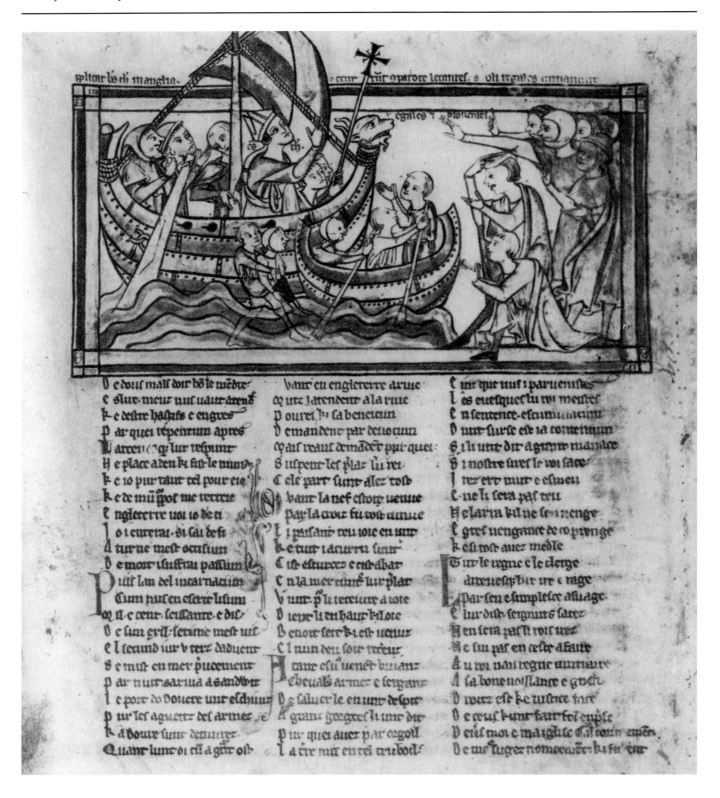

The Pope and the two kings of England and France began to try and effect a reconciliation between Henry and Becket. They believed that if Canterbury was restored to Becket, they could form an alliance to start a new crusade to the Holy Land. Meanwhile, Becket heard that back in England the bishops were preparing to cross the channel to join King Henry – who had set up court at Bur-le-Roi, near Bayeux – and form an alliance against Becket. Determined to avert what he saw as an affront to the Holy See, Becket decided to return to England and on what was believed to be 30 November, he crossed at night to Sandwich, Kent.

On his return to Canterbury, Becket began to instil discipline in his monks. He also sent a trusted minion to the Pope, to tell Alexander that Henry had broken the terms of the peace.

At Henry's court, the events were regarded very differently. On more than one occasion Henry was heard to cry out, "Will no one rid me of this turbulent priest?" and "What a band of loathsome vipers I have nursed in my bosom who will let their lord be insulted by this low-born cleric!" Overhearing him were four knights – Reginald Fitzurse, Hugh de Morville, William de Tracy and Richard le Breton – and they set out to assassinate the archbishop.

The four men left the court separately and made their way stealthily back to England. When their disappearance was noted, envoys were despatched to overtake them and stop their plan. It was apparent to the knights that the king might well change his mind and they did not want to be stopped, hence the secrecy with which they plotted. They arranged to meet at Saltwood Castle in Kent, the home of a fifth knight Ranulf de Broc, on 28 December 1170.

Date and Place of Assassination

29 December 1170, Canterbury Cathedral, Kent, England.

The Event

With a body of men, the four knights set off for Canterbury on the morning of Tuesday 29 December 1170. At St Augustine's Abbey, more forces joined them. Becket lunched at 2pm and retired to his room with some of his closest aides. The assassins arrived at the cathedral at about 5pm and pushed their way into Becket's chamber. He did not acknowledge their presence – possibly affronted that they had burst into the church – but when more of the band arrived, the monks feared for their master's safety and forced Becket further into the church, telling him that vespers was about to begin. He was calm and collected, unlike the monks who were surprised to see him, having heard that he had already been killed. They made to bolt the doors but Becket stopped them, telling them the house of God should not be turned into a fortress. Had he wished, Becket could have saved his own life and hidden in the vast church but he stayed – perhaps foolishly, more likely bravely, certainly sanguinely – to face his killers.

While the majority of the band of killers kept watch in the main cathedral lest the monks try to engineer Becket's escape, the four knights drew closer – with them was one of Becket's own monks, Hugh de Horsea – later to be named Hugh Evil-Clerk for his part in the killing. Hugh de Morville kept the crowd at bay with his sword. Fitzurse shouted, "Where is Thomas Becket, traitor to the king and the kingdom?" It was dark in the cathedral so it is entirely possible that the assassins could not make out Becket in the gloom. The archbishop stepped forward and spoke, "Here I am, no traitor to the king, but a priest. Why do you seek me? God forbid that I should flee on account of your swords or that I should depart from righteousness." Becket stood in the centre of the transept and turned to face the altars dedicated to the Virgin Mary and St Benedict. The knights rushed towards him. Fitzurse tried to hoist Becket onto de Tracy's shoulders so they could carry him outside, but

The knights kill Thomas Becket in Canterbury Cathedral, ridding Henry II of his "turbulent priest". Engraving by Opie Stowe, 1793.

the archbishop fought back fiercely. Fitzurse raised his sword to strike Becket who lifted his hands in prayer, "I commend myself and the Church of God, St Mary and the blessed martyr St Denis." At this point, those monks who had been near Becket fled except for one Edward Grim, who put his arms around Becket. Fitzurse's sword struck Becket's head removing his tonsure and slicing into his left shoulder and into Grim's arm down to the bone. Another blow rained down on Becket and then a third before he fell face forward with his head to the north and the altar of St Benedict to his right. The killer blow was administered by le Breton who sliced off the top of Becket's head. Hugh de Horsea put his foot on Becket's neck and pushed his sword into the head, forcing brain matter on to the floor. Their job done, the assassins left Canterbury Cathedral.

Edward Grim's account, albeit written some years later, is the only first-hand version of the events that day. He recalled:

The murderers followed him, "Absolve," they cried, "and restore to communion those whom you have excommunicated, and restore their powers to those whom you have suspended."

He answered, "There has been no satisfaction, and I will not absolve them."

"Then you shall die," they cried, "and receive what you deserve."

"I am ready," he replied, "to die for my Lord, that in my blood the Church may obtain liberty and peace. But in the name of Almighty God, I forbid you to hurt my people whether clerk or lay."

Then they lay sacrilegious hands on him, pulling and dragging him that they may kill him outside the church, or carry him away a prisoner, as they afterwards confessed. But when he could not be forced away from the pillar, one of them pressed on him and clung to him more closely. Him he pushed off calling him "Pander" and saying, "Touch me not,

Reginald; you owe me fealty and subjection; you and your accomplices act like madmen."

The knight, fired with a terrible rage at this severe repulse, waved his sword over the sacred head. "No faith," he cried, "nor subjection do I owe you against my fealty to my lord the king."

The Assassins

The knights were really barons. Oddly, despite the fact that they carried out the most famous assassination of the Middle Ages, very little is known about them. Reginald Fitzurse was probably born in 1130. He owned lands in Somerset, Kent and Northamptonshire. Hugh de Morville was the owner of Knaresborough Castle and a regular at Henry's court. He was one of the signatories to the Constitutions of Clarendon. The sword with which he held back the crowds at Becket's murder became a holy relic.

The Aftermath

Thomas Becket's valet, Osbert, tore his own shirt and covered the fallen archbishop's head with it. The monks emerged from their hiding places as a thunderstorm began. As the rain lashed down the monks prayed silently (the church having been desecrated) as they washed and cleaned the archbishop's corpse. They discovered that under his robes he was wearing a monk's habit and a vermin-infested sackcloth. The next morning, a relative of Ranulf de Broc returned to Canterbury and told the monks to bury Becket secretly. He was fearful of a cult beginning around the slain archbishop. The monks interred Becket in the crypt but kept his bloodstained clothing as relics. A tomb was built between two pillars of Purbeck marble. It is now an empty spot. On 7 July 1220, an impressive shrine was translated behind the high altar and filled with precious jewels. It, too, is now an empty space thanks to King Henry VIII. Today, a lighted candle marks the place where the shrine stood.

MIRACLES AT CANTERBURY

It was not long after his death that miracles were claimed at Canterbury. The first recorded miraculous cure in the city was on 4 January 1171, although the nature of the cure was not recorded.

The assassins were excommunicated by the Pope but escaped retribution from King Henry II. He told them to flee to Scotland for their own safety but when they arrived north of the border the king of Scotland and his people wanted to hang them. They fled south to Knaresborough in north Yorkshire, where they kept a low profile for a year, reviled by the local people. Despite a popular appeal for the assassins to be executed, they were not. Instead, they were banished to the Holy Land. Before he left, Fitzurse divided his estate equally between his brother and the Knights of St John. Within three years of Becket's death, Reginald Fitzurse, too, was dead and he was buried in Jerusalem. William de Tracy founded a chantry in Devon after returning from banishment, where he died in or before 1174. Richard le Breton retired to Jersey. Hugh de Morville died in 1173.

Thomas Becket was canonized by Pope Alexander on 21 February 1173. On 12 July 1174, Henry did penance at Becket's tomb. He walked barefoot into Canterbury Cathedral, clad only in a shirt. He kissed the spot where Becket fell and then each of the 80 monks beat him three times. The bishop and abbots administered five strokes, before Henry retired to the cathedral crypt where he fasted and prayed for a day.

The story of Thomas Becket has been used in many great works of literature. Geoffrey Chaucer's pilgrims in *The Canterbury Tales* meet at the Tabard Inn in Southwark before beginning their journey to Becket's tomb to pay homage. Modern works based on the story include T. S. Eliot's play *Murder in the Cathedral* and Jean Anouilh's play *Becket*, which was made into a film with the same title. Ken Follett's novel, *The Pillars of the Earth*, is a fictional account of the struggles between the church and gentry, culminating in the assassination and martyrdom of Becket by Henry's men.

Becket's cult lasted until the sixteenth century. On 16 November 1538, King Henry VIII declared that the death of Becket was "untruly called martyrdom" and that "there appeareth nothing in his life and exterior conversation where he should be called a saint, but rather esteemed to have been a rebel and a traitor to his prince." It was not until the twentieth century that a revision was ordered of Becket's reputation. However, in 2005, Becket was chosen as Britain's worst villain of the twelfth century in the "Worst Britons" poll by the *BBC History Magazine*. Professor John Hudson of St Andrews University, who chose Becket said, "He divided England in a way that even many churchmen who shared some of his views thought unnecessary and self-indulgent. He was a founder of gesture politics."

Jean-Paul Marat (1743–1793)

The Victim

One of the leading figures in the French Revolution, Jean-Paul Marat was born at Boudry, in the principality of Neuchâtel, Switzerland, on 24 May 1743. Prior to the revolution, he was a well-known doctor and scholar. His interests included aeronautics, optics and electrical therapy. The establishment did not take Marat seriously, seeing him as something of an eccentric. He developed an interest in politics and, in 1774, he published *The Chains of Slavery*, a revolutionary tract. In September 1789, he founded a newspaper *Moniteur Patriote* (*Patriotic Watch*), changed four days later to *Publiciste Parisien* (*Parisian Publicist*) and finally *L'Ami du Peuple* (*The Friend of the People*). Marat used the paper to attack his enemies and took up the cudgels on behalf of anyone who he thought had been wronged, whether or not this was actually the case. As a result, this often meant that an innocent suffered merely because the paper took the side of someone with a grudge.

Marat was an independent revolutionary – he never aligned himself to any group or faction or belief. It was a risky strategy and certainly one that made him lots of enemies. To avoid them, he spent much of his time hidden in cellars or sewers. It was there that he picked up an unfortunate skin disease.

Following the execution of Louis XVI on 21 January, 1793, there was a five-month battle between Marat and the Girondins (see box on right). They attempted to have Marat tried before the Revolutionary Council but he was acquitted on 24 April 1793. The Girondins had overstepped their mark and the people of Paris rose up on 27 May and again four days later. A final revolt occurred on 2 June 1793, and François Hanriot, a revolutionary leader with the National Guards, purged the Girondins from the Convention.

By this time Marat's skin complaint had worsened and he had to spend long periods in the bath to alleviate the itching. He wrote in the tub, leaning on a board that rested on the sides.

Date and Place of Assassination

13 July 1793, Rue des Cordeliers, Paris, France.

The Event

On 9 July 1793, Charlotte Corday left her cousin's home in Caen, carrying a copy of Plutarch's *Parallel Lives*, and caught the post coach to Paris. When she arrived two days later, she booked into the Hotel de Procidence. She bought a 6-inch (15-centimetre) dinner knife at the Palais-Royal, and wrote her *Adresse aux Français Amis des Lois et de la Paix* (*Speech to the French who are Friends of Law and Peace*), in which she sought to explain what she was about to do.

On the day of the assassination, Marat was, as usual, working in his bath. Corday arrived at Marat's home at 11.30am and told his two female aides that she must see him so as "to put him in a condition to render a great service to France". But they refused her admission saying that he was simply too ill to receive visitors. That evening at 7pm, she returned and shouted that she had important news of the Girondins in Caen. Marat overheard her and asked his associates to admit her. For 15 minutes they sat, Marat in his tub, Corday at his side, discussing the revolution. Marat asked her for the names of Girondin deputies in Caen and wrote them down, adding, "They shall be guillotined." At this, she pulled out her knife and stabbed Marat behind the right shoulder blade, severing the carotid artery. He called out, "Aidez, ma chère amie!" ("Help, my dear friend!") before he died.

THE GIRONDINS

The Girondins, also known as the Brissotins and Baguettes, were a group of individuals holding similar opinions rather than an organized political party. Their name came about because the most eloquent advocates of their view were deputies from the Gironde.

The Assassin

Marie Anne Charlotte de Corday d'Armont was born on a farm in Saint-Saturnin-des-Ligneries, Normandy, France, on 27 July 1768, the fourth child of an impoverished aristocratic family. She was a distant relative of the dramatist Pierre Corneille. After the Catholic convent in which she was educated closed, she moved in with a cousin at 148 Rue St-Jean, Caen. She was an impetuous woman – she supported the Girondins but, two years earlier, had been a fervent monarchist. When she realised that the Girondins were losing the battle to rule France to the militant Jacobins, she blamed Marat personally. However, while Marat preferred the Jacobins to the Girondins, he had no connection with them.

The Aftermath

Six policemen examined Charlotte Corday in Marat's home before she was taken to the Abbaye Prison and then to the Conciergerie where she continued to claim that she had acted alone, "Even the women of the country are capable of firmness." At her trial, which began on the same day as the assassination, she stated, "It is only in Paris that people have eyes for Marat. In the provinces he is regarded as a monster," adding "I killed one man to save one hundred thousand". Corday appeared before Judge Jacques Montané and was defended by Chauveau-Lagarde, while prosecuting was Antoine Fouquier-Tinville. She was condemned to death and executed at 7pm on 17 July 1793.

After Marat's assassination, his tub vanished. Some believe that his wife, Simonne Evrard, might have sold it to a journalist – it was found among the writer's belongings at his death. The monarchist Monsieur de Sainte-Hilaire bought the bath, taking it to Sarzeau in Normandy. His daughter Capriole de Sainte-Hilaire inherited it when he died in 1805 and she bequeathed it to the curate of Sarzeau when she died in 1862 without heirs. He sold it to the waxworks, the Grévin Museum, for FF5,000.

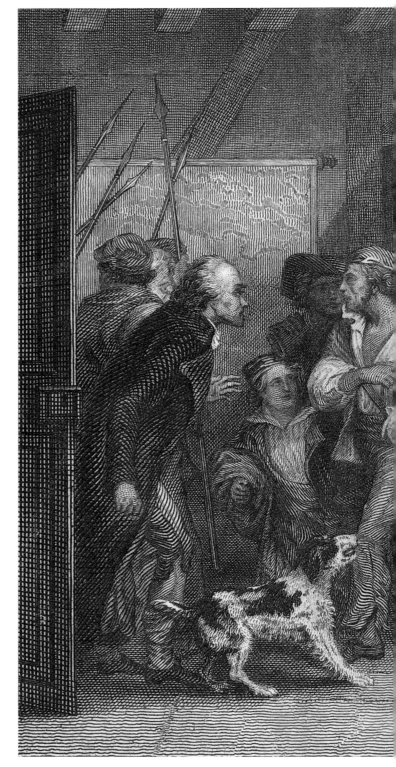

The revolutionary Marat was killed in his bath.
A crowd discover the crime.

Joseph Smith, Jr (1805–1844)

The Victim

The founder of the Church of Jesus Christ of Latter-day Saints was born on 23 December 1805 in Sharon, Windsor County, Vermont, USA, the fourth of 11 children of Joseph Smith, Sr and Lucy Mack. The family was, to say the least, peripatetic – they moved ten times in 19 years.

In 1820, when he was 14, Joseph fell victim to depression. During this time he saw his first vision, also called the "grove experience", in a forested area now called the Sacred Grove, near his home in western New York. He had two more visions on 21 and 22 September 1823. He claimed that he saw the angel Nephi (later Moroni), who told him that none of the religions or cults then on earth truly represented the word of God. Further, the church of Christ had been removed from the earth and God had chosen Smith to restore it.

On 20 March 1826, Smith was convicted after an alleged admission to being a "disorderly person" and an "impostor" for an unspecified misdemeanour charge in a court in Bainbridge, New York. Meanwhile, the visions reoccurred annually until 22 September 1827 when Smith claimed that he had found "plates" of gold in Hill Cumorah, near Manchester, New York. These "plates" told the story of the American church from its migration from Jerusalem to the continent. Naturally, the story was not written in English and Smith spent three years laboriously translating it. His finished work was published in July 1830 as *The Book of Mormon*. (Mormon is the author/prophet of the *Book of Mormon*) Scholars think it odd that someone as lacking in education as Smith could have written the book. (There is a long-held but unestablished theory that *The Book of Mormon* was actually based on a novel by Solomon Spaulding.) The book contains autobiographical material and the subject is indigenous to the community in which Smith was raised. One authority described it as "a catch-all of frontier Protestant doctrine [which] touches on practically every controversial belief of the time".

Before its publication, Smith had founded the Church of Jesus Christ of Latter-day Saints on 6 April 1830 at Fayette, Seneca County, New York. The members were made up entirely of Smith's relatives, neighbours and friends until 14 November 1830, when Sidney Rigdon, the first outsider, was baptized. The church became a cooperative society led by an ecclesiastical oligarchy. Rigdon was the official spokesman for both the church and Smith. It worked well for the Mormons but on occasion caused friction with others in the locale.

In 1831, Smith took his flock to Kirtland, Ohio, where Rigdon had a church. Seven years later, on 12 January 1838, Rigdon and Smith fled to Missouri on the run from the authorities for a banking scam. In the autumn of that year the two men were imprisoned and sentenced to death, but escaped when a general refused to carry out the order. The locals in Missouri drove the Mormons out to a remote part of the state and then (in 1839) to Commerce, Illinois, which Smith renamed Nauvoo. The commune grew both from an American influx and from European converts.

With the increase in population, politicians began to take notice because there were votes to be had. Smith revelled in his role as leader, enjoying the status, publicity and power. However, he and Rigdon fell out (the cause of the argument may have been Smith's suggestion that Rigdon's daughter, Nancy, become one of his "spiritual wives", that is to say, not a legal wife). On 15 February 1844, Smith announced his candidature for the presidency of the United States, with Rigdon as his running mate (despite the men's animosity). However, his megalomania made the Mormons unpopular and the unpopularity was enhanced when it was discovered that his followers practised polygamy. It produced a schism within the church.

On 7 June 1844, the first and only edition of the *Nauvoo Expositor* was published by the printer William Law, a Canadian convert. It featured a vicious attack on Smith by Law. "We are earnestly seeking to explode the

Like many founders of religions, Joseph Smith was a controversial figure, eliciting as much hatred as love.

vicious principles of Joseph Smith, and those who practice the same abominations and whoredoms," the article began. The reason for the attack was that Smith had made romantic overtures to Mrs Law. Three days later, Smith ordered the destruction of the printing presses belonging to Law. The order was carried out peacefully, but on 12 June, Charles A. Foster, a co-publisher of the *Expositor*, claimed that the building had been damaged as well. This was untrue but some claimed that Smith was violating the freedom of the press. Threats were made against Smith. Warrants from outside Nauvoo were dismissed in Nauvoo courts on a writ of *habeas corpus*. Smith declared martial law on 18 June.

Thomas Ford, the governor of Illinois, suggested a trial in Carthage by a non-Mormon jury. Smith originally intended to flee but changed his mind and stayed. He said, "If my life is of no value to my friends it is of none to myself. I am going like a lamb to the slaughter; but I am calm as a summer's morning; I have a conscience void of offence towards God, and towards all men. I shall die innocent, and it shall be said of me – he was murdered in cold blood." He was arrested on 25 June, along with his brother, Hyrum, the other 15 city council members and some friends on the original charge of rioting. Joseph and Hyrum

Smith was shot as he jumped out of a jail window but, to make sure he was dead, the mob "executed" him again.

were charged with treason against the state of Illinois for declaring martial law in Nauvoo. The councillors were freed on $500 bail but the Smith brothers were held on the treason charge.

Date and Place of Assassination

27 June 1844, Carthage, Hancock County, Illinois, USA.

The Event

Smith was put in a spacious cell on the second floor of the jail in Carthage. In the late afternoon he was drinking wine with his brother, Hyrum, and some friends when he heard a furious mob approaching. Arming himself with a six-chambered pistol that had been smuggled in, Smith awaited his fate. The mob broke down the cell door and shot Hyrum in the face. He called, "I am a dead man!" and fell to the floor where he was shot five more times.

Smith's friends, Dr Willard Richards and John Taylor, tried to fight back. Taylor was shot four or five times, but survived, one shot being stopped by his pocket watch (the hands stopped at 5.16pm). Richards escaped unhurt as he was pushed behind the door when it was forced open. Abandoning his fight, Smith jumped out of the jail window in a hail of bullets from inside and below. He was dead before his body hit the ground but just to make sure, the mob propped him in a chair and shot him again. One man tried to decapitate Smith for a bounty, but was prevented from doing so by "divine intervention" when a thunderstorm began.

The Assassins

A 200-strong mob of men with faces blacked with wet gunpowder.

The Aftermath

Had Smith lived, it is likely that the Mormon church would have split; his martyrdom had the affect of consolidating the faithful.

Less than two months after Smith's assassination, Brigham Young (1801–1877), a 43-year-old former caretaker and house-painter was the new leader of the Mormons. Under his leadership, the Mormons trekked west in 1846–1847 and settled in Salt Lake City.

Abraham Lincoln (1809–1865)

The Victim

The sixteenth and tallest president of the USA, Abraham Lincoln was born at dawn on 12 February 1809 in a one-room, dirt-floor log cabin on the 348-acre (141-hectare) Sinking Spring Farm, in Nolin Creek, 3 miles (5 kilometres) south of Hodgenville, in southeast Hardin County, Kentucky. He was the second of three children and eldest son of Thomas Lincoln and Nancy Hanks. In December 1816, the family moved to Indiana after Thomas Lincoln got into financial difficulties. A year after his wife died, Thomas Lincoln married Sarah Bush Johnston, a widow with three children, on 2 December 1819.

Abraham Lincoln was an autodidact whose political career began in the spring of 1832 when he campaigned unsuccessfully for the Illinois General Assembly as a member of the Whig Party. In the meantime, on 9 May 1832, he was sworn into federal military service and served under Captain Zachary Taylor in the Black Hawk War. He left the army on 10 July and, on 6 August 1832, he came eighth in a field of 13 candidates. He received 277 votes – this was the only direct election he lost.

That same year he went into business with a general store in New Salem selling tea, coffee, sugar, salt, blue calico, brown muslin, straw hats and whisky. On 7 May 1833, he was appointed postmaster in New Salem and in the autumn of 1833 began work as a surveyor. On 4 August 1834 he was elected to the State Legislature and around this time began studying law. In December 1834, he took his seat in Vandalia, then the capital of Illinois. He was re-elected to the State Legislature on 1 August 1836 and the following month, on 9 September, received his law licence. On 1 March 1837, he was admitted to the Bar. Six weeks later he moved to Springfield, Illinois and on 5 August 1838 was again re-elected to the State Legislature. Exactly two years later, he was re-elected for a fourth term. In December 1840, he fell ill with a depression that lasted three weeks.

On 27 August 1842, the *Sangamo Journal* published a satirical letter about the leading Democrat and state auditor, James Shields. Supposedly written by "Rebecca", it was, in fact, written by Lincoln as a joke. Then a second letter was published in which she offered to marry Shields. When Shields discovered that the second letter was written by the future Mrs Abraham Lincoln, Mary Todd, and her friend Julia Jayne, he challenged Lincoln to a duel, but it never happened. On 4 November 1842, at the home of the bride's sister at Springfield, Illinois, Lincoln married Mary. She was born at Lexington, Kentucky, on 13 December 1818, the daughter of a banker. (Mary was argumentative, mentally unstable and on 20 May 1875 she was sectioned. She died on 16 July 1882 at Springfield, Illinois.) The couple had four sons (see box on page 28).

Lincoln was nominated for the House of Representatives on 1 May 1846 and was elected on 3 August. He took his seat on 6 December 1847, serving in the Thirtieth Congress. In January 1848, he voted on an anti-war amendment and later that year damaged his growing reputation with a foolish speech in the House. The local parties denounced him and Lincoln decided not to run for re-election. From August to November 1848, he campaigned for his old military colleague Zachary Taylor in his successful bid for the presidency. Having turned down jobs in the far-flung Oregon territory, Lincoln returned to Springfield and gave up politics for several years while he earned a living as a lawyer. Lincoln was involved in more than 5,100 cases in Illinois alone during a 23-year legal practice. Lincoln and his partners appeared before the Illinois State Supreme Court more than 400 times. In May 1849, he received a patent (the only president to do so) for "an improved method of lifting vessels over shoals" by means of "adjustable buoyant chambers".

Despite the success of his legal practice, Lincoln felt that he was not being stretched professionally so decided to return to politics. On 7 November 1854 he

Legend has it that Lincoln grew his beard after receiving a letter from Grace Bedell, a member of the public. However, others claim that this story may have been an early example of political spindoctoring.

was elected to a fifth term in the State Legislature but resigned almost immediately to run for the Senate. On 8 February 1855, he lost to Lyman Trumbull. (Trumbull was married to Julia Jayne, the co-author of the second letter to James Shields.) The following year he left the Whigs and joined the anti-slavery Republican Party. On 17 June 1856, he was the favourite for the vice presidential nomination at the first Republican Convention but lost to William L. Dayton. On 16 June 1858, he was nominated unanimously for the Senate at the Republican Convention in Springfield. His acceptance speech became known as "The House Divided Speech". It was not the first time he had used the expression – he had employed it in a Whig campaign

LINCOLN'S SONS

Robert Todd: born in the Globe Tavern, Springfield, Illinois on 1 August 1843; died in Manchester, Vermont, 25 July 1926. He has a unique and unwanted claim to fame; he is the only man to have been present at the assassinations of three American presidents – his father, Garfield and McKinley. His grandson died in 1985, the last direct living descendant of Abraham Lincoln.

Edward Baker: born in Springfield, Illinois on 10 March 1846; died in Springfield, Illinois, 1 February 1850.

William Wallace: born in Springfield, Illinois on 21 December 1850; died at the White House, 1600 Pennsylvania Avenue, Washington DC, 20 February 1862. Like his elder brother, Robert, Willie also has a unique and unwanted claim to fame; he is the only child to have died in the White House.

Thomas "Tad": born in Springfield, Illinois on 4 April 1853; died in Chicago, Illinois, 16 July 1871. He was born with a lisp and a cleft palate.

circular on 4 March 1843. Lincoln quoted the Bible "A house divided against itself cannot stand." (Mark 3:25) "I believe this government cannot endure permanently half slave and half free. I do not expect the Union to be dissolved – I do not expect the house to fall – but I do expect it will cease to be divided. It will become all one thing, or all the other."

Democratic senator Stephen A. Douglas, one of the most powerful men in the Senate, broke away from President James Buchanan during 1857 and 1858 and Lincoln stood against him for his Senate seat. On 24 July 1858, Lincoln challenged Douglas to a series of debates, which occurred between 21 August and 15 October 1858. By the last debate, Lincoln had reduced the argument to the moral question of slavery. Douglas said, "If you desire Negro citizenship ... if you desire them to vote on an equality with yourselves ... then support Mr Lincoln and the Black Republican party, who are in favour of the citizenship of the Negro." The verbal contests brought Lincoln to the notice of the wider public. However, on 5 January 1859, it was Douglas and not Lincoln who was victorious.

In April 1859, Lincoln said that he was "not fit for the presidency," a view much of the populace did not share. On 18 May 1860, on the third ballot, he became the first Republican nominee for president. Lincoln did not go out on the stump and give speeches the way candidates usually do. The campaign was held at local level but virtually no one bothered to go to the southern states. However, Lincoln's supporters claimed that if he was elected, secession of the southern states was not an inevitability.

In October 1860, he began to grow the beard by which he is most recognizable. On 6 November 1860, Lincoln was elected the first Republican president, beating Democrat Stephen A. Douglas, John C. Breckinridge of the Southern Democrats, and John Bell of the new Constitutional Union Party. The election was won totally on northern support. Lincoln was not even on the ballot in nine southern states and won only two

Lincoln arrives at The Capitol for his inauguration on 4 March 1861.

Baltimore, Maryland, on 23 February. A distraction would engage the police while an assassin killed the president-elect. Allan Pinkerton, who was assigned to protect Lincoln, discovered the plan and foiled the attempt.

Lincoln arrived in Washington nine days before his inauguration, which was held on 4 March 1861 on the east portico of the Capitol. Former president James Buchanan said to Lincoln, "If you are as happy, my dear sir, on entering this house as I am on leaving it and returning home, you are the happiest man on earth." In his inauguration address, Lincoln said that he had no lawful right to interfere with slavery and nor did he intend to do so. Lincoln did not attend his inauguration ball. A large army contingent was assembled to protect the president-elect and to make sure there was no Confederate uprising.

Lincoln, as a believer in the Constitution, would not make a move against the southern states that had seceded. On 12 April 1861, the Union battlement at Fort Sumter was attacked and the inhabitants surrendered at 7pm that day. The American Civil War had begun. On 15 April, the president demanded that state governors send a total of 75,000 militia to recapture forts, protect the capital and "preserve the Union". On 17 April, Virginia seceded, along with Arkansas (5 May), North Carolina (the last Confederate state to secede, 20 May) and Tennessee (the last of 11 Southern states to secede, 8 June). On 19 April, Lincoln ordered a blockade of all seceded ports. On 3 May, he called for 42,000 volunteers to join the army and 18,000 to join the navy. A week later, on 10 May, he declared martial law. On 29 June, the decision was made to attack Manassas, the Confederate headquarters. The first battle of Bull Run, Manassas Junction, Virginia, took place on 21 July and resulted in a victory for the

of 996 counties in the other southern states. Lincoln won 180 Electoral College votes and 18 states. As Lincoln's election victory became more likely the southern states prepared to secede from the US Union. South Carolina was the first to go followed by six other southern states. Delaware, Maryland, Virginia, North Carolina, Tennessee, Kentucky, Missouri and Arkansas all decided to stay in the Union. The seven Confederate states seceded before Lincoln took office, declaring themselves an entirely new nation, the Confederate States of America.

On 11 February 1861, Lincoln left Springfield for the White House. A plot was hatched to kill Lincoln when his train stopped at the Calvert Street Depot in

Lincoln addresses troops during the Civil War.

Confederacy. On 6 April 1862, the Battle of Shiloh began and ended the following day with a Union victory. Several times during the war, Lincoln made it clear that he was not fighting to end slavery but to save the Union. On 22 August 1862, he wrote, "I would save the Union. I would save it the shortest way under the Constitution. The sooner the national authority can be restored; the nearer the Union will be 'the Union as it was' ... My paramount object in this struggle is to save the Union, and is not either to save or to destroy slavery. If I could save the Union without freeing any slave I would do it, and if I could save it by freeing all the slaves I would do it; and if I could save it by freeing some and leaving others alone I would also do that."

The freeing of slaves was an economic policy to undermine the power bases of slave owners, his opponents.

On 17 September 1862, the Battle of Antietam was fought north of the small town of Sharpsburg in Maryland. Beginning at dawn and lasting until night fell, it was the bloodiest battle of the war with more than 22,000 casualties. Five days later, Lincoln issued a preliminary Emancipation Proclamation, effective 1 January 1863. In reality, the Emancipation Proclamation did not actually free any slaves since it exempted all areas under Union military occupation and the Confederacy simply ignored it.

Lincoln believed that the presidency was there only to rubber-stamp laws made by Congress and only

Andrew Johnson, who became president on the death of Lincoln, ran away from home aged 16 and became a tailor before finding his true vocation in politics. He became an alderman aged just 20 and a mayor two years later.

vetoed those he thought harmed his war efforts. He signed the Homestead Act on 20 May 1862, making available 160 acres (65 hectares) of government-held land in the west to each adult head of a family for between $26 and $34; the Morrill Land-Grant Colleges Act, on 2 July 1862, which awarded each loyal senator 30,000 acres (12,140 hectares) and established agricultural universities in each state; the Pacific Railway Act of 1 July 1862 and the National Banking Acts of 1863, 1864 and 1865.

On 17 October 1863, Lincoln called for 300,000 volunteers for the duration of the conflict and on 1 February 1864, called for half a million more. On 19 November 1863, he gave his Gettysburg Address at the dedication of the Soldiers' National Cemetery. He said:

Four score and seven years ago our fathers brought forth on this continent a new nation, conceived in Liberty, and dedicated to the proposition that all men are created equal. Now we are engaged in a great civil war, testing whether that nation, or any nation, so conceived and so dedicated, can long endure. We are met on a great battlefield of that war. We have come to dedicate a portion of that field, as a final resting place for those who here gave their lives that that nation might live. It is altogether fitting and proper that we should do this. But, in a larger sense, we can not dedicate – we can not consecrate – we can not hallow – this ground. The brave men, living and dead, who

struggled here, have consecrated it, far above our poor power to add or detract. The world will little note, nor long remember what we say here, but it can never forget what they did here. It is for us the living, rather, to be dedicated here to the unfinished work which they who fought here have thus far so nobly advanced. It is rather for us to be here dedicated to the great task remaining before us – that from these honoured dead we take increased devotion to that cause for which they gave the last full measure of devotion – that we here highly resolve that these dead shall not have died in vain – that this nation, under God, shall have a new birth of freedom – and that government of the people, by the people, for the people, shall not perish from the earth."

On 9 March 1864, Lincoln promoted Ulysses S. Grant making him lieutenant general, the highest rank in the army. On 7 June 1864, at the Front Street Theatre in Baltimore, Maryland, Lincoln was re-nominated for president. Andrew Johnson of Tennessee was chosen as the vice presidential nominee after Lincoln dropped his vice president Hannibal Hamlin from the ticket. On 8 November 1864, Lincoln was re-elected despite fears, groundless as it turned out, that he would lose. He won 212 Electoral College votes and 22 states. Democrat General George B. McClellan won just three states and 21 Electoral College votes. On 4 March 1865, Lincoln was inaugurated for the second time on the east portico of the Capitol. In a picture taken at the inauguration can be seen John Wilkes Booth, David Herold, Lewis Powell, George Atzerodt, John Surratt and Edmund Spangler, who would all play a leading role in Lincoln's life (and death) the following month.

A week later, the president announced that all deserters from the forces had 60 days to report back or they would no longer be American citizens. On 9 April 1865, the American Civil War came to an end when General Robert E. Lee surrendered at Appomattox Court House in Virginia.

Date and Place of Assassination
14 April 1865, Ford Theatre, 511 10th Street, NW Washington DC, USA.

The Event
In September 1864, with conspirators Samuel Bland Arnold, Michael O'Laughlen, George Andreas Atzerodt, David Edgar Herold, Lewis Thornton Powell (aka Lewis Paine) and John Harrison Surratt, Jr, actor John Wilkes Booth formulated a plan to kidnap Lincoln and exchange him for Confederate prisoners of war. The conspirators met at a bed and breakfast run by Mary Surratt, the widowed mother of John. One of the residents, Louis J. Weichmann, was also suspected of being part of the kidnapping attempt.

On 4 March 1865, Booth was present at Lincoln's second inauguration as the guest of his secret fiancée Lucy Hale, the daughter of John P. Hale, then the United States ambassador to Spain. A little under two weeks after the inauguration, on 17 March 1865, Booth discovered that the president would be watching the play *Still Waters Run Deep* at Campbell Military Hospital. The gang hid along a road that led to the hospital but their plan came to nought when Lincoln did not show up. The president was instead giving a speech at the National Hotel in the capital, which, ironically, was where Booth lived.

On 11 April 1865, Lincoln gave his last public speech. He spoke outside the White House in favour of enfran-chising blacks. Booth became so enraged by the idea that he changed his mind about kidnapping Lincoln and decided to assassinate him instead.

The president, Mrs Lincoln and Major Henry R. Rathbone and his fiancée Clara Harris were to attend a performance of the play *Our American Cousin* starring Laura Keene at Ford's Theatre on Good Friday 1865. Booth told his gang that he intended to kill Lincoln and assigned others to murder the vice president, Andrew Johnson, and Secretary of State William H. Seward.

Herold and Powell were given the task of killing Seward, who was bedridden at his home in Lafayette Park in Washington following a carriage accident. Powell was armed with an 1858 Whitney revolver and a huge silver-mounted bowie knife. The two men arrived at Seward's home just after 10pm and William Bell, Seward's butler, answered the door. Powell said that he was bringing medicine from Dr Verdi and had to personally show Seward the correct dosages. Powell was shown up to Seward's bedroom on the third floor, where he was met by Seward's son and Assistant Secretary of State, Frederick. Powell told the son the same story he had told the butler but Frederick Seward was not so easily swayed and told Powell that his father was sleeping. Frederick Seward's sister, Fanny, opened the door and said, "Fred, Father is awake now." Powell pulled his gun and placed the barrel against Frederick Seward's head. He pulled the trigger but the gun misfired so he clubbed the assistant secretary over the head until he collapsed. Powell ran into William Seward's room and stabbed him repeatedly. Seward's life was saved by the metal neck restraint he was wearing. Another son, Augustus, and a Sergeant Robinson dragged Powell away, although both men and Fanny Seward were stabbed in the process. Waiting outside, Herold heard Fanny's screams and ran away. As Powell rushed down the stairs to the front door, a telegram boy, Emerick Hansell, arrived with a cable for Seward. Hansell, too, was stabbed by Powell who then jumped on a horse that had been tethered nearby by Herold.

George Atzerodt was tasked with killing Vice President Andrew Johnson at 10.15pm. On 14 April 1865, Atzerodt booked into room 126 at the Kirkwood House Hotel in Washington, immediately above the vice president's suite. Having washed and changed, Atzerodt went down to the bar where he asked the barman about Vice President Johnson's itinerary and movements. Atzerodt contemplated what he was about to do and then rose from his seat at the bar and walked out of the hotel. Booth had feared that his co-conspirator would not have the bravery to go through with the plan and on his way to Ford's Theatre, Booth stopped at the vice president's house and left a note, "Don't wish to disturb you. Are you at home? J. Wilkes Booth."

It has long been reported that on the days leading up to his death, President Lincoln had recurring dreams of his own death. His bodyguard, Ward Hill Lamon, recalled Lincoln saying:

About ten days ago, I retired very late. I had been up waiting for important dispatches from the front. I could not have been long in bed when I fell into a slumber, for I was weary. I soon began to dream. There seemed to be a death-like stillness about me. Then I heard subdued sobs, as if a number of people were weeping. I thought I left my bed and wandered downstairs. There the silence was broken by the same pitiful sobbing, but the mourners were invisible. I went from room to room; no living person was in sight, but the same mournful sounds of distress met me as I passed along. I saw light in all the rooms; every object was familiar to me; but where were all the people who were grieving as if their hearts would break? I was puzzled and alarmed. What could be the meaning of all this? Determined to find the cause of a state of things so mysterious and so shocking, I kept on until I arrived at the East Room, which I entered. There I met with a sickening surprise. Before me was a catafalque, on which rested a corpse wrapped in funeral vestments. Around it were stationed soldiers who were acting as guards; and there was a throng of people, gazing mournfully upon the corpse, whose face was covered, others weeping pitifully. 'Who is dead in the White House?' I demanded of one of the soldiers, 'The president,' was his answer, 'he was killed by an assassin.' Then came a loud burst of grief from the crowd, which woke me from my dream. I slept no more that night; and although it was only a dream, I have been strangely annoyed by it ever since.

It should be pointed out that Lincoln himself did not believe that the dream referred to his own death, but that of another, unknown president.

President and Mrs Lincoln arrived at the theatre at 9pm and were taken to the presidential box (number seven) along with Rathbone and Harris. Lincoln sat in a rocking chair on the left of the box. Around this time Booth arrived at the back of the theatre where he was known to the stage door staff. Booth crept into a narrow passageway between Lincoln's box and the theatre balcony, and barricaded the door. Meanwhile, Lincoln's bodyguard, John F. Parker, was no longer in position having left to get a better view of the play, although some believe that he abandoned his post to sate his thirst. The president and Mrs Lincoln held hands as they watched the play. Mary Lincoln whispered to her husband, "What will Miss Harris think of my hanging on to you so?" To which Lincoln responded, "She won't think anything about it." Booth waited for the biggest laugh of the night to shoot Lincoln. A few moments later, Booth silently entered the box and as the big laugh came he shot Lincoln in the back of the head with a .44 calibre Deringer. Major Rathbone tried to stop Booth escaping, but was stabbed in the arm for his troubles. Booth climbed onto the parapet to jump but was again grabbed by the major

John Wilkes Booth waited for the loudest laugh in the play to cover the sound of him shooting President Lincoln in the back of the head.

who was again stabbed. As Booth jumped, his spur caught on the Treasury flag and he fell awkwardly breaking his left leg. He yelled out, "*Sic semper tyrannis*" before limping away. His words mean "Thus always to tyrants" and are the state motto of Virginia. Despite some of the crowd's best efforts he managed to escape. The cry went up for a doctor in the house and was answered by an army surgeon, Charles Leale. He removed a blood clot but said it was unlikely that Lincoln would survive. The mortally wounded president was taken to the William Petersen House at 516 10th Street. Doctors, including the US Army Surgeon General Joseph K. Barnes of the Army Medical Museum, attended Lincoln but nothing could be done. Lincoln never regained consciousness and was officially pronounced dead at 7.22am the following day. He was 56.

The Assassin

John Wilkes Booth was born the ninth child of an acting family on 10 May 1838, in a large log cabin at his father's farm near Bel Air, Maryland. He was named for the English politician John Wilkes. He was an impetuous boy, often running away from home to find adventure, and many have assumed he was tainted with his father Junius's insanity. His father's farm was a sanctuary for animals of all kinds and on more than one occasion Junius performed a burial ceremony for a deceased four-legged friend. His love of animals was not shared by John Wilkes Booth, who bore a hatred of cats and would kill any he saw on their land.

He followed in the family tradition, making his acting debut aged 17 at the St Charles Theatre in Baltimore in the role of Richmond in Shakespeare's *Henry VI, Part*

Three. In 1860, his career took off and he became a success on the stage. His fame allowed him to enjoy the attentions of many ladies. In May 1861, in Madison, Indiana, one such admirer stabbed him and then herself when she discovered she was not his favourite. The outbreak of the American Civil War separated Booth from his family – he supported the South believing that slavery was "one of the greatest blessings (both for [the slaves] and us) that God ever bestowed upon a favoured nation". Two years earlier, Booth had been part of the militia that had executed abolitionist John Brown. Booth did not join the Confederate army, supposedly because of a promise to his mother, but more likely because he did not want to serve as a private.

The Aftermath

A manhunt began for the assassin, organized by Secretary of War Edwin Stanton. Booth met Herold and went to collect weapons and food that they had previously hidden at Surattsville. They then went to the home of Dr Samuel Alexander Mudd whom Booth knew. Mudd put Booth's leg in splints. Never has the following of the Hippocratic oath had such unfortunate results; as well as being imprisoned for his role, Mudd's name is said to live on in the expression "his name is mud". The conspirators spent a day at Mudd's house before paying a local to take them to Samuel Cox's house and then to Thomas A. Jones, who hid the fugitives in a swamp near his house for six days and five nights until they were able to escape across the Potomac. On 23 April, they made it across the

---

MUSEUM EXHIBITS

The bullet that killed Lincoln, pieces of his skull and hair and the surgeon's cuff stained with the president's blood are all at the Army Medical Museum, now the National Museum of Health and Medicine, Washington DC, USA.

---

river and on 24 April crossed the Rappahannock and travelled to a barn belonging to Richard H. Garrett. On 26 April, they were found by soldiers, locked in the barn. Called upon to surrender, Herold gave himself up but Booth refused to leave the barn. The troops set the barn on fire and Sergeant Boston Corbett, a religious monomaniac, moved in close and shot Booth in the neck despite orders not to fire. Booth was carried to the porch of Garrett's house and lingered until around 7pm when he died. His last words were, "Tell Mother – tell Mother – I died for my country."

It was not long before the other conspirators were arrested and tried by a military tribunal headed by Major-General David Hunter. They were accused of conspiring with Jefferson Davis, president of the Confederate States of America, and Confederate officials in Canada to murder the American president, although Davis explicitly denounced the assassination plot, believing it would bring disgrace to the south and make Lincoln a martyr. Many believed that the defendants should have been tried before a civilian court and to bring the Confederacy into the event was simply wrong. The trial lasted seven weeks from 10 May until 29 June 1865 and 366 witnesses – many irrelevant to the proceedings – were called to testify. On 5 July, all of the defendants were found guilty. Mary Surratt, Lewis Powell, David Herold and George Atzerodt were sentenced to death by hanging and went to the gallows in the Old Arsenal Penitentiary on 7 July. Mary Surratt was the first woman to be hanged by the US government. Samuel Mudd, Samuel Arnold and Michael O'Laughlen were given life in prison. Edmund Spangler, a scenery mover at Ford's Theatre, was sentenced to six years in prison.

Michael O'Laughlen died in prison of yellow fever on 23 September 1867. President Johnson pardoned Mudd, Arnold and Spangler on 4 March 1869. John Surratt stayed in hiding in Canada, went to Europe and returned to America in December 1866. His trial began on 10 June 1867 and ended on 10 August 1867 with the jury voting eight to four for acquittal. Despite this verdict, Surratt was kept in prison until 22 June 1868 when he was released on bail. He became a teacher and died of pneumonia at 9pm on Friday 21 April 1916.

Abraham Lincoln's corpse was taken to the White House where he became the first president to lie in state (in the East Room). The funeral cortege, consisting of 300 people, travelled 1,654 miles (2,662 kilometres) to Illinois, beginning on 19 April. It also carried the casket of his son, William Lincoln. President Lincoln was buried at Oak Ridge Cemetery in Springfield, Illinois. His tomb measures 177 feet (54 metres) in height. In 1901, Robert Lincoln exhumed his father's body and it was reburied in several feet of concrete to deter grave robbers.

Andrew Johnson was inaugurated on 15 April 1865, aged 56, in his suite at the Kirkwood House Hotel. On 21 December 1865, President Johnson signed an act that paid $25,000 to Mrs Lincoln for expenses.

In 1867, Congress vetoed President Johnson's own veto of the Tenure of Office Act, which forbade the president from sacking certain public officials without the prior consent of the Senate. In February 1868, Johnson sacked Edwin Stanton as Secretary of War because Stanton had been undermining him. On 24 February 1868, the House of Representatives voted by 126–47 to impeach President Johnson for "high crimes and misdemeanours". The president asked for 40 days to prepare his defence but was allowed just ten. The House filed 11 articles of impeachment against Johnson. The Senate voted three times 35–19 to convict Johnson, just one short of the necessary two-thirds margin. Johnson survived thanks to the bravery of seven Republican senators who voted with the Democrats.

William Seward recovered from his injuries and continued to serve as Secretary of State. On 30 March 1867, he signed the deal that bought Alaska from Russia for $7.2 million. Critics called it "Seward's Folly" but Alaska was to yield more than $750 million of gold, as well as oil, timber, minerals and fish.

THE KENNEDY-LINCOLN ASSASSINATION COINCIDENCES

• Abraham Lincoln was elected to Congress in 1846. John F. Kennedy was elected to Congress in 1946.

• Abraham Lincoln was elected president in 1860. John F. Kennedy was elected president in 1960.

• In 1860, Lincoln was elected with less than 50 percent of the popular vote over Stephen A. Douglas (born 1813). In 1960, Kennedy was elected with less than 50 percent of the popular vote over Richard Nixon (born 1913).

• The names Lincoln and Kennedy each contain seven letters.

• Both men lost children while they were living in the White House.

• Both were married in their thirties to women in their early twenties.

• Both presidents were shot on a Friday.

• Both were shot in the head.

• Both were assassinated by Southerners.

• Both were succeeded by Southerners.

• Both successors were named Johnson.

• Andrew Johnson, who succeeded Lincoln, was born in 1808; Lyndon Johnson, who succeeded Kennedy, was born in 1908.

• Lincoln and Kennedy were both younger than their vice presidents.

• Both assassins were known by three names.

• Both assassins' names are comprised of 15 letters.

• Booth ran from a theatre and was caught in a warehouse; Oswald ran from a warehouse and was caught in a movie theatre.

• Booth and Oswald were assassinated before their trials.

William McKinley (1843–1901)

The Victim

William McKinley, Jr (he dropped the "Jr" on his father's death), the 25th president of the United States, was born at Niles, Ohio, the third son and seventh child of nine of William McKinley (1807–1892), a pig iron manufacturer, and Nancy Allison (1809–1897), on 29 January 1843. When he was 17, McKinley enrolled at Allegheny College in Meadville, Pennsylvania, but a brief illness and money worries forced him to drop out after a single term.

On 11 June 1861, near the start of the American Civil War, he joined the Twenty-third Regiment, Ohio Volunteer Infantry, which was commanded by Rutherford B. Hayes. William McKinley was the first man in his town to enlist. After the war he became a lawyer, being admitted to the Ohio Bar in 1867. He also developed an interest in politics and became active in the Republican Party. On 25 January 1871, at the First Presbyterian Church at Canton, he married Ida Saxton (born at Canton, 8 June 1847), the daughter of James Asbury Saxton, a local banker. The couple had two daughters, one of whom, Ida (born 31 March 1873), died on 22 August 1873, aged just four months, and the other, Katherine (born 25 January 1872), died on 25 July 1875 at the age of three. The grief and a bout of epilepsy transformed Mrs McKinley into a chronic invalid.

On 5 October 1876, McKinley was elected to Congress and marked out as a rising star. On 6 October 1890, Congress passed the McKinley Tariff, which raised customs duties but authorised trade reciprocity. The measure was not popular and in the 1890 election, the Republicans were swept from office and McKinley lost his seat. He remained personally popular within the party, however and in October 1891, he was elected governor of Ohio. In February 1892, Robert L. Walker, a friend for whom McKinley stood as guarantor, was declared bankrupt and McKinley found himself saddled with debts of $130,000. Wealthy friends rallied round and met his obligations and in the autumn of 1893 the fiasco elicited sympathy for him and he was re-elected as governor.

McKinley had resisted attempts to get him to run for the presidency in June 1892, while lumbered with the debt, but on 3 November 1896, he was elected president with Garret A. Hobart of New Jersey as his vice president. McKinley won 271 Electoral College votes and carried 23 states against William Jennings Bryan's 176 votes and 22 states. McKinley's inauguration was on 4 March 1897. He spent the early part of his presidency travelling, explaining his policies to the people and he introduced the media to the White House, where they received daily briefings from a press secretary.

One of the biggest events in McKinley's presidency came on 15 February 1898 at 9.40pm, when the 6,680-ton American ship *Maine* sank in Havana harbour. Of the 354 personnel aboard, 262 were killed. The Spanish claimed that it was accidental while America claimed it was the result of a mine. An inquiry called by McKinley concluded on 15 March that the *Maine* had suffered an explosion on the port side but did not decide what had caused it. It absolved the navy of any "fault or negligence", and it did not lay the blame on either the Spanish or the Cubans. Some newspaper proprietors such as William Randolph Hearst alleged that the Spanish were responsible for atrocities against America and used the sinking of the *Maine* as an excuse to engender anti-Spanish feelings in America.

On 25 April Congress declared that a state of war between the United States and Spain had existed since 20 April (later changed to 21 April). The first battle, on 1 May in the Philippines, saw the Americans victorious. On 1 July, about 15,000 American troops, including Theodore Roosevelt and his "Rough Riders", attacked

---

AN ALTERNATIVE OPINION

Theodore Roosevelt said, "The *Maine* was sunk by an act of dirty treachery on the part of the Spaniards."

William McKinley was the third US president to be assassinated.

1,270 entrenched Spaniards at the Battle of El Caney and Battle of San Juan Hill outside of Santiago. More than 200 US soldiers were killed and close to 1,200 wounded in the fighting. The war ended on 12 August 1898 and a peace treaty was signed in Paris on 10 December.

Vice President Hobart died aged 55 at Paterson, New Jersey, on 21 November 1899, which led to Theodore Roosevelt's appointment. On 6 November 1900, McKinley was re-elected with 292 Electoral College votes and 28 states to William Jennings Bryan's 155 votes and 17 states. McKinley said, "I am now the president of the whole people." An unwritten convention then existed that American presidents did not travel abroad while in office but McKinley decided to ignore that edict and travelled widely. In the summer of 1901 he toured the States and then decided to visit the Pan-American Exposition in Buffalo. His trip was delayed until early September because of Ida McKinley's ill health.

Date and Place of Assassination

6 September 1901, Temple of Music, Pan-American Exposition, Buffalo, New York, USA.

The Event

William McKinley gave a speech at Buffalo on 5 September, President's Day, in which he spoke in favour of reciprocity treaties. In the audience was a man called Leon Czolgosz who was angry. "I thought it wasn't right for any one man to get so much ceremony," he said later. The next day, a group of happy visitors to the Pan-American Exposition in Buffalo queued up to shake hands with McKinley at the Temple of Music.

Czolgosz, his hand swathed in a fake bandage, waited patiently. When he reached the front of the line at 4.07pm, he pulled out his .32 calibre Iver Johnson revolver and shot McKinley twice at point-blank range. The first bullet hit a button and was deflected, but the second hit McKinley in the abdomen between the navel and left nipple. The bullet clipped the top of the left kidney and wedged in the pancreas. McKinley stiffened and then slumped into the arms of his aide. "Be easy with him, boys!" McKinley called out as he saw Czolgosz being attacked. The president was taken to a

39

hospital in the exhibition grounds. Doctors opened McKinley up and spent an hour looking for the bullet. They washed the abdominal cavity with a saline solution and sewed the entry wound shut. Four days later, a second operation was performed to remove a piece of cloth that the bullet had pushed into the abdomen. President McKinley was taken to the home of exhibition president John G. Milburn to recover.

It did indeed seem that he was on the road to recovery. On 11 September, his temperature fell to 37.4°C (100°F) from 38.5°C (102°F) and he asked for a cigar, which was denied, and some solid food, a request that was granted. On 12 September he suffered a relapse and his doctors administered digitalis but it was of no use. The next day, McKinley weakened further and he passed away at 2.15am. His last words were, "It is God's way. His will, not ours, be done." The cause of death was gangrene of the pancreas, although it is believed his demise was as much to do with sloppy surgery as his actual wound.

PROTECTING PRESIDENTS

In 1902, the Secret Service (formed on 5 July 1865 to suppress counterfeit money) assigned two agents to protect the president full-time. In 1994, Congress passed laws stating that presidents elected to office after 1 January 1997 (George W. Bush), will receive Secret Service protection for ten years after leaving office. Those elected before that date (Jimmy Carter, George Bush and Bill Clinton) will receive lifetime protection, as will Senator Hillary Clinton, as do Betty Ford, Rosalynn Carter, Nancy Reagan and Barbara Bush. On 1 March 2003, responsibility for the Secret Service was transferred from the Department of the Treasury to the newly established Department of Homeland Security.

The Assassin

Leon Czolgosz was born in 1873 in Detroit, Michigan, the son of Paul Czolgosz, a Polish labourer. As a boy, the devoutly Catholic Czolgosz earned money by shining shoes and selling newspapers. In 1880, when Leon was seven, the family moved to Rogers City in northern Michigan, but stayed for only five months before relocating to the Polish community in Posen. In 1885, when he was 12, his mother died in childbirth. He got a job looking after machinery at the Newberg Wire Mills in Cleveland. He saved $400 and put it towards buying a family farm. His face was slashed and scarred when a wire spool snapped and hit him. In 1893, he was sacked after he and other workers went on strike. As well as losing his job, he lost his faith and was drawn to radical groups.

In 1898, Czolgosz suffered a breakdown and went to recover at the family farm. He spent his time reading newspapers, especially the anarchist *Free Society*. He was intrigued by reports of Gaetano Bresci, an anarchist from Paterson, New Jersey, who, in 1900, shot and killed King Umberto I of Italy (see Appendix, page 183). In April of 1901, Czolgosz asked his family to repay the money he had saved to help them buy the farm so that he could seek work in the West. Rather begrudgingly they gave him $70. On 5 May, he set off for Cleveland and met various anarchists and told them his name was Fred Nieman but they were dismayed by his attitude, specifically when he asked whether they were "plotting something like Bresci".

In July he travelled to Buffalo and took a room in a small hotel in West Seneca, just outside Buffalo. He probably hoped to find work. In late July, the anarchists discovered that Czolgosz had lied to them about his name but assumed that he was a government spy sent to infiltrate them. They even published a warning about him in the 1 September issue of their journal *Free Society*. It may have been this that prompted Czolgosz to prove his loyalty. On 2 September, he bought an Iver Johnson revolver for $4.50.

McKinley (left) and his successor Theodore Roosevelt (right).

The Aftermath

On 14 September 1901, Theodore Roosevelt was sworn in as president, at 42 the youngest man ever to hold the office of president.

William McKinley was buried at Westlawn Cemetery in Canton before his remains were transferred to the McKinley National Memorial in Canton in 1907. He left his entire estate, worth more than $200,000, to his wife.

Czolgosz was convicted and sentenced to death on 23 September 1901, in a trial that lasted just 8 hours and 26 minutes from jury selection to verdict. When doctors, who wanted to assess his sanity, examined him, he freely admitted, "I fully understood what I was doing when I shot the president." At the trial, he said just one word, "Guilty." As an anarchist, he did not recognize the authority of the court. Czolgosz was electrocuted by three jolts at 1700 volts each, on 29 October 1901, in Auburn prison, New York. His last words were "I killed the president because he was the enemy of the good people – the good working people. I am not sorry for my crime." As the prison guards strapped him into the chair, however, he did say through clenched teeth, "I am sorry I could not see my father." Sulphuric acid was poured over his corpse to speed up decomposition.

Franz Ferdinand (1863–1914)

The Victim

Franz Ferdinand Karl Ludwig Josef von Habsburg-Lothringen was born on 18 December 1863 at Graz, Austria, the eldest son of Archduke Karl Ludwig of Austria (1833–1896) (who was the younger brother of the Emperor Franz Joseph) and of his second wife, Princess Maria Annunciata (1843–1871) of the Two Sicilies. On 20 November 1875, Duke Francis V of Modena died and named Franz Ferdinand his heir, on condition that he added the name Este to his own. Eight years later, Franz Ferdinand joined the army as a third lieutenant. On 30 January 1889, he became the heir presumptive to the Austro-Hungarian throne when his cousin, Crown Prince Rudolf, committed suicide aged 40 at his hunting lodge in Mayerling (see box below).

On 1 July 1900, despite familial opposition, Franz Ferdinand married morganatically Countess Sophie Maria Josephina Albina Chotek von Chotkowa and they had four children. Meanwhile, in that same year, King Alexander of Serbia (born at Belgrade on 15 August 1876) was also facing opposition to his marriage plans. He had fallen for Draga Mashin, a widow some nine years older than him. When he went ahead and married her on 5 August 1900, he was disowned by his father, Milan IV, who died, it was said, of a broken heart a few months later, on 11 February 1901. Queen Draga tried her utmost to be a popular queen but was fighting a losing battle. A conspiracy was hatched to depose Alexander and Draga and place Peter Karageorgevitj (son of Prince Alexander Karageorgevitj who reigned 1841–1858) on the throne.

Alexander knew that his throne and likely his life were in danger and he did not know who to trust. On 10 June 1903 soldiers stormed the Royal Palace in Belgrade and, on finding the king and queen hiding in a room off their bedroom, shot them and slashed them with sabres. The bodies were then thrown out of the palace window and lay naked in the garden as the conspirators drank to the health of the new king. Over the course of the next ten years Serbia engaged in a number of disputes with its neighbours. In 1906, it fought a customs battle, known as the Pig War (pigs being the largest export) with Austria-Hungary. In 1908 Austria-Hungary annexed Bosnia-Herzegovina, to protests from Serbia. A climb-down from Serbia followed in March 1909. In 1912–1913 Serbia took Macedonia and Kosovo from the Ottoman Empire and Bulgaria. It was against this volatile background that Franz Ferdinand visited Bosnia in order to observe military manoeuvres at the invitation of General Oskar Potiorek, the governor of Bosnia, and to open a museum in Sarajevo.

Many living in Bosnia-Herzegovina wanted union with Serbia, rather than rule by Austria-Hungary. They saw in Franz Ferdinand someone who would maintain the status quo and prevent union. The visit was scheduled for 28 June 1914. The date was perceived as a further insult. It was the anniversary of the Battle of Kosovo (or Battle of Amselfeld) in 1389 in which the Turks conquered the old Serbian kingdom.

Date and Place of Assassination

28 June 1914, Franz Joseph Street, Sarajevo, Bosnia.

CROWN PRINCE RUDOLF

The death of Crown Prince Rudolf continues to elicit controversy. Officially, Rudolf died in a double suicide pact with his mistress, the 17-year-old Baroness Marie Vetsera, in Mayerling, the hunting lodge that he had bought in 1887. He shot her in the head and then himself. His father, Emperor Franz Joseph I, had Mayerling converted into a Carmelite nunnery after the deaths. In 1992, the remains of Marie Vetsera were stolen and when they were returned, an examination showed that there was no bullet-hole in her head. The case remains a mystery.

The archduke and archduchess in Sarajevo, photographed a few minutes before their deaths.

The Event

The perceived insult of the date, added to the negative view of Franz Ferdinand, made for a powder-keg of emotion. The Serbian Black Hand, a terrorist group, decided to assassinate him. However, the day turned out to be almost a comedy of errors, albeit with fatal results.

Black Hand leader Colonel Dragutin Dimitrijevic, the chief of the Intelligence Department of the Serbian General Staff, and his fellow conspirators Milan Ciganovic and Major Voja Tankosic, hired three young Black Hand gang members to kill Franz Ferdinand. They were Gavrilo Princip, Nedeljko Cabrinovic and Trifko Grabez. All three were suffering from tuberculosis and not expected to live much longer. Each of them was handed a pistol, two bombs and a phial of cyanide with which to commit suicide after the event.

The three arrived in Bosnia-Herzegovina and were met by six more assassins: Vaso Cubrilovic, Veljko Cubrilovic – a schoolboy, Danilo Ilic – a radical intellectual and the chief technical organizer, Misko Jovanovic, Muhamed Mehmedbasic – a Muslim carpenter, and Cvijetko Popovic – also still at school. Prior to the arrival of Franz Ferdinand at Sarajevo station, 35 agitators had been arrested and taken into custody. One hundred and twenty policemen were on crowd duty. There were also 70,000 Austro-Hungarian troops in Sarajevo, but they were confined to barracks. When the train pulled into the station, General Potiorek met Franz Ferdinand and his wife, Sophie. They joined a motorcade to the City Hall for an official reception.

Franz Ferdinand travelled in a 1911 Gräf & Stift Rois De Blougne tourer, which had the roof rolled back to allow the crowds a better view of the royal couple. Seven would-be assassins mingled with the crowd. The first opportunity fell to Muhamed Mehmedbasic who was by the Austro-Hungarian Bank, but he lost his nerve and stood watching the motorcade pass safely by. He was to later claim that a policeman stood near him and would have intervened had he produced his bomb.

THE MOTORCADE IN DETAIL

First car: Chief detective of Sarajevo and three local policemen.

Second car: Fehim Efendi Curcic, the mayor of Sarajevo and Dr Edmund Gerde, the commissioner of police.

Third car: Franz Ferdinand, his wife Sophie, Oskar Potiorek – governor of Bosnia, and Lieutenant-Colonel Count Franz von Harrach – Franz Ferdinand's bodyguard.

Fourth car: Baron Carl von Rumerskirch – head of Franz Ferdinand's military chancery, Countess Wilma Lanyus von Wellenberg – Sophie's lady-in-waiting, Lieutenant-Colonel Erich Edler von Merizzi – Potiorek's chief adjutant and Lieutenant-Colonel Count Alexander Boos-Waldeck.

Fifth car: Adolf Egger – director of Fiat Factory in Vienna, Major Paul Höger, Colonel Karl Bardolff and Dr Ferdinand Fischer.

Sixth car: Baron Andreas von Morsey, Captain Pilz and other members of Franz Ferdinand's staff and Bosnian officials.

Seventh car: Major Erich Ritter von Hüttenbrenner, Count Josef zu Erbach-Fürstenau and Lieutenant Robert Grein.

The second assassin was Vaso Cubrilovic, armed with a revolver and a bomb. He, too, did nothing. Nedeljko Cabrinovic was next and he threw his bomb. The chauffeur saw the bomb flying towards the car and put his foot on the accelerator. The bomb hit the roof of Franz Ferdinand's car and bounced off, exploding under the following car, wounding two of the occupants and 20 members of the crowd. Cabrinovic swallowed his cyanide pill and jumped into the Miljacka River. However, the cyanide did not work. The water at the point at which he jumped in the river was only 4 inches (10 centimetres) deep and four men jumped in after him and dragged him out. The crowd beat him before the police arrested him.

Some way further down the route Princip heard the explosion and, believing that the assassination had been a success, adjourned to a nearby café, Schiller's Delicatessen, to celebrate with a coffee and a sandwich.

The motorcade made it safely to the hall where the mayor, Fehim Efendi Curcic, gave a speech of welcome, only for Franz Ferdinand, understandably tense, to interrupt, "What is the good of your speeches? I come to Sarajevo on a visit, and I get bombs thrown at me. It is outrageous!" As the reception proceeded, Franz Ferdinand expressed his concern for the injured and insisted on going to the hospital to see them. Baron Andreas von Morsey advised against the visit, sensing that the danger had not completely passed. However, General Potiorek overruled him saying, "Do you think Sarajevo is full of assassins?" The general decided the party should travel along the Appel Quay, the city's central riverside road, to Sarajevo Hospital, but for some reason forgot to tell the driver, Franz Urban, of the change of plan. Urban drove into Franz Joseph Street before Potiorek spotted his mistake and shouted, "This is the wrong way! We're supposed to take the Appel Quay." By an absolute coincidence, the car was now in the street where Princip was in the café. As the driver began to reverse, Princip strode up to the car and fired his Belgian-made Fabrique Nationale M1910 semi-auto-

The police moved quickly to arrest suspects following the death of Franz Ferdinand.

matic pistol (serial number 19074) twice from less than 1 metre (1 yard) away. The first bullet hit Franz Ferdinand in the throat and severed his jugular vein; the second hit Sophie in the abdomen. Ferdinand called out, "Sopherl! Sopherl! Sterbe nicht! Bleibe am Leben für unsere Kinder!" ("Soferl! Soferl! Don't die! Live for my children!") Franz Urban drove them to the governor's mansion for medical attention. It was too late. Sophie died 15 minutes after being shot, the archduke shortly afterwards. At the scene, Princip turned the gun on himself, but was prevented from pulling the trigger by two bystanders, Ante Velic and Danilo Pusic. The police quickly arrived and, as with Cabrinovic, administered a

beating to Princip. Cabrinovic and Princip were tortured and gave the police the names of their fellow conspirators. Grabez, Vaso Cubrilovic, Veljko Cubrilovic, Ilic, Jovanovic and Popovic were all arrested and charged with treason and murder. Muhamed Mehmedbasic escaped to Serbia before he was taken into custody.

The Assassin

Gavrilo Princip was born in the village of Obljaj, near Bosansko Grahovo, Bosnia-Herzegovina, on 25 July 1894, the son of Marija and her husband, Peter, a postman. Princip was one of nine children, five sons and four daughters, six of whom died in infancy. Always in poor health, he contracted tuberculosis when he was a teenager. He was sent to live with an older brother in Sarajevo. Historians are divided on whether Princip was a member of the Black Hand, some believe he belonged to an organization called Young Bosnia. Young Bosnia was a group made up of Serbs, Croats and Bosnian Muslims, committed to the independence of the South Slavic peoples from Austria-Hungary. In February 1912, Princip was expelled from school for taking part in a demonstration against the Sarajevo authorities. He went to Belgrade in May 1912 where he tried to enrol in the First Belgrade Gymnasium but failed the entrance exam. That same year he attempted to join a Serbian guerrilla force under Serbian Major Vojislav Tankosic but was turned down because of his slight build.

Princip was tried in Sarajevo in 1915, found guilty and sentenced to the maximum of 20 years in prison. He died of tuberculosis of the bone on 28 April 1918 in Bohemia's Terezin prison.

The Aftermath

Europe in the summer of 1914 was a simmering cauldron waiting to boil over (see box below). In May of that year the American president, Woodrow Wilson, had sent Colonel Edward M. House, his personal envoy, to assess the situation and determine if war was likely or even inevitable. House had reported that "militarism [had] run stark mad … It only needs a spark to set the whole thing off." Princip's action was the spark that fuelled the First World War.

LEADERS ASSASSINATED

In the years between 1900 and 1913, 40 heads of state, politicians and diplomats were murdered, including four kings, six prime ministers and three presidents. In the Balkans alone there were eight assassinations.

The trial of the conspirators opened on 12 October 1914 at Sarajevo, before President of the Court Luigi von Curinaldi, who sat with no jury but was assisted by Bogdan Naumowicz and Dr Mayer Hoffmann. Murder was a capital offence but accessory to murder was not, so the charge was changed to high treason, which did carry the death sentence. The trial, conducted in Serbo-Croat, lasted 11 days and although nominally open to the public, seats were very difficult to come by – to view the proceedings required a special invitation. The verdicts were announced on 28 October with 16 defendants found guilty, none acquitted and five facing the death penalty. Two of those had their sentences commuted to life imprisonment. The three who did not, Danilo Ilic, Misko Jovanovic and Veljko Cubrilovic, were hanged on 3 February 1915.

Trifko Grabez, who had been born to a Serbian-Orthodox priest at Pale, a small town in Bosnia-Herzegovina, was sentenced to 20 years in prison. He died of tuberculosis in February 1918.

Nedeljko Cabrinovic was also sentenced to 20 years in prison. He died on 23 January 1916 of tuberculosis.

Vaso Cubrilovic, who had been born at Bosnia-Herzegovina in 1897, received a sentence of 16 years. He was released in November 1918 after the Allied victory and became a teacher in Sarajevo, then a university professor in Belgrade. After the Second World War, Vaso Cubrilovic served as Minister of Forests in Yugoslavia's government. He died in 1990.

Cvijetko Popovic was sent to prison for 13 years. He was also released in November 1918, whereupon he returned to teaching and eventually became the curator of the Ethnographic Department of the Sarajevo Museum.

After the First World War, Muhamed Mehmedbasic returned to Sarajevo. In 1919, he received a pardon for his role in the assassination. During the Second World War, he was killed by the Ustace (a Croatian organization founded in 1929 to create an independent Croatian state), in Sarajevo, on 29 May 1943.

The assassination of Franz Ferdinand led to the "war to end all wars" but just over 20 years later the world was at war again.

Under torture, the conspirators confessed that the plot to assassinate Franz Ferdinand had been organized by Dimitrijevic, Ciganovic and Tankosic. On 23 July 1914, the Austro-Hungarian government demanded that the Serbian authorities arrest the men and send them to face trial in Vienna. On 25 July, Nikola Pasic, the Serbian premier, told the Austro-Hungarian government that he was unable to hand over the three men as it "would be a violation of Serbia's Constitution and criminal in law". On 28 July the Austro-Hungarian Empire declared war on Serbia. The arms race of the previous decade had precipitated treaties and alliances. In consequence, countries began declaring war on each other, so that by the second week of August 1914, most of Europe was involved in a bloody conflict that would cost millions of lives and last for more than four years.

The Black Hand was officially disbanded and Dimitrijevic and several of his military colleagues were arrested. On 23 May 1917, Dimitrijevic was found guilty of treason and sentenced to death. A month later, he was executed by firing squad.

The bullet fired by Princip is stored as a museum exhibit in the Konopiste Castle near the town of Benesov, Czech Republic.

Princip's gun, Franz Ferdinand's car, his bloodstained light blue uniform and plumed cocked hat, and the chaise longue on which he was placed while being attended to by doctors, are kept as a permanent exhibit in the Museum of Military History, Vienna, Austria.

Oscar Potiorek, who was born on 20 November 1853, died on 17 December 1933.

After the war ended in 1918, Bosnia-Herzegovina became part of the new Kingdom of the Serbs, Croats and Slovenes. The kingdom was renamed Yugoslavia in 1929. In March 1992, Bosnia declared its independence from Yugoslavia.

Grigori Rasputin (1869–1916)

The Victim

On 21 January (Old Style Julian calendar) 1862, 22-year-old Anna Egorovna married Efim Aklovlevich Rasputin (the surname does not mean "the licentious one" as is often reported), a carter and farmer, two years her junior. Between 1862 and 1867 the couple had six daughters but all died in infancy. On 7 August (OS) 1867, a son Andrei, known as Mischa, was born. Two years later, another son, Grigori Efimovich was born on 10 January (OS) 1869 at Pokrovskoe, Tobolsk, western Siberia. Almost nothing is known about his childhood and early years. In August (OS) 1877, Mischa fell into a pond and young Grigori jumped in to to save him but both boys were pulled out by a passer-by. Mischa developed pneumonia and died. By some accounts, his sister, Maria, an epileptic, drowned in a river.

When Grigori was 18 he spent three months in a monastery but despite a later nickname of "The Mad Monk" never took holy orders. He married Praskovia Fyodorovna Dubrovina in 1889 and had three children with her, Dmitri (born at Pokrovskoe 1897, who was retarded), Maria (born at Pokrovskoe 26 March (OS) 1898) and Varvara (born at Pokrovskoe 1900). Another son, also called Dmitri, died aged just six months. In 1901, Grigori went on a pilgrimage to Greece and Jerusalem and two years later arrived at St Petersburg where he quickly gained a reputation as a mystic with healing powers.

On 30 July (OS) 1904, Alexei, the tsarevich, was born at Peterhof and, like many of Queen Victoria's descendants (his father the tsar, Nicholas II, was Victoria's grandson), was stricken with haemophilia. In 1905, Tsarina Alexandra, desperately fearful that her son would die, asked a friend to make contact with Rasputin whose reputation had even reached royal circles. From his home in Siberia Rasputin prayed for the boy and Alexei recovered. Each time the boy fell ill, the tsarina contacted Rasputin, and each time he "cured" the boy. Thus Rasputin's influence at court grew. He also used his position to indulge in inappropriate sexual behaviour (he is said to have raped a nun) knowing that the tsar's friendship protected him.

The Russian Orthodox Church regularly condemned Rasputin. On 29 June 1914, he was at Pokrovskoe visiting his family when Khionia Gusyeva stabbed him several times in the stomach. The attacker was a deformed (she was said to be noseless thanks to the effects of syphilis) former prostitute and a follower of Iliodor the monk, an ex-friend of Rasputin. His entrails spilled out and Gusyeva shouted, "I have killed the Antichrist." Rasputin lay near death for some time but survived thanks to rapid surgery. The event added to Rasputin's mystique and air of mystery, although his daughter said that her father was not the same after the attack; he tired quickly and often took opium to cope with the pain.

Rasputin was deeply opposed to war, both from a moral point of view and because he felt that it was likely to lead to political catastrophe. At that time, Rasputin's increasing drunkenness, sexual promiscuity, willingness to accept bribes in return for helping petitioners who flocked to his apartment and efforts to have his critics dismissed from their posts, made him appear increasingly cynical. The German tsarina was accused of being a spy and her friendship with Rasputin (was it more than mere friendship wondered her enemies with a lack of subtlety?) made her all the more cause for suspicion. Rasputin then claimed that he had a revelation that the Russian armies would not be successful until the tsar took command. Nicholas, who would have made a very good constitutional monarch but was not a natural autocrat, took control of his army. The consequences were awful for himself and for Russia. While the tsar was away at the Front, Rasputin's influence over Alexandra grew. He soon became her confidant and personal advisor. He also convinced her to fill some government offices with his own handpicked candidates. It was a recipe for disaster.

Rasputin's huge influence over the imperial family, particularly Tsarina Alexandra, was a reason cited for his assassination.

Date and Place of Assassination

16 December (OS) 1916, 94 Moika, Petrograd, Russia.

The Event

The facts of what happened on the night that Rasputin died, and why, are still in dispute more than 90 years after the event. According to one theory, Rasputin's influence on the imperial family, especially the tsarina, was becoming too great, and so it was decided he should die.

For many years the accepted story of the assassination was the one told by Prince Felix Yussopoff, even though he changed his tale on more than one occasion. It seems likely that Yussopoff collected Rasputin in a car from his home, Apartment 20, 64 Gorokhovaya Street, not long after midnight on the pretence that he would meet a beautiful Russian Romanov woman who was married to a homosexual transvestite. Yussopoff took Rasputin to the basement of 94 Moika, his luxury home where there were at least two women present. Also there, by his own later admission, were the Oxford-educated Lieutenant Oswald Rayner (born November 1888) and Captain (later Major) Stephen J. Alley (born 1876 at Krivo, a Yussopoff palace in Moscow, died 6 April 1969), British soldiers attached to the Secret Intelligence Service Station in St Petersburg.

Rayner and another soldier, Captain John Dymoke Scale (died at Battle, East Sussex, 22 April 1949), had met Yussopoff several times in the lead up to the assassination, a fact confirmed by the diary of their chauffeur, William Compton. According to Compton, "It is a little known fact that Rasputin was shot not by a Russian but by an Englishman." Back in the cellar Rasputin was offered cakes and red wine liberally laced with cyanide. (In the autopsy, Professor Kossorotov revealed that Rasputin had not eaten immediately prior to his death.) To the assassins' horror, Rasputin refused the poisoned treats. It now seems probable that an attempt was made to beat him to death as the autopsy shows that, among other injuries, the right eye was detached from its socket, the genitals had been crushed, there was a gaping wound in the back and the right ear was almost ripped off. Assuming Rasputin was dead, the assassins carried him outside, or he may have attempted to escape as they went upstairs. He groaned and was put into a sitting position against a snowdrift and was shot twice. The body was wrapped in a cloth and carried to a waiting car. As the assassins made for the car, Rasputin made a noise, alerting them to the fact that he was still alive. He was placed on the ground and shot through the forehead, killing him instantly.

The autopsy by Professor Kossorotov reported that the three bullets were of different calibres. The bullet that finally killed him was reported to be a Webley .455 inch unjacketed round. Rasputin was taken to the icy River Neva and thrown in. The only man present at the killing who owned a Webley was Oswald Rayner. At a later meeting between the tsar and the British ambassador, Sir George Buchanan, Nicholas said he believed Rayner was Rasputin's assassin. Rayner burned all his papers before his death from cancer at Oxford on 6 March 1961. His only son, John Felix Hamilton Rayner (born 1 February 1924), who was named after Oswald Rayner's school and

---

THE BRITISH SOLDIERS

It is thought that the British soldiers were there to make sure the assassination went as planned, not to play a major role in it. Intelligence reports from St Petersburg at the time show that the British were concerned that Rasputin was using his influence to replace pro-British ministers in the Russian government and his apparent insistence on withdrawing Russian troops from the battlefield. If this had been allowed the Germans would have moved their troops from the Eastern Front to the Western one, where they would have outnumbered the Allies and probably won the conflict.

Prince Felix Yussopoff and wife Irina.

university friend Yussopoff, died four years later, aged just 41.

That the assassination had not gone quite to plan is hinted at in a letter that Alley wrote to Scale eight days after the murder, "Although matters here have not proceeded entirely to plan, our objective has clearly been achieved … a few awkward questions have already been asked about wider involvement. Rayner is attending to loose ends and will no doubt brief you."

At 8.40am on Monday 19 December (OS) Rasputin's body was retrieved from the river. The corpse took two days to thaw sufficiently for a post-mortem to be performed. The face was black and the eyes and nose swollen. The legs, from the knees down, were tied in a sack but the arms were free and bent at the elbows as if clawing for air.

The Assassins

A conspiracy existed to kill Rasputin; the plotters included Prince Felix Yussopoff, the British Army officers and Grand Duke Dmitri Pavlovich. Pavlovich (died Davos, Switzerland 5 March 1941) was one of the few Romanovs to escape the 1917 Revolution alive. His life was saved because he was sent to the Persian front for his part in Rasputin's murder and thus escaped the Bolshevik killers. Little is known of the other murderers, Lieutenant Sergei Sukhotin (died Paris June 1939), Vladimir Purishkevich (died 1920) and Stanislaus Lazovert (died Paris 1934).

The Aftermath

No one was charged with the murder of Rasputin. Tsar Nicholas exiled Yussopoff to Kursk and Grand Duke Dmitri Pavlovich to Persia. The tsarina arranged for Rasputin's body to be buried in the ground of Tsarkoye Selo at 8.30am on 21 December (OS). Following the February Revolution, his body was dug up and burned in a nearby wood. Another long-standing story has it that

Rasputin foresaw his own death. Not long before his assassination, Rasputin is supposed to have written:

I write and leave behind me this letter at St Petersburg. I feel that I shall leave life before January 1. I wish to make known to the Russian people, to Papa, to the Russian Mother and to the Children, to the land of Russia, what they must understand. If I am killed by common assassins, and especially by my brothers the Russian peasants, you, Tsar of Russia, will have nothing to fear for your children, they will reign for hundreds of years in Russia. But if I am murdered by boyars, nobles, and if they shed my blood, their hands will remain soiled with my blood, for twenty-five years they will not wash their hands from my blood. They will leave Russia. Brothers will kill brothers, and they will kill each other and hate each other, and for twenty-five years there will be no nobles in the country. Tsar of the land of Russia, if you hear the sound of the bell which will tell you that Grigori has been killed, you must know this: if it was your relations who have wrought my death, then no one in the family, that is to say, none of your children or relations, will remain alive for more than two years. They will be killed by the Russian people. I go, and I feel in me the divine command to tell the Russian Tsar how he must live if I have disappeared. You must reflect and act prudently. Think of your safety and tell your relations that I have paid for them with my blood. I shall be killed. I am no longer among the living. Pray, pray, be strong, think of your blessed family. Grigori.

However, the original letter has never been found (if indeed it ever existed) and scholars point to its startling lack of similarities with Rasputin's known writings.

In February 1917, the first revolution of the year took place and with Nicholas at the front he was unable to influence events at home. On 2 March (OS) he abdicated. The following month the revolutionary Lenin arrived in Petrograd from Switzerland, aboard a sealed train. The popularity of the Bolsheviks increased exponentially. The Provisional Government under Alexander Kerensky put the Romanovs under house arrest in the Alexander Palace at Tsarskoe Selo, 15 miles (24 kilometres) south of Petrograd. In August, Nicholas and his family were evacuated to the Urals for their own safety. On 25 October (OS) 1917, Lenin led his Bolsheviks in an uprising against the Provisional Government. Many of the revolutionaries called for Nicholas to be put on trial. In April 1918, the Romanovs were taken to the House of Special Purpose in Ekaterinburg. At 2.33am on 17 July (New Style Gregorian calendar), Nicholas, Alexandra, Alexei the 13-year-old tsarevich, their four daughters – Olga (22), Tatiana (21), Maria (19) and Anastasia (17), their doctor – Yevgeny Botkin (53), and three servants – footman Alexei Trupp (60), cook Ivan Kharitonov (46) and Alexandra's maid Anna Demidova (40), were taken into the basement and executed. Despite many rumours to the contrary that have surfaced over the years, no member of the immediate imperial family survived the night in the cellar.

SAINTS

In 1981 Nicholas, his slain family and servants were canonized as saints by the Russian Orthodox Church Outside Russia as martyrs. In fact, Alexei Trupp was a Roman Catholic. Nineteen years later, on 14 August 2000, the Romanov family was canonized by the synod of the Russian Orthodox Church. They were not named martyrs as their deaths did not result from their Christian faith; instead they were canonized as passion bearers.

Tsar Nicholas, seated with his wife Tsarina Alexandra Fyodorovna and surrounded by their children (clockwise, from left) Maria, Olga, Tatiana, Anastasia and Alexei, referred to Rasputin as "our friend".

In 1932 MGM released the film *Rasputin and the Empress*. Although the studio changed the names of the protagonists, Yussopoff was easily identifiable as Chegodieff and the film claimed that Rasputin had slept with his wife Irina (called Natasha in the movie) – they had never met – so Yussopoff sued for libel. On 27 February 1934, the Yussopoffs' libel case opened in London. In March they won their suit and were awarded £25,000 and the character of Natasha was cut from future releases. In 1965, Yussopoff again sued for libel (over a CBS television programme) but this time he lost the case. He died in Paris on 27 September 1967. He was 80.

After the October Revolution, Rasputin's daughter Maria left Russia for France and then America. She worked as a dancer and then a tiger trainer in a circus. She wrote a biography of her father, but it is not regarded as a reliable source. She died in Los Angeles, California in September 1977.

One of the more unusual aspects of the aftermath concerns Rasputin's penis. It was said that Yussopoff was bisexual and sexually abused Rasputin during the assassination. Another assassin is said to have castrated Rasputin. A servant supposedly collected the severed member and gave it to a maid who apparently kept the organ which looked "like a blackened, overripe banana, about a foot long" in a wooden box. In 2004, Igor Knyazkin, the chief of the prostate research centre of the Russian Academy of Natural Sciences, announced that he was opening a Russian museum of erotica and claimed that he would exhibit Rasputin's penis. It is not known whether the genitalia is actually that of Rasputin.

Leon Trotsky (1879–1940)

The Victim

One of the leading forces in the Russian Revolution, Leon Trotsky was born as Lev Davidovich Bronstein on 26 October (Old Style Julian calendar) 1879 at Yanovka, Kherson Province, Russia. He was the fifth child of a wealthy, yet illiterate, Jewish farmer, David Leontyevich Bronstein (1847–1922) and Anna Bronstein (died 1910).

In 1888, he was sent to school in Odessa. Eight years later, he became a revolutionary, later turning to Marxism. In 1897, he organized the South Russian Workers' Union in Nikolayev proselytizing students and factory workers to Marxism. The following year, in January 1898, Trotsky, and 200 other members of the union, were arrested; he spent the next two years in jail awaiting trial. In March of that year, the inaugural congress of the Russian Social Democratic Labour Party was held. While he was in prison he married Alexandra Sokolovskaya (1872–c. 1938), a fellow Marxist, and began to study philosophy. In 1900, he was sent into exile for four years, in Ust-Kut and Verkholensk in the Irkutsk region of Siberia. It was there that his daughters, Zinaida (born 1901) and Nina (born 1902), were born.

In the summer of the year his second daughter was born, Trotsky fled, hidden in a lorry of hay, from Siberia to London, where he became a writer on the newspaper *Iskra* (*Spark*). Towards the end of 1902, he met Natalia Sedova whom he married in 1903. They had two sons: Leon (born February 1906) and Sergei (born 1908). The editorial board of *Iskra* was divided into two camps: the "old guard" led by Georgy Plekhanov and the "new guard" led by V. I. Lenin and Julius Martov. The new guard then split into the Bolsheviks (the majority) led by Lenin and the Mensheviks (the minority) by Martov. It was assumed that Trotsky would side with Lenin but that was not the case and he aligned himself with the Menshevik faction of the Russian Social Democratic Labour Party. The alliance only lasted a year but Trotsky spent the next ten years attempting to unite the two factions.

On Sunday 9 January (OS) 1905, a Russian Orthodox priest named George Gapon led a gathering of working class people to protest to the tsar. Tsarist troops opened fire on the demonstrators and around 1,000 people died. In the October 1905 revolution, Trotsky became the leader of the St Petersburg Soviet of Workers' Deputies, the first democratic institution ever seen in Russia. The Soviet lasted for 50 days and on 2 December, Trotsky and other Soviet leaders were arrested and put on trial. He was convicted and sentenced to deportation. On his way to Siberia, Trotsky again escaped and once more surfaced in London before settling in Vienna. In October 1908, Trotsky founded and co-edited a bi-weekly newspaper called *Pravda*, which ran until April 1912.

At the outbreak of the First World War, Trotsky fled Vienna to avoid internment. Lenin and Trotsky were opposed to the war but many Bolsheviks and Mensheviks supported the Russian government. On 19 November 1914, Trotsky moved to France where he worked as a war reporter for *Kievskaya Mysl*. In September 1915, he was a delegate at the Zimmerwald Conference of anti-war socialists. A year later in October 1916, France deported Trotsky because of his anti-war stance. Spain refused to let him stay and on Christmas Day 1916 he was sent to America, landing in New York on 13 January 1917.

Trotsky was still in America when Tsar Nicholas II abdicated on 2 March (OS) 1917. On 4 May, he arrived in Russia but did not join the Bolsheviks immediately. After he finally joined, he was arrested on 7 August (New Style Julian calendar) after a failed uprising in Petrograd and spent 40 days in prison. After the 7 November (NS) revolution, Trotsky was second only to Lenin in the Bolshevik hierarchy. The new Soviet Union legalized homosexuality and abortion, abolished the concept of illegitimacy, opened more libraries, got rid of university tuition fees and gave women the vote and equal pay. Trotsky's first official job was as commissar of foreign affairs and he negotiated a peace treaty with Germany.

Leon Trotsky's reputation has not been rehabilitated in Russia, unlike many of those who suffered or died in the Stalin purges.

On 13 March 1918, he resigned and became commissar of war and head of the Red Army.

His troops defeated the White Army but this was not good enough for some of the top ranking Bolsheviks who heavily criticized him. In 1920–1921, Lenin and Trotsky's political and personal differences again came to the surface. Although the Reds had won the civil war the country was in a state of economic collapse. In the mêlée, the people who prospered were the state officials – the bureaucracy. Both Lenin and Trotsky were worried by the rise of this officialdom and both railed against it, but its rise was encouraged by one man: Joseph Stalin, the General Secretary of the Central Committee. When Lenin's health began to fail, Stalin formed a pact with Gregori Zinoviev and Lev Kamenev to ensure that Trotsky did not succeed Lenin. The trio offered Trotsky a number of low influence jobs knowing that he would refuse them so they could use them as an excuse to oust

him. Lenin spent his last months trying to ensure that Stalin did not succeed him and in his political testament he advised that Stalin should be removed from power.

However, at the 12th Communist Party Congress in April 1923, as Lenin lay ill, the keynote speech was delivered by Stalin, not the nominal deputy leader Trotsky. In 1923, Trotsky formed the Left Opposition to combat the Stalinism that was sweeping the Soviet Union. After the 14th Congress, Trotsky was on holiday in the Caucasus when he learned of Lenin's death on 21 January 1924. Stalin stage-managed Lenin's funeral and positioned himself as the true heir, much to the dismay of Lenin's widow. Infighting was rife in the party afterwards with alliances being made and broken. Stalin used the secret police to undermine his political opponents.

Despite their apparent easy manner, there was a *froideur* between Lenin (left) and Stalin (right) and the former did his best to ensure that the "Man of Steel" did not succeed him.

In 1926, Trotsky, Zinoviev and Kamenev formed the United Opposition. In October 1927, Trotsky and Zinoviev were expelled from the Central Committee. On 12 November, the two men were expelled from the Communist Party. On 31 January 1928, Trotsky was exiled to Alma Ata in Kazakhstan and in February 1929 expelled from the Soviet Union, along with his wife, Natalia Sedova, and son, Leon. He spent four years in Turkey before the French prime minister, Edouard Daladier, offered Trotsky political asylum in France in 1933, but after two years it was suggested that he find a home elsewhere and he moved to Norway. In 1937, he was placed under house arrest, thought to be at the behest of the Soviet Union. He moved to Mexico at the invitation of the painter Diego Rivera.

Date and Place of Assassination

21 August 1940, Viena 45, Coyoacán, Mexico.

The Event

When Stalin fell out with someone, he arranged for them to be killed. He even arranged for an attempt to be made on the life of the actor John Wayne because of "The Duke"'s hatred of communism. Stalin announced that Trotsky and Zinoviev had plotted to have him (Stalin) killed. He ordered Trotsky's assassination. In 1939, Trotsky had moved into Coyoacán, a suburb of Mexico City. At 4am on 24 May 1940, Stalinist agent Iosif Romualdovich Grigulevich, aided by David Alfaro Siqueiros, Vittorio Vidale and 17 other men, attacked Trotsky's house, riddling the building with hundreds of bullets. Although Trotsky survived, a bodyguard and an American visitor were killed. (In later life Grigulevich became a respected historian and his secret life as a spy was not revealed until after his death on 2 June 1988.)

In the summer of 1940, Trotsky met a man calling himself Jacques Mornard who was the lover of Sylvia Ageloff, one of Trotsky's followers. Mornard claimed to be interested in Trotsky's political ideas and the two men had many long conversations. On 20 August 1940, Trotsky invited Mornard for tea and because he was a guest, Trotsky's bodyguards did not search him nor did they think it odd that he was wearing a raincoat in the heat of summer. These were to be fatal mistakes. Without warning, Mornard pulled an ice pick and thrust it into Trotsky's skull, his right shoulder and right knee. The attack was not immediately fatal and when Trotsky's bodyguards heard the commotion, they rushed to their boss's aide. Trotsky, still conscious, called out, "Do not kill him! This man has a story to tell." The former Soviet official was taken to hospital where he lingered for a day before dying, aged 61. According to James P. Cannon, the secretary of the Socialist Workers' Party (USA), Trotsky's last words were, "I will not survive this attack. Stalin has finally accomplished the task he attempted unsuccessfully before."

ANIMAL FARM

Trotsky was the basis for the character of Snowball in George Orwell's allegoric *Animal Farm* (published on 17 August 1945). The other characters were Napoleon (Stalin), Mr Jones (Tsar Nicholas II), Mr Frederick (Hitler), Squealer (Molotov), Mr Pilkington (the UK and the USA), Mr Whymper (George Bernard Shaw), Minimus (Gorky), Old Major (Lenin and Marx), Moses (the Russian Orthodox Church) and the rebel pigs (Bukharin, Rykov, Zinoviev and Kamenev).

The Assassin

Jaume Ramón Mercader del Rio Hernández was born on 7 February 1914 in Barcelona, Spain. He was raised mainly in France after his parents, Eustacia María Caridad del Río Hernández and Don Pablo Mercader Marina split up. He embraced Communism while still young and was briefly imprisoned for his activities. His mother became a Soviet agent and it was not long before he followed her lead, with the codename "Gnome".

In October 1939, Mercader arrived in Mexico on a fake passport in the name of Frank Jacson, a Canadian. When he was arrested for Trotsky's murder, he insisted his name was Jacques Mornard and his real name did not emerge until 20 August 1953.

The Aftermath

Trotsky's house in Coyoacán is now a museum and is maintained much as it was on the day of the assassination. His grave is in the museum grounds.

Unlike many of the Soviet politicians who died under Stalin, Trotsky's reputation was never formally rehabilitated, although Mikhail Gorbachev did call him "a hero and martyr" in 1987. That year, he featured on a commemorative postage stamp. Trotsky's books were banned until 1987 and have been published in Russian since 1989.

Mercader's trial technically began on 22 August 1940, 48 hours after the arrest, in Mexico City. Three judges heard the case and there was no jury. On 16 April 1943, Mercader was convicted of the murder of Trotsky and sentenced to 20 years in prison – 19 years and 6 months for premeditated murder and 6 months for illegally carrying a weapon. He was released from Mexico City's Palacio de Lecumberri prison on 6 May 1960 and moved to Havana. In 1961, he relocated to the Soviet Union where he became one of only 21 non-Soviet citizens to receive the Hero of the Soviet Union medal. He died at Havana on 18 October 1978 and is buried (under the name of Ramón Ivanovich López) in Kuntsevo Cemetery, Moscow.

Adolf Hitler (1889–1945)

The Victim

Adolf Hitler was born in the Gasthof zum Ponner at Branau-am-inn, Austria, at 6.30pm on Saturday 20 April 1889, the third son and fourth child of six of Alois Hitler. Hitler's mother was Klara Pozl, Alois's third wife. Despite propaganda, his name was never Schicklgruber. Alois Hitler had changed the family name on 6 January 1877, and he was never a house-painter. On 22 May 1904, Hitler was confirmed a Catholic. He left school at 16 with no qualifications. From 1905, he lived a bohemian life on an orphan's pension and support from his mother. He was rejected by the Academy of Fine Arts in Vienna in October 1907 due to "unfitness for painting" but was told he had talent as an architect. After his mother's death, Hitler worked as an artist in Vienna. After a second rejection from the Academy of Fine Arts in Vienna in October 1908, he became a down-and-out and lived in a homeless shelter.

On 16 August 1914, he enlisted in the Bavarian army. During the First World War, he served in Belgium and France. Hitler was twice decorated for bravery. He received the Iron Cross, Second Class, on 2 December 1914 and the Iron Cross, First Class, on 4 August 1918. Five months earlier, in March 1918, the last major offensive of the First World War began at the village of La Fère on the Oise River in France. The Germans outnumbered the Allies by ten to one. A young British adjutant rallied his troops against the bombardment. On the other side, a German corporal with an Iron Cross, Second Class, was determined to win the battle for his side. The two men met again in February 1934 at a banquet in Berlin. Anthony Eden, for that was the British adjutant, wrote in his memoirs, "It emerged we must have been opposite each other … Together we drew a map on the back of a dinner card, which I still have, signed by both of us, Hitler marking in some places and I in others. The corporal on the German side had as clear a recollection of place names and dispositions as the young staff officer, as I had then just become, on the British."

On 11 November 1918, Hitler cried on hearing that Germany had lost the First World War. (It was said that he only ever wept twice. The other occasion was over the grave of his mother. She died of breast cancer on 21 December 1907.) At the Battle of Ypres on 15 October, he had been temporarily blinded by a British chlorine gas attack. As Hitler lay in a field hospital, he recalled, "I stumbled back with burning eyes, taking with me my last report of the war. A few hours later, my eyes had turned to burning coals; it had grown dark around me." The defeat of his country lit a fire in Hitler. "In these nights hatred grew in me, hatred for those responsible for this deed… Miserable and degenerate criminals! The more I tried to achieve clarity on the monstrous event of this hour, the more the shame of indignation and disgrace burned my brow. What was the pain in my eyes compared to this misery?" Hitler became an obsessive believer in the Dolchstoßlegende ("dagger-stab" or "stab in the back legend"), which claimed that the army, "undefeated in the field", had been "stabbed in the back" by civilian leaders and Marxists back on the home front. These politicians were later called the November Criminals, although the Treaty of Versailles (21 June 1919) left them with very little choice.

In March 1920, Hitler was demobbed and became active in the German Workers' Party. The following year, he began speaking out against the Treaty of Versailles. His polemics criticized Jews, Marxists and other politicians. His fame, or rather notoriety, grew, and the party hierarchy attempted to dilute his power by making an alliance with a group of socialists from Augsburg. On 11 July 1921, Hitler resigned from the party knowing that his popularity meant that the party would collapse without him. When he was asked to return, he agreed but on his own terms, and those terms basically meant that he was in charge. Party members balloted on the decision and Hitler won 543 votes with just one dissenter. On 29 July 1921, at the next meeting, Hitler was introduced as *führer* of the National Socialist Party,

the first time that title was used publicly. Hitler then changed the name of the party to the Nationalsozialistische Deutsche Arbeiterpartei (National Socialist German Workers Party).

On Thursday 8 November 1923, Hitler awoke with a sore head and a toothache but refused aides' suggestions that he see a doctor and dentist, saying that he was too busy. Later that day, he attempted to seize power in the Munich "Beer Hall Putsch". Around 3,000 Germans gathered in the Bürgerbräukeller, a Munich beer hall, to listen to a speech by Gustav Ritter von Kahr, the state commissioner of Bavaria. At 8.30pm, as von Kahr spoke, around 600 storm troopers surrounded the hall. Hitler walked up the aisle of the hall and jumped on a chair. He fired a shot in the air and shouted, "The national revolution has broken out. The Bavarian government and the government at Berlin are hereby deposed. A new government will be formed at once." Hitler took von Kahr and other dignitaries into a side room and told them that he and the war hero General Erich Ludendorff would form a new administration. Ludendorff appeared at the hall to cheers at 11pm.

Early the next morning, Hitler began to realise that his plot may not have been successful. At 11am, with Ludendorff, Hermann Goering and Julius Streicher, he began a demonstration towards the centre of Munich. When the 3,000 or so protesters reached their

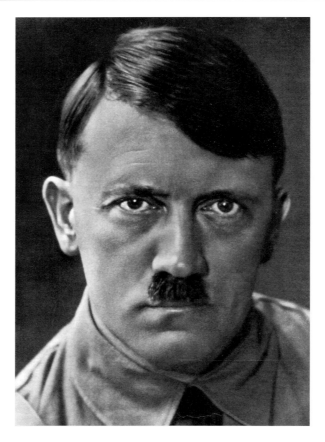

Hitler was careful to present an idealized image of himself as this flatteringly lit photograph exemplifies.

destination, 100 armed policemen met them at 12.20pm. Hitler ordered the police to lay down their weapons. They responded by opening fire. In seconds, 16 Nazis (to whom he dedicated *Mein Kampf*) and three policemen were dead. Goering was shot in the thigh and Hitler fled in a car. Three days after the putsch, he was arrested and charged with treason. He was taken to Landsberg prison fortress where he briefly went on hunger strike.

On 26 February 1924, the trial of Hitler and ten others, including Ludendorff, opened in a lecture hall at the Infantry Officer's School in Munich. Chief Justice Georg Neithardt presided with a panel of two professional and three lay judges. Virtually all the judges had sympathy for Hitler and the other defendants and Hitler began to swing public and media opinion his way. By the time closing arguments were made on 27 March, millions of Germans supported Hitler. The verdict was delivered on April Fool's Day, 1924. Ludendorff, unsurprisingly, was acquitted but the others were found guilty. Hitler was sentenced to five years in prison, with the possibility of parole after six months.

While in Landsberg, he feasted on the many boxes of chocolates sent to him by his female admirers. He also dictated (his amanuensis was Rudolf Hess) the ponderously prolix *Mein Kampf* (volume one was published on 18 July 1925 and a second volume, in which he expanded his views in three more chapters, appeared two years later) in which he outlined his beliefs on race: "It is never by war that nations are ruined, but by the loss of their powers of resistance, which are exclusively a characteristic of pure racial blood. In this world, everything that is not of sound racial stock is like chaff"; and his anti-Semitism: "One cannot be surprised if in the imagination of our people the Jew is pictured as the incarnation of Satan and the symbol of evil"; and propaganda: "The broad masses of a nation are always more easily corrupted in the deeper strata of their emotional nature than consciously or voluntarily, and thus in the primitive simplicity of their minds they more readily fall victims to the big lie than the small lie." He served nine months and was released as part of a general amnesty for political prisoners on 20 December 1924.

Out of jail, Hitler spent time rallying his party. In the December 1924 election, the Nazis garnered just over 907,300 votes and won 14 seats. On New Year's Eve 1924, Hitler was invited to a party at the home of the photographer Heinrich Hoffman. It took some persuasion for Hitler to accept, but finally he agreed to attend. However, a pretty girl manoeuvred him under the mistletoe whereupon she kissed him. Hitler shook with absolute fury before storming out of the gathering. In the May 1928 elections, the Nazis' share of the votes and seats dropped. In September 1930, after the financial crisis, they rose again and won 107 seats. There were two elections in 1932 – one in July and another in November – and the Nazis won 230 and 196 seats respectively. That year, Hitler wrote to Benito Mussolini to ask for an autographed picture but received a reply via their embassy in Berlin from the Italian foreign office: "Please thank the above-named gentleman for his sentiment and tell him in whatever terms you think best that the Duce does not think fit to accede to his request."

Hitler had intended to challenge President Paul von Hindenburg but was unable to because he was not a German citizen. This was rectified on 25 February 1932. His campaign was called "Hitler über Deutschland" (Hitler over Germany). He lost to Hindenburg, but established himself as a viable alternative. Despite losing some seats in the second election, the Nazis remained the largest party in the Reichstag. Hindenburg appointed the nobleman Franz von Papen as chancellor, but Hitler demanded that he, as the leader of the largest party, should hold that position. When von Papen resigned, Hindenburg turned to General Kurt von Schleicher but he was unable to form an administration.

On 30 January 1933, Hitler became Chancellor and began meeting other world leaders. Their opinions of him were mixed. American president, Herbert Hoover, said that Hitler was "forceful, highly intelligent, had a remarkable and accurate memory, a wider range of information, and a capacity for lucid exposition… From his clothing and hairdo he was obviously a great deal of an exhibitionist. He seemed to have trigger spots in his mind which, when touched, set him off like a man in a furious anger." Anthony Eden recalled in his memoirs *Facing the Dictators* (1962), "I was most unfavourably impressed with Hitler's personality. Unlike Stalin as I was to know him, or Mussolini, he appeared negative to me, certainly not compelling; he was also rather shifty. Stalin and Mussolini were, in their separate ways, men whose personality could be felt in any company. Hitler was essentially the man who could pass in the crowd." In 1936, the former British prime minister, David Lloyd George, met Hitler at Obersalsburg and hailed him as a

WEALTHY AUTHOR

Mein Kampf sold 9,473 copies in 1925, but when Hitler came to power eight years later, sales leapt to more than a million. Royalties made him Germany's wealthiest author. By 1940 more than six million copies had been sold in Germany.

"great man". Lord Halifax, the man many Conservatives wanted to be prime minister instead of Churchill on the resignation of Neville Chamberlain in May 1940, mistook Hitler for a footman on a visit to Berchtesgaden in 1937. Chamberlain found him to be "the commonest little dog" yet wrote to his sister, "I get the impression that here was a man who could be relied upon when he had given his word." The Duke of Windsor said, "His eyes were piercing and magnetic. I confess frankly that he took me in. I believed him when he implied that he sought no war with Britain." – he had sent a telegram to Hitler in August 1939 appealing for peace. Harold Macmillan wrote, "The British people found it difficult to take Hitler too seriously with his Charlie Chaplin moustache and his everlasting raincoat. Naturally, nobody read *Mein Kampf*. Nor could anybody see below the apparent insignificance of his appearance the deep, cunning, malignant brain."

At 10pm on 27 February 1933, the authorities were informed that the Reichstag was on fire. By 11.30pm, the conflagration had been extinguished. German police arrested a Dutch communist, Marinus van der Lubbe, who claimed that he alone had started the fire. Later, four other men, Ernst Torgler, and three Bulgarian communists Georgi M. Dimitrov, Blagoi Popov and Vasily Tanev were also taken into custody. Their trial began at Leipzig at 8.45am on 21 September and ended on 21 December 1933. Van der Lubbe, a 24-year-old, was brought into the courtroom in chains, while the other four defendants were unfettered. When the verdict was delivered, van der Lubbe was found guilty of high treason, insurrectionary arson and attempted common arson. The other four men were acquitted. Marinus van der Lubbe was beheaded in a Leipzig prison yard on 10 January 1934, three days before his 25th birthday. (In 1981, a West Berlin court posthumously overturned the 1933 verdict and declared him not guilty.) Seventy years on, historians are still debating the origins of the Reichstag fire. Some, including Alan Bullock and William

L. Shirer, believe that despite the court case, the Nazis burned down the parliament building so that Hitler could consolidate his hold on power. However, Fritz Tobias wrote a detailed account of the event, which came to the conclusion that van der Lubbe *was* the sole arsonist. Yet in June 1931, Hitler had given an interview to Richard Breitling, the editor of *Leipziger Neueste Nachrichten*, giving two reasons in favour of burning down the building. The first was aesthetic and the second was because the Reichstag represented the degenerate bourgeoisie and the deluded working class.

In March 1935, Hitler violated the Treaty of Versailles by reintroducing conscription in Germany, building a massive military machine, including a new navy and an air force. In March 1936, Hitler again violated the treaty by reoccupying the demilitarized zone in the Rhineland. Hitler kept a careful eye on Britain and France and was emboldened when they did nothing. On 25 October 1936, Hitler formed an alliance with Mussolini. On 27 April 1937, German planes bombed Guernica in support of General Franco. On 5 November 1937, at the Reich Chancellory, Adolf Hitler held a secret meeting, the Hossbach Conference, and stated his plans for acquiring *lebensraum* ("living space") for the German people. On 12 March 1938, German troops entered Austria, the Anschluss. On 26 September 1938, Hitler announced that the Sudetenland was Germany's last acquisition in Europe. Three days later, Hitler, Mussolini, Chamberlain and Edouard Daladier of France signed the Munich Agreement agreeing to German occupation of the Sudetenland. A month later, on 28 October, the first Polish Jews were deported from the Third Reich. On 9 November, Kristallnacht, mobs attacked 1,574 synagogues and 8,000 Jewish businesses. Thirty thousand Jews were arrested and taken to concentration camps. On 4 July 1939, German Jews were denied the right to hold government jobs. Seventeen days later, Adolf Eichmann was appointed director of the Prague Office of Jewish Emigration. On 1 September 1939, Germany invaded Poland.

From the time he became German Chancellor in January 1933, there were many plots against Hitler (see box on page 64), but only two ever came close to success – one on 8 November 1939 (see below) and a second on 20 July 1944 (see pages 64–68).

THE BÜRGERBRÄUKELLER ATTEMPT

Date and Place of Attempted Assassination

8 November 1939, Bürgerbräukeller, Munich, Germany.

The Event

Every 8 November Hitler gave a speech in the Bürgerbräukeller where the Munich Putsch had occurred. In 1939, because of the outbreak of war, Hitler decided to cancel the speech. Then he changed his mind, but announced that he would need to return to Berlin that same night. Hitler intended to fly to Munich, but it was foggy that night, so he travelled by train. It meant that he would have to leave the Bürgerbräukeller early. It was his habit to speak from 8:30–10pm and then stay behind to drink and reminisce with his colleagues. That night he began to speak at 8:10pm before a backdrop of huge swastikas. He gave a sarcastic speech about the British, which delighted the party faithful. At 9.20pm, 13 minutes after Hitler had left, a bomb exploded behind the speaker's stand and killed eight Germans and wounded 63 others, 16 seriously.

Hitler believed that the British Secret Service was behind the attempt but others were unsure. Many thought that it, like the Reichstag fire, was a Nazi invention. Fingers were pointed at Heinrich Himmler, the leader of the SS, and Reinhard Heydrich (see pages 86–91). However, investigations showed it was a genuine attempt. By fluke, Johann Georg Elser had been arrested 35 minutes before the bomb went off.

The customs border police in Konstanz had been suspicious when he tried to cross the border into Switzerland and stopped him. In his coat were pictures of the Bürgerbräukeller and he was taken to Munich, where the Gestapo interrogated him. Elser denied all knowledge of the assassination attempt, but when the evidence against him mounted he confessed. Himmler did not believe that Elser had acted alone and tortured him to find his accomplices.

The Would-be Assassin

Johann Georg Elser was born on 4 January 1903 in Hermaringen, Württemberg, the illegitimate son of Ludwig Elser and Maria Müller. In 1910 he began schooling in Königsbronn. Seven years later, on leaving school, he became a lathe operator apprentice but ill health forced him to choose another career. He became a carpenter in 1922. For four years from 1925, he worked in a watch factory in Konstanz where he learned the skills he would use in the assassination attempt. In 1928, he joined the Red Front Fighters' Association, a militant organisation affiliated with the Communist Party. In 1929, he moved to Switzerland where he worked as a carpenter. In 1930, his girlfriend Mathilde Niedermann gave birth to his son Manfred, but Elser left her soon afterwards. Two years later, he returned to Königsbronn and in 1936 he began work in a fitting factory in Heidenheim.

After Hitler came to power, Elser refused to raise his right arm in salute and would not listen to Hitler's radio speeches. He was opposed to the curtailing of religious freedoms and the legislation introduced by the Nazis, especially their total control of the educational system. On 8 November 1938, Elser travelled to Munich to listen to Hitler at the Bürgerbräukeller. What he heard that night solidified his view that Hitler must die and the night of the Bürgerbräukeller would be the perfect night to commit the act. In October 1939, Elser went back to Munich and began to patronize the Bürgerbräukeller every night for a month. He hid as last orders were called and the venue was closed and, in the time when the bar was empty, Elser spent time hollowing out the pillar behind the speaker's rostrum. In it, he placed a bomb.

The Aftermath

Georg Elser was sent to Sachsenhausen and then Dachau where he was kept as a special privilege prisoner. It seemed that Hitler was convinced that evidence would be discovered proving that the British Secret Service was behind the attempt and Elser could be subject to a show trial. Later research showed that Elser was indeed acting alone. As it became apparent that the Nazis were losing the war Hitler had no interest in a show trial for Elser. In April 1945, Hitler ordered the execution of "special security prisoner Eller", the name by which Elser was known in Dachau. The head of the Gestapo, SS-Gruppenführer Heinrich Müller delivered the order to the commandant of Dachau, Obersturmbannführer Eduard Weiter. On 9 April, Elser was shot in Dachau.

> ## OTHER PLOTS
>
> On 13 March 1943, 1st Lieutenant von Schlabrendorff, a junior officer attached to Henning von Tresckow, placed a bomb disguised as a bottle of brandy on Hitler's plane as it took off from Smolensk. The bomb did not go off and, at the time, the plot was not discovered.
>
> On 21 March, Colonel Freiherr Rudolf von Gersdorf offered to place two bombs with a 10-minute fuse in his overcoat pocket while with Hitler at an exhibition, but abandoned the attempt when he learned that Hitler intended to spend just eight minutes at the exhibition.
>
> In January and February 1944, three young officers offered themselves as suicide bombers but the plot failed when Hitler changed his schedule.

A plaque is dedicated to Elser's memory at Königsbronn. It reads: "'I wanted through my deed to prevent even greater bloodshed.' In remembrance of Johann Georg Elser, who spent his youth in Königsbronn. On 8 November 1939, he wanted to thwart genocide with his assassination attempt on Hitler. On 9 April 1945, Johann Georg Elser was murdered at Dachau concentration camp."

A concert venue – the Georg Elser Halle – is named after him in Munich.

THE 20 JULY PLOT – OPERATION VALKYRIE

Date and Place of Attempted Assassination

20 July 1944, Wolfsschanze (Wolf's Lair), near Rastenburg, East Prussia (now Ketrzyn, Poland).

The Event

On 19 October 1938, Colonel-General Ludwig Beck resigned as Chief of the General Staff in protest at Hitler's plan to annexe Czechoslovakia. Beck had been for a time trying to assemble a group of high-ranking officers to support him in a plan to overthrow Hitler. He created a small organization to effect this plan. Over the next six years, more and more officers began to join covertly. The plotters included Major-General von Tresckow, the chief of staff in Army Group Centre on the Russian Front; Colonel-General Erich Hoepner, an army chief who had been sacked by Hitler in December 1941; Colonel-General Friedrich Olbricht, the head of the supply section of the Reserve Army; Colonel-General Karl Heinrich von Stuelpnagel, a military governor in France; Major-General Hans Oster, the chief of staff of the Abwehr; and Field Marshal Erwin von Witzleber who had retired in 1942.

On 6 June 1944, the Allies launched the D-Day invasion of France. A number of Germans began to

The Axis Powers high command (from left): the bombastic Hermann Goering, Benito Mussolini, Rudolf Hess (behind), Adolf Hitler and Henrich Himmler (behind, in black uniform).

plot against Hitler believing that the war was lost. Co-ordinating the plan was Claus Philipp Maria Schenk Graf von Stauffenberg. His idea was to remain at the Bendlerstrasse offices in Berlin. He was to call army units all over Europe and the Reich to try to convince them to arrest leaders of Nazi political organizations, such as the Sicherheitsdienst and the Gestapo. He was the only officer (he was a colonel) among the conspirators who knew most of the German military leaders personally and the only one with regular access to Hitler, so he agreed to carry out the assassination. It was set for the Führer's briefing hut at the military high command in Rastenburg, Eastern Prussia, called the Wolf's Lair.

Stauffenberg put two small bombs in his briefcase. Each was equipped with a simple, soundless chemical timer that could be set to explode either at a 10- or 15-minute delay. When he arrived at 10.15am on 20 July, Stauffenberg was surprised to find that Hitler's headquarters had been moved from the underground Führerbunker to the Lagebaracke, a wooden hut that was normally used by Albert Speer, Minister for Armaments and War Production. Stauffenberg told Hitler's butler that he needed to use the bathroom and took his briefcase with him. He locked the door and opened his briefcase and began to prime the bombs. It was difficult because of the injuries he had suffered the previous year: on 7 April 1943, near the

Kasserine Pass in Tunisia, the British strafed his vehicle; he spent three months in hospital in Munich and lost his left eye, his right hand and the fourth and fifth fingers of his left hand.

Stauffenberg had only managed to prime one bomb before he was called back into the room. He handed the other, unprimed bomb to his aide de camp. He put his case under the conference table not far from Hitler. The meeting went ahead 30 minutes earlier than planned at 12.30pm because Mussolini was due to arrive at 3pm. After a few minutes, Stauffenberg excused himself saying that he had to make an urgent telephone call to Berlin. He waited in a nearby shelter for the explosion. The bomb went off at precisely 12.42pm and the hut was virtually destroyed. Every one of the 24 men were injured – one died later that afternoon and three more a few days later. Hitler was saved because the heavy, solid oak conference table deflected the blast. Hitler suffered concussion, singed hair, cuts to his forehead, a bruised back, burned right calf and left hand and hurt eardrums; but the main injury was to his dignity – the blast had ruined his new trousers.

The Would-be Assassin

Claus Philipp Maria Schenk Graf von Stauffenberg was born on 15 November 1907, the third of three sons (the others being the twins Berthold and Alexander), of Alfred Schenk Graf von Stauffenberg and Countess Caroline Schenk von Üxküll-Gyllenband. A devout Catholic, he joined the army in 1926. Although loyal, he was disgusted by Kristallnacht and in 1939 when his uncle, Nikolaus Graf von Üxküll, asked him to join the movement against Hitler, he was tempted. Count Peter Yorck von Wartenburg and Ulrich Wilhelm Graf Schwerin von Schwanenfeld urged him to become the adjutant of Walther von Brauchitsch, then Supreme Commander of the Army, in order to participate in a coup against Hitler. He refused because the army had sworn allegiance not to the presidency of the German Reich, but to Hitler personally.

For his bravery in France, Stauffenberg was awarded the Iron Cross, First Class. On 22 June 1941, the Germans launched Operation Barbarossa (the invasion of the USSR). To achieve their objective, the Germans almost casually murdered, or sent to the camps, Jews, Poles and Russians. It was this cruelty that finally persuaded Stauffenberg to throw his lot in with the resistance groups within the Wehrmacht in 1942. They bided their time as Hitler was then at the peak of his power. However, they did begin to plan for life in a post-Hitler Germany. In 1943, Stauffenberg was promoted to Oberstleutnant i.G. (im Generalstab) (Lieutenant-Colonel on a general staff), and was sent to Africa to join the 10th Panzer Division as its "First Officer in the General Staff". After he was injured, he was sent home to recuperate and in September 1943 was posted as a staff officer to the Ersatzheer (home army), located in an office on Berlin's Bendlerstrasse. The planning for Hitler's assassination, known as Operation Valkyrie, continued.

The Aftermath

Believing that Hitler was dead, Stauffenberg and his aide-de-camp, Leutnant Werner von Haeften, left the scene and talked their way out of the heavily guarded compound – it was protected by soldiers, electric fences and barbed wire. Their chauffeur drove them to an airfield. Before they boarded the Heinkel He111 that was to take them to Berlin, they disposed of the second bomb in a nearby forest. While the plane was in the air at 1pm, an order was given by Hitler to shoot Stauffenberg and Haeften immediately they landed. Friedrich Georgi of the air staff, who was in on the conspiracy, received the instruction so it was not passed on. Stauffenberg arrived in Berlin at 4.30pm and, still mistakenly believing Hitler to be dead, began the second phase of the project: to organize the military coup against Nazi leaders.

Propaganda minister Joseph Goebbels went on the radio at 6.30pm to announce that Hitler had survived an assassination attempt. Hitler himself later broadcast on state radio. At their Bendlerstrasse offices, the conspirators realised the plot had failed and tried to flee. In a shoot-out, Stauffenberg was hit in the shoulder. General Friedrich Fromm, one of the conspirators, attempted to save his own life by arresting other conspirators. He held an impromptu court martial and condemned the ringleaders to death. Stauffenberg, along with fellow officers General Olbricht, Leutnant von Haeften and Oberst Albrecht Mertz von Quirnheim, was shot late that night by a makeshift firing squad in the courtyard of the Bendlerblock, the army headquarters. Stauffenberg and the rest were buried in the Matthäus Churchyard in Schöneberg, Berlin. The next day, however, Stauffenberg's body was exhumed by the SS, stripped of his medals and cremated.

Stauffenberg's eldest brother, Berthold Schenk Graf von Stauffenberg, was also involved in the plot. On 10 August, he and eight more conspirators were tried before Roland Freisler (a prominent and notorious Nazi judge) in the Volksgericht, the People's Court. They were all executed by slow strangulation that night in Plötzensee Prison, Berlin (reputedly with piano wire used as the garot). More than a thousand fellow conspirators were condemned in show trials and executed. The SS arrested members of the Stauffenberg family, including Stauffenberg's wife and children.

Between 100 and 200 people died as a result of the 20 July plot. Other plotters who supported the plan but did not play an active role included Field Marshal Erwin Rommel, Lieutenant-General Adolf Heusinger and Field Marshal Günther Hans von Kluge.

Colonel-General Ludwig Beck, who had had an operation for cancer in 1943, made two attempts to kill himself after the plot failed. He asked a sergeant to administer the *coup de grâce* in the Bendlerstrasse on 20 July 1944.

General Erich Hoepner had been slated to take command of the army following the success of the plot.

After its failure, he was arrested, tried by the People's Court, and found guilty. He was offered a pistol to kill himself but he refused. He was hanged at Berlin on 8 August 1944.

Friedrich Olbricht was arrested by his superior, General Friedrich Fromm, immediately it was discovered Hitler had survived the assassination attempt. He was shot by firing squad the same day.

Hans Oster was arrested after the plot. He was executed at Flossenburg concentration camp on 9 April 1945, along with Admiral Wilhelm Canaris and Pastor Dietrich Bonhoeffer.

On 20 July 1944, Colonel-General Karl von Stuelpnagel arrested 1,200 leading Gestapo and SS men in Paris but when he learned that the plot had failed, he calmly destroyed his papers. He was ordered to return to Berlin the next day. He took a leisurely stroll before setting off under escort. Near Sedan, he stopped and asked to walk a little. Away from the convoy, he shot himself in the face. Although he had shot his own eye out, he survived the suicide attempt. He was hanged at Berlin on 30 August 1944.

After the war, the German government transformed the Bendlerblock into a memorial to the events of 20 July. It features an exhibition of more than 5,000 photographs and documents. The courtyard where the executions took place now has a plaque commemorating the events.

The D-Day landings heralded the beginning of the end of Hitler's Third Reich, which, far from lasting the much-vaunted thousand years, had managed just 12. As the Allies began to gather around Berlin, Hitler took refuge in his bunker. "After a six years' war which, in spite of all setbacks will one day go down in history as the most glorious and heroic manifestation of a people's will to live, I cannot forsake the city which is the capital of this state," he said.

At 4.10pm on Saturday 28 April 1945 in the village of Giulino di Mezzegra, Como, his sometime ally Benito

Reichsmarschall Hermann Goering (left) and Hitler's former deputy, Rudolf Hess (centre), at the Nuremberg trials. Goering escaped the hangman's noose by taking poison in his prison cell. Hess was sentenced to life in prison in Spandau, Berlin. He died in 1987.

Mussolini and his mistress Clara Petacci were shot by a mob of Communist partisans and then hanged upside down from lampposts in front of a petrol station in Milan. On 29 April, some time between 1 and 3am, Hitler married his long-time mistress, Eva Braun. The witnesses were Joseph Goebbels and Martin Bormann. Hitler then dictated his will to his secretary Traudl Junge. He named Bormann as executor. In his political testament, he opined, "It is untrue that I, or anybody else in Germany, wanted war in 1939. It was wanted and provoked by those international politicians who either came of Jewish stock or worked for Jewish interests." He also expelled Goering and Himmler from the Nazi Party and stripped them of all their official titles.

Hitler ordered his Alsatian bitch, Blondi, to be poisoned. He and Eva locked themselves in the bunker beneath the Chancellery at 3.30pm on 30 April and, after a lunch of spaghetti with vegetarian sauce, committed suicide. He shot himself in the mouth and she took cyanide. With more than two hundred litres of petrol, the SS then burnt their bodies as Hitler had decreed but his last order was bungled and the corpses were not completely consumed by the flames. Joseph and Magda Goebbels also committed suicide after first poisoning their six children.

At the Nuremberg trials, it was estimated that the Germans had murdered 5,750,000 Jews and that the war had cost the lives of 54,800,000 people.

Michael Collins (1890–1922)

The Victim

Michael Collins (Mícheál Seán Ó Coileáin) was born on 16 October 1890 (his tombstone lists his birthdate as 12 October) in Woodfield, near Clonakilty, in County Cork, Ireland, the third son and youngest of eight children of Michael John Collins (1815–7 March 1897) and Mary Anne O'Brien (1855–April 1907). The Collinses were wealthier than most working class Irish families of the time and Collins was a precocious boy intellectually and on the sports field. His childhood was not always an easy one, though; his father, who was 75 when Michael was born, died when the boy was just six.

When he left school, his mother set out to find him a job with the post office. He studied for the post office examinations with a teacher who was also an avowed nationalist, which had an enormous influence on Collins. In July 1906, he landed a temporary boy clerkship in the Postal Savings Bank in West Kensington, London. Collins spent the next nine and a half years living with his sister, Johanna ("Hannie") and her illegitimate son Daniel, at 5 Netherwood Road, West Kensington. He attempted to join the Civil Service but failed the examinations several times. In 1910, he got a job with an accounting firm, moving later to a stockbroker's, Horne and Company, based at 23 Moorgate. On 1 September 1914, he moved on again, joining the Board of Trade as a clerk. In May 1915, he joined the bills department of the Guarantee Trust Company of New York's London branch in Lombard Street.

Like many immigrants, Collins spent much of his time with his own kind. He joined the Gaelic League and studied Irish. He played hurling and football with a Gaelic Athletic Association club. It was among the London Irish that his radicalism was fomented. In 1908, he joined Sinn Féin (see box on right) and in November 1909 he joined the Irish Republican Brotherhood. This organization was created in the 1860s and "swore to free Ireland through violent revolution, and to set up an independent republic". He was sworn in at Barnsbury Hall, Barnsbury Street, Islington, London N1 by Sam Maguire, a post office colleague and worker for the Irish Republican Brotherhood in London until 1921. Why he left London is unknown. The Irish Republican Brotherhood was an organization that his father had once belonged to and one that Collins would eventually lead.

On 25 April 1914, Collins became an Irish Volunteer and was appointed treasurer of the Irish Republican Brotherhood for southern England; he became privy to its plans for a rising in 1916. On 15 January 1916, he fled to Dublin to avoid being conscripted into the British army. He found work with an accountancy firm and moved into lodgings at 44 Mountjoy Street, where he began the preparations for the uprising. When the delayed Easter Rising finally began at noon on 24 April he was an aide to Joseph Plunkett, its tubercular chief planner. Under the leadership of Padraic Pearse and James Connolly, 1,600 Irish rebels, most of whom were members of the Irish Volunteers, rose up in Dublin and seized key points in the city. They failed to gain popular support. The rebellion lasted for five days and resulted in the destruction of large portions of the city before the

---

SINN FÉIN

Founded by Arthur Griffith on 28 November 1905, the name means "We ourselves". The organization had nothing to do with the Easter Rising (see page 69), apart from a desire of separation stronger than Home Rule. After 1920, Sinn Féin underwent successive splits (1922, 1926, 1970 and 1986), from which emerged a range of parties: Cumann na nGaedheal (now known as Fine Gael), Fianna Fáil, Official Sinn Féin (later Sinn Féin The Workers Party, then The Workers Party, then Democratic Left, which finally joined the Labour Party after serving in government with them) and Republican Sinn Féin.

Dublin after the storm: locals inspect the bomb damage to their city
in the wake of the Easter Rising.

British military crushed it. Fifteen of its leaders were arrested, summarily tried and sentenced to death. All 15 were executed by firing squad.

After its failure, Collins was arrested and sent to Frongoch internment camp, 3 miles (5 kilometres) from Bala in Merionethshire in north Wales. He became de facto leader of the contingent. The Frongoch prisoners were released on 23 December 1916. Encouraged by their release, which they interpreted as a victory, Collins and his comrades became embroiled in local politics, winning several by-elections. On 19 February 1917, Collins became secretary of the Irish National Aid Association, a front organization for the Irish Republican Brotherhood, through which Collins channelled contributions from America.

On 25 September 1917, Thomas Patrick Ashe, the president of the Irish Republican Brotherhood, died while on hunger strike at Mater Hospital, Dublin City. His funeral was a paramilitary affair at which Collins played a prominent role. After a volley was fired at the graveside, Collins, ever the showman, remarked, "Nothing additional remains to be said."

Sinn Féin was officially relaunched at a national convention in October 1917. By this time Collins was unique in being on the national executives of the Irish Republican Brotherhood, the Irish Volunteers and Sinn Féin. In the general election of 14 December 1918, Sinn Féin won 73 of the 105 Irish seats. Collins was elected MP for South Cork but, as with his later compatriots Adams, McGuinness et al, refused to take his seat at Westminster and was part of an independent parliament in Dublin, Dáil Éireann (Assembly of Ireland), formed on 21 January 1919. Eamon de Valera, Chief Minister of the Dáil Éireann, appointed him Minister for Home Affairs, a job he held only until April when he became Minister for Finance. Collins was no mere rhetorical politician – in 1919 he officially assumed the title of director of intelligence, as well as that of president of the Irish Republican Brotherhood. From July he spent his time plotting to kill British agents and gunrunning.

In September 1919, all political organizations were banned. Sinn Féin went underground. On the 19th of the

Michael Collins in IRA uniform. He plotted to kill British agents.

month, Collins organized a killing force that was known as "The Twelve Apostles". On 19 December 1919, Field Marshal Lord French, the Lord Lieutenant of Ireland, escaped an assassination attempt. The only fatality was one of the assassins who got shot in the crossfire.

On the morning of 21 November 1920 – Bloody Sunday – 14 British officers were murdered in their beds, a concerted operation mainly in south inner city Dublin. Collins justified the killings:

My one intention was the destruction of the undesirables who continued to make miserable the lives of ordinary decent citizens. I have proof enough to assure myself of the atrocities which this gang of spies and informers have committed. If I had a second motive it was no more than a feeling such as I would have for a dangerous reptile. By their destruction the very air is made sweeter ... For myself, my conscience is clear. There is no crime in detecting in wartime the spy and the informer. They have destroyed without trial. I have paid them back in their own coin.

The murders were the legitimate acts of self-defence which had been forced upon the Irish people by English aggression.

After two years of forbearance, we had begun to defend ourselves and the life of our nation. We did not initiate the war, nor were we allowed to select the battleground. When the British Government, as far as lay in its power, deprived the Irish people of arms, and employed every means to prevent them securing arms, and made it a criminal (in large areas a capital) offence to carry arms, and, at the same time, began and carried out a brutal and murderous campaign against them and against their national government, they deprived themselves of any excuse for their violence and of any cause of complaint against the Irish people for the means they took for their protection.

Later that day, at 3.25pm, the Black and Tans, the Royal Irish Constabulary Reserve Force, had their revenge, opening fire on the 8,000-strong crowd at a Gaelic football match between Dublin and Tipperary at Croke Park in north Dublin. Seven people died immediately including one of the players, Michael Hogan, and five were fatally wounded. That night, two high-ranking IRA officers, Dick McKee, brigade commander, and his deputy Peadar Clancy, who had helped plan the killings of the British agents, were arrested. Also taken into custody was their civilian friend Conor Clune, a clerk from the west of Ireland, who was mistaken for another IRA volunteer. They were brought to Dublin Castle, tortured with bayonets and shot while allegedly trying to escape.

In 1920, Collins went on the run but the canard that a bounty of £10,000 was placed on his head is not true. It was certainly suggested, but the idea was not acted upon. This did not deter him and he cycled to numerous meetings with couriers, agents, guerrillas and friends without disguises, bodyguards or a gun. Eamon de Valera had returned to Dublin in December 1920 as the undisputed leader but he and others including Charles Burgess, the Minister of Defence, and Austin Stack, the Minister for Home Affairs, while appreciative of Collins's efforts were, to put it mildly, suspicious of him.

On 11 December 1920, Sinn Féin ambushed the Police Auxiliary Cadets, known as Auxiliaries, killing one and wounding 11. That night, Auxiliaries and Black and Tans arrived in Cork and burned many of the buildings including the Carnegie Library, the City Hall and about 50 private houses. They also shot two members of the

IRA

A legacy of Collins is the formation in 1920 of the Irish Republican Army from members of the Irish Volunteers and Irish Republican Brotherhood.

IRA. Martial law was declared over a large part of the country. Between January and April 1921, rebels shot 73 alleged spies and informers. The Black and Tans and Auxiliaries fought a war of reprisals. British newspapers began editorializing, condemning the government's behaviour. Worldwide, the tide turned against the British government. In April 1921, Lloyd George, the British prime minister, sent Lord Derby to secretly negotiate a ceasefire with the rebels. On 25 May 1921, the IRA burned the Dublin Customs House. Seventy-two policemen and soldiers were killed that month by the terrorists. On 22 June, de Valera was arrested but was released, to his surprise, two days later. A ceasefire was signed on 11 July 1921.

Three months later and rather surprisingly, Collins was sent to London to negotiate a peace treaty. The conference opened on 1 October. In the capital he kept his distance from his colleagues, even lodging in a different place. When he appended his name to it at 2.15am on 6 December 1921, under threat of immediate military action from Lloyd George, he also signed his own death warrant because some Republicans saw it as a sell-out. He wrote to a friend, "When you have sweated, toiled, had mad dreams, hopeless nightmares, you find yourself in London's streets, cold and dank in the night air. Think – what have I got for Ireland? Something which she has wanted these past seven hundred years. Will anyone be satisfied at the bargain? Will anyone? I tell you this; early this morning I signed my death warrant. I thought at the time how odd, how ridiculous – a bullet may just as well have done the job five years ago." A shorter version has it that Lord Birkenhead remarked to Michael Collins, "I may have just signed my political death-warrant," whereupon Collins replied, "I may have signed my actual death-warrant."

On 19 December 1921, the Dáil Éireann met to ratify the treaty. Arthur Griffith was accused of conspiring with Lloyd George against the Irish; Collins was called a traitor and a renegade and de Valera made an impassioned plea to the Dáil to reject the treaty. On 7 January 1922, the Dáil ignored de Valera and ratified the treaty by a vote of 64–57. The next day, Eamon de Valera resigned as president because he did not support the treaty. Collins became chairman and finance minister of the transitional provisional government. Collins spent the next seven months holding together his new government while at the same time undermining elements of the treaty he disliked through his IRA contacts. Collins was determined to create a treaty that lead to a quasi-Republican constitution for the free state but in June 1922 the British Government rejected Collins' draft. Most of his fellow cabinet members and the IRA were hostile to his intriguing. On 28 June 1922, Collins agreed to an attack on the IRA leadership and after a brief struggle took over as commander-in-chief of the Irish Free State Army in July. It was to be the start of the civil war.

Date and Place of Assassination

22 August 1922, Béal na mBláth, near Bandon, County Cork, Ireland.

The Event

Like many political assassinations, Michael Collins' death is shrouded in mystery. On Friday 18 August, Collins announced his intention to continue his inspection tour of the south, despite protests from intelligence officers concerning the potential dangers of such a trip. He was also in poor physical and mental health. Collins went to Curragh, then Limerick and Mallow. Having arrived in Cork City on Sunday 20 August, Collins met his close friend, General Emmet Dalton, the commander of the Cork region's Free State troops, in the military headquarters of the Imperial Hotel. It was decided here that Tuesday be spent on an inspection tour of the full command area of west Cork.

Michael Collins had a most peculiar habit of challenging his friends to "a bit of ear", which was a wrestling competition that usually ended with Collins sinking his teeth into his friend's ear and drawing blood. Before he set off on his final journey, Collins and a friend from Frongoch had "a bit of ear". (It is probably this unusual activity that led to persistent rumours that Collins was homosexually inclined.)

Accompanied by Dalton and Commandant O'Connell and other members of his headquarters staff, Collins set off at 6.15am on 22 August. Collins headed for Macroom via Coachford and then on to Bandon. The journey was an obstacle course of destroyed bridges and potted roads. Having lost sight of the scout leader momentarily, upon reaching a crossroads near Bandon, the convoy asked a man outside Long's Pub for directions. Denny "The Dane" Long helpfully pointed out the route to Bandon. He was an IRA sentry and many prominent Republicans were in the pub. The site chosen for the ambush was south of the Béal na mBláth crossroads, where an elevated narrow country road overlooked the main road along which the convoy was to pass. Three mines were laid along the road and some 37 armed men were allotted ambush positions.

They waited for Collins to return. However, as light began to fade at 7.30pm, the assassins began to wonder if Collins would travel again that evening. Commander Liam Deasy, thinking that the convoy had stopped for the night, ordered that the mines be disconnected and the party disperse. Not long afterwards, Collins's convoy trundled along the road and was ambushed. The fighting lasted anything between 20 and 40 minutes and at the end, Michael Collins was the only man to die. Theories range from a direct hit to an unlucky ricocheting bullet. Perhaps rashly, he had ordered his convoy to stop and return fire, instead of choosing the safer option of driving on in the safety of his armoured car. According to Emmett Dalton, the convoy consisted of a Crossley tender armed with a Lewis machine gun and eight rifled men, one motorcyclist, an armoured car and the car that Collins and he

A guard stands over Michael Collins' body.

were in when they came under heavy fire from the front and behind.

A cart in the middle of the road hindered their escape. Collins's driver, M. J. Corry, claims that the Collins convoy consisted of three Crossley tenders, one Rolls Royce Whippet armoured car, a motorcyclist and a Leyland Tomas racing car that had Collins in it as the convoy left Bandon. Corry also says there was a single shot fired and the convoy stopped on the orders of Collins. There was no cart in their way on the road in Béal na mBláth. Corry further states that the firing was coming from the front only. Collins stood in the road a few yards from the vehicles to get a better view of the men on the hillside. A shot rang out and Collins fell. He was just 31 years old.

The Assassins

Who killed Michael Collins? Was it the British Secret Service? Was it a group of anti-peace-treaty IRA men? If so, then Denis "Sonny" O'Neill, a former British army marksman who died in 1950, takes the credit for firing the bullet that killed Collins. Or did his own men kill Michael Collins?

The Aftermath

Collins's death did not stop the bloodletting in Ireland. In fact, more died in the civil war than in the fighting with the British.

His body was taken to Dublin on 24 August and lay in state in the City Hall where thousands filed past his coffin to pay their respects. He was buried in Glasnevin

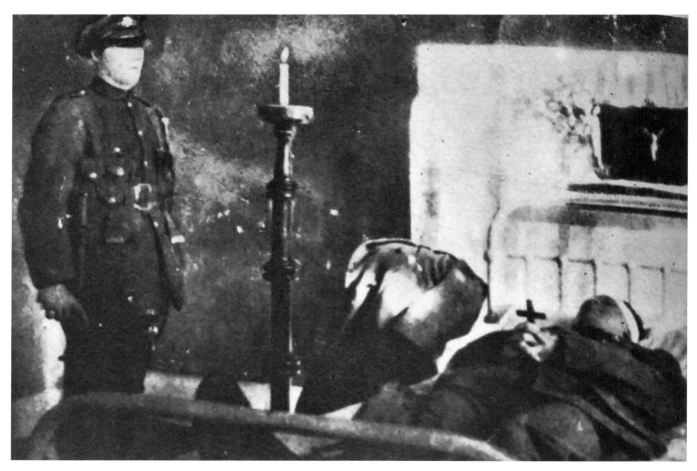

Michael Collins was buried in Glasnevin Cemetery in Dublin.

Cemetery in Dublin. A monument stands in Béal na mBláth marking the spot where Collins met his death.

On 9 September 1922, the Dáil elected William Cosgrave as president. It passed the constitution of the Irish Free State although the Republican members abstained from attending. The new Irish government extended the death penalty for possession of materiel. Several leading Republicans were executed, including the novelist Erskine Childers. The IRA gave up the struggle on 30 April 1923 and in November 1925 the Dáil formally recognized the separation of the country.

Eamon de Valera was no admirer of Michael Collins, even long after the latter's assassination. Aged 85, de Valera said, "I can't see my way to becoming patron of the Michael Collins Foundation. It's my considered opinion that in the fullness of time history will record the greatness of Collins, and it will be recorded at my expense."

Earl Mountbatten (1900–1979)

The Victim

Admiral of the Fleet Louis Francis Albert Victor Nicholas, 1st Earl Mountbatten of Burma, KG, GCB, OM, GCSI, GCIE, GCVO, DSO, PC, was born at Frogmore House, Windsor, Berkshire, at 6am on 25 June 1900. He was the second son and fourth and youngest child of Prince Louis of Battenberg (later 1st Marquess of Milford Haven, born at Graz, Austria 24 May 1854, died at 42 Half Moon Street, Piccadilly, London, in the annexe of the Naval & Military Club on 11 September 1921 of heart failure following influenza) and Princess Victoria of Hesse (born at Windsor Castle, Berkshire 5 April 1863, died at Kensington Palace, London 24 September 1950). The newborn child was Queen Victoria's great-grandson. At the start of the First World War, his father was the First Sea Lord but resigned on 29 October 1914 at Winston Churchill's behest as anti-German feeling rose. The family quietly anglicized their name on 14 July 1917, three days before the House of Saxe-Coburg-Gotha became the House of Windsor.

During the Great War, Mountbatten served in Admiral Beatty's flagship. After the Armistice he went up to Cambridge for five months where he became friends with Edward, Prince of Wales. He accompanied the prince on a tour of the empire and took great pleasure in recording in his diary of the trip the social solecisms of the locals who incorrectly addressed His Royal Highness. In March 1920 in the West Indies, Mountbatten recorded that "one fat old woman" in a "crowd of niggers" made a basic error. Historian Andrew Roberts commented that

Handsome, heroic and high-minded – at least that's what Mountbatten thought of himself.

Mountbatten's remark "at least has the distinction of offending against every canon of political correctness". Mountbatten was careful to cultivate a close relationship with the prince, so much so that it saved him from dismissal from the Royal Navy in 1922 when many other officers were forced to leave the senior service. His friend, the Prince of Wales, put in a good word for him.

That year he went to India with the prince and met Edwina Cynthia Annette Ashley; they became engaged on St Valentine's Day. Marriage followed shortly afterwards on 18 July with, unsurprisingly, the Prince of Wales as the best man. She was wealthy, having been left £2 million by her grandfather, Sir Ernest Cassel, and he had a social cachet through his royal connections. They had two daughters: Patricia Edwina Victoria, 2nd Countess Mountbatten of Burma (born 14 February 1924), and Pamela Carmen Louise (born 19 April 1929). He was a doting father, she less than a doting mother. In fact, Edwina preferred spending her time with her myriad lovers – male and female – to looking after her children.

In 1936, during the abdication crisis, Mountbatten had to choose between his friendship with the man who was now King Edward VIII and his ambition. Not for the first time, Mountbatten's ambition won and he shifted his loyalties from the old monarch to Bertie, the younger brother, who would become King George VI. In March 1937, Mountbatten visited the former king and his future wife in exile in Austria to assure them of the royal family's attendance at their forthcoming nuptials that June. Not only did the royals boycott the wedding, but Mountbatten did not bother to attend either. He later claimed that he had not been invited. This was a lie as on 5 May 1937 he had written to thank the Duke (and future Duchess) of Windsor for their "kind invitation". When the duke died, Mountbatten went on the BBC and claimed that the duke had been "more than my best man, he was my best friend all my life…".

Unlike many of his ilk, indeed some in his family, Mountbatten was opposed to the appeasement of Germany. During the war he commanded the 5th Destroyer Flotilla. Despite the legend, Mountbatten's captaincy of the destroyer HMS *Kelly* (launched on 28 October 1938) was not particularly heroic. Mountbatten liked to do everything at breakneck speed; this trait is problematic when you have charge of a destroyer. One who served in *Kelly* noted that in the first eight months of the war, the ship spent only 57 days out of the dockyard. Those who served below him adored Mountbatten but he was not so highly regarded by the Admiralty or other commanders. On 9 March 1940, the *Kelly* struck another destroyer, HMS *Gurkha*. It resulted in another six weeks in dry dock being repaired. In early May 1940, Mountbatten led a convoy of four destroyers to rescue troops sent to the "botched and ill-conceived" Namsos campaign. On 23 May 1941, *Kelly* was sunk during the Battle of Crete. Mountbatten was to later claim that the Germans had machine gunned the survivors in the water as they swam for safety, However, other crew members report no such action.

In August 1941, Mountbatten was appointed captain of the aircraft carrier HMS *Illustrious*. On 27 October 1941, he replaced Roger Keyes as chief of combined operations. Mountbatten asked Churchill to be allowed to stay in the navy, only to be met with the rejoinder, "What could you hope to achieve except to be sunk in a bigger and more expensive ship this time?" On 19 August 1942, the Allies launched the disastrous Dieppe

ON THE SILVER SCREEN

A fictionalized biopic was made of the *Kelly*. *In Which We Serve* (1942) starred (Sir) Noel Coward, (Sir) John Mills, (Lord) Bernard Miles and (Dame) Celia Johnson, and was directed by (Sir) David Lean. Coward wore Mountbatten's own cap in the film.

Raid. Among the troops who crossed the Channel in Operation Jubilee were 4,963 men of the Canadian Second Division. In nine hours, 3,369 were killed, captured or wounded. The raid was the largest operation on the French coast between Dunkirk and D-Day and was Mountbatten's personal responsibility. One of his colleagues called the raid "demented", another said, "It was a terribly bad plan." General Eisenhower thought it a "fiasco". Bernard Montgomery, later the victor at El Alamein, abandoned the Dieppe Raid only for Mountbatten to resurrect it.

In October 1943, Churchill appointed Mountbatten as the Supreme Allied Commander South East Asia Theatre. Montgomery said, "Dickie Mountbatten is, of course, quite unfit to be Supreme Commander. He is a delightful person, has a quick and alert brain and has many good ideas. But his knowledge of how to make war is really NIL." As with politicians in Whitehall, Mountbatten realised the strength he would have if he created a large personal staff and he set up an elaborate headquarters in the Royal Palace at Kandy, Sri Lanka, nearly 2,000 miles (3,218 kilometres) from the front line. His staff grew from 23 to 540, an increase of more than 2,200 percent. One aspect of life in the military that Mountbatten excelled at was public relations – he was great at taking the credit for other people's work and blaming others for his own mistakes. Professional soldiers never believed in publicly blaming their senior officers, which allowed Mountbatten – who had no such scruples – to benefit as much as he did. He also made the Chiefs of Staff back in London think that he was busy and achieving by regularly dismissing his senior commanders.

When Japan surrendered, Mountbatten claimed that it had been he who rushed across Horse Guards Parade and alerted the prime minister to the news. In fact, it had been Jock Colville, Churchill's private secretary, who had told Clement Attlee. It was Attlee, who had come to a power with a landslide that would not be bet-

tered until Tony Blair's triumph on 1 May 1997, who appointed Mountbatten Viceroy of India on 24 March 1947. It was a necessity for political and financial reasons for Britain to divest itself of India and it was thought that the previous viceroy, Field Marshal the Lord Wavell, was not up to the task. He had suggested that soldiers should be sent to the disputed Muslim areas in the north and power transferred immediately to the Congress Party in the Hindu areas. Attlee believed that this plan was defeatist, although in hindsight it may well have saved more lives than Mountbatten's transfer.

Attlee made the announcement of Mountbatten's appointment on 20 February 1947, adding that Britain would withdraw from India no later than June 1948. Mountbatten was to claim that the date was his idea and that he had to work hard to persuade Attlee to agree. Rather than concentrating Indian minds, as had been the intention, all the time limit did was to exacerbate the problem facing the country and made partition inevitable. Three and a half centuries of British rule in India was to be wound up, thanks to Mountbatten, in 16 months. Non-Hindus – Sikhs, Untouchables, Muslims and princes – realised that they had little time to establish their positions – by violence if necessary – or face dictatorship under the Hindu majority. The Mountbattens had been in India only a week before rumours began that Edwina was having an affair with Jawaharlal Nehru (1889–1964), who was to become the first prime minister of independent India. Mountbatten and Nehru had known each other since their time in Singapore at the end of the war.

On 5 April, Mountbatten met for the first time Mohammed Ali Jinnah (1876–1948), known as "the father of Pakistan", who was the leader of the Muslim League. The two men did not get on. Jinnah asked for more time and wondered if Mountbatten intended "to turn this country over to chaos and bloodshed and civil war". Mountbatten's bias against Jinnah and Muslims was apparent, although in public Mountbatten continued to insist that he was impartial. In private and to journalists, Mountbatten called Jinnah "a lunatic", "most frigid, haughty and disdainful", an "evil genius", a "psychopathic case", a "clot" and a "bastard". Unsurprisingly, Muslims felt justifiably aggrieved at the viceroy. Mountbatten was warned that bloodshed could be expected in the Punjab but later claimed that no one could have foreseen the loss of life. He chose to ignore the warnings with terrible consequences.

It seems that Mountbatten spent much of his time in India concerned with his own image. Historian Andrew Roberts writes, "Discussions about flags, titles, salutes, honours, cars, uniforms, medals and toasts … had to be settled at the very highest level. In matters relating to his own prestige, Mountbatten never delegated." On 25 April, Jinnah told Mountbatten that, should there be a referendum in Calcutta to decide its future, the Muslim League would triumph. Just a fortnight earlier, Mountbatten had said that areas within provinces would have the right to self-determination. Fearing that Calcutta could become a city in Pakistan, Mountbatten came up with several reasons as to why this was no longer a good idea. Mountbatten told his staff that "It would be most undesirable to lay down a procedure for self-determination that would give the wrong answer." Muslims were not even invited to meetings to discuss probable or possible difficulties after partition, only members of the Hindu Congress Party. Mountbatten also wanted to be Governor-General of India and Pakistan after partition and wanted a Union Jack in the corner of the Pakistan flag. Neither of these outlandish ideas came to pass.

In May, Mountbatten began to consider withdrawal in August 1947 rather than June 1948. The Attlee government wanted to keep India in the Commonwealth but were less concerned whether Pakistan stayed. Mountbatten claimed that the day chosen for independence – 14/15 August – was purely arbitrary when he announced it at a press conference. This was another lie

– the date had been cleared with the Secretary of State the day before the conference. It was also the date of a Muslim religious festival – another slap in the face for followers of Islam, or an unfortunate coincidence? Sir Cyril Radcliffe, a London barrister, who had never been to India, was given the onerous task of drawing up the new borders – known as Awards. He later said that he could have done the job properly if he had been given two years – Mountbatten allowed him 40 days. Until recently, historians and writers have believed that the viceroy took no part in the decisions as to which parts of the country were in India and which in Pakistan. In fact, he spent much time ensuring that India was represented favourably in the Awards. It seems quite odd that Mountbatten was so pro-India since the Indian leader, Nehru, was sleeping with his wife. However, there are allegations that both Mountbattens were sleeping with Nehru.

After Independence (midnight of 14/15 August 1947, celebrated on the 14th in Pakistan and the 15th in India), Mountbatten remained in New Delhi for ten months, serving as the first of independent India's two governors general until June 1948. It is impossible to say how many died after partition – Mountbatten at the royal wedding in November 1947 claimed it was "only 100,000". He later said the figure was close to 200,000, but civil servant Sir Algernon Rumbold of the India Office estimated the death toll at closer to 600,000. Others suggested the true figure was 800,000, while some, including Churchill and fellow Tory politicians Rab Butler and Julian Amery, believed nearer to a million people had perished.

Mountbatten had been created a viscount on 23 August 1946, then earl and baron on 28 October 1947. A year later, in October 1948, Mountbatten returned to active naval service. On 18 April 1955 he was appointed First Sea Lord, the position that his father had once held. On 30 April 1959 he became Chief of the Defence Staff, a job he held for six years. On

21 February 1960 Edwina Mountbatten died at Jesselton, Borneo, while on tour for the St John Ambulance Brigade.

Three years after he left active service, Mountbatten became involved in a most bizarre incident. It was at his Knightsbridge home, 2 Kinnerton Street, London SW1X 8AE, on 8 May 1968, that Mountbatten, the press barons Cecil Harmsworth King and Hugh Cudlipp, and Sir Solly Zuckerman, the chief scientific advisor to the government, held a meeting about deposing Harold Wilson, the prime minister, and placing Mountbatten at the head of a military government. King was convinced that Wilson was leading the country to anarchy and civil war and that only a cabal of business leaders, politicians and soldiers could prevent the coming storm. He believed that Mountbatten, as both a member of the Royal Family and a former chief of the defence staff, would be able to command public support as leader of a non-democratic government. Mountbatten insisted that Zuckerman should be present at the meeting. (For his part Zuckerman later claimed that he was urged to attend by Mountbatten's son-in-law, Lord Brabourne, who was worried about King's influence over Mountbatten.) After King explained his view that the country was headed toward civil collapse, he asked Mountbatten if he would be willing to head an emergency government. Zuckerman said that the idea was treachery and that Mountbatten should have nothing to do with it. Mountbatten took his friend's advice and turned down King. Two days later, King published an article in the *Daily Mirror* under his own name entitled "Enough is enough". It read, "Mr Wilson and his government have lost all credit and we are now threatened with the greatest financial crisis in history. It is not to be resolved by lies about our reserves but only by a fresh start under a fresh leader." The City was aghast and three weeks later, on 30 May 1968, King was sacked as the head of the International Publishing Corporation. In 1974, Mountbatten was appointed the first Lord Lieutenant of the Isle of Wight. Mountbatten spent many of his declining years ensuring the preservation of his own legacy.

Date and Place of Assassination

27 August 1979, Mullaghmore, County Sligo, Republic of Ireland.

The Event

In July 1970, Mountbatten carried the Sword of State at the Opening of Parliament and almost fainted. That night he became angry when a doctor told him that his arteries were furred and he should go to bed for a fortnight. In 1976 he was forbidden from carrying the Sword of State after a medical showed up a heart problem. He hated growing old but it was the fear of becoming senile or helpless that really scared him, rather than death.

Mountbatten usually holidayed at Classiebawn, his summer home in Mullaghmore, County Sligo, a small seaside village between Bundoran, County Donegal and Sligo Town in the Republic of Ireland on the far northwest coast. He was not unaware of danger. In 1960, Mountbatten's estate manager, Patrick O'Grady, raised questions with the Garda about the earl's safety. "While everything points to the fact that no attack of any kind on the earl by subversive elements was at any time contemplated," the reply went, "it would in my opinion be asking too much to say in effect that we can guarantee his safety while in this country." By 1971, 12 policemen were on duty, Mountbatten said, "in case the IRA try to take me as a hostage". The following year he asked the Cabinet Office if he should go. The reply said that no visit to Ireland was completely safe. In 1974, Sir Robert Mark, the Commissioner of the Metropolitan Police Force, said that he would prefer Mountbatten not to go to Ireland. That year there were 28 policemen assigned to protect Mountbatten. Each year, he wrote to the commissioner to announce that he would be holidaying, as usual, in Ireland. As each year passed the danger for Mountbatten seemed to pass.

In 1979, he was nearly 80 years old and, although he was the uncle of the queen's husband, he had not had any real power for 14 years. The family mentioned to the Garda Síochána that their 9-metre (29-foot) long fishing boat, *Shadow V*, was left unattended, moored in the small harbour at Mullaghmore for long periods, but surely there was no real danger. At 11.30am on Monday 27 August 1979, Mountbatten and his party climbed aboard the *Shadow V*. He was accompanied by his daughter, Patricia, son-in-law, Lord Brabourne, twin grandsons, Nicholas and Timothy, their grandmother, the 83-year-old Doreen, Dowager Baroness Brabourne and a local boy, Paul Maxwell, a 15-year-old Protestant youth from County Fermanagh. Usually, a member of the Garda had accompanied them, but the previous year the policeman had been so seasick that Mountbatten said that his presence on board would no longer be necessary. The boat, steered by Mountbatten, raced to the first of the lobster pots, the point of the expedition. Before he could cut the engine, a 50-pound (22.5-kilogram) bomb blew the boat apart. It appeared that the device had been activated remotely from the shore.

Mountbatten died immediately, as did his grandson, Nicholas, and the local boy, Paul Maxwell. Doreen Brabourne died of her injuries the following day. Lord and Lady Brabourne suffered broken legs and various splinter injuries. Timothy suffered serious injuries but survived. On the same day that Mountbatten died, the Provisional IRA also killed 18 British army soldiers from the Parachute Regiment at the Warrenpoint Ambush in County Down.

The Assassins

Thomas McMahon was born at Monaghan Town, County Monaghan, Ireland in 1948. He joined Sinn Féin in 1966 and was the leader of the South Armagh Brigade of the Provisional IRA despite being acquitted twice (1972 and 1975) of membership of a proscribed organization. At 9.40am on the day of the assassination, the car he was driving was stopped by police for a routine tax disk check. The driver, Francie McGirl of Ballinamore, County Leitrim, gave a false name to police. Shortly before noon, while both men were being questioned, *Shadow V* was ripped apart by an explosion activated by a timer. When McGirl said, "I put no bomb in the boat", before the fact that it was a bomb and not a rocket launched from the shore was released to the public, Irish police knew that they had caught the perpetrators.

The Aftermath

A memorial service was held for Mountbatten in St Patrick's Cathedral in Dublin. He was buried in Romsey Abbey after a televised funeral in Westminster Abbey, which he himself had comprehensively planned.

Thomas McMahon and Francie McGirl were tried for the murder. McMahon was convicted on 23 November 1979, McGirl acquitted. In 1985, McMahon was among 11 IRA prisoners who used smuggled guns, explosives and fake prison officer uniforms to try to break out of Portlaoise prison. In 1988, he fired a pistol while being held in a cell at Dublin High Court, but the bullet hit the ceiling and McMahon was overpowered. McMahon was released in 1998 under the terms of the Good Friday Agreement. McGirl died in a farming accident in 1995.

Albert Anastasia (1902–1957)

The Victim

Known as the The Lord High Executioner of Murder Inc. (see box below), Albert Anastasia was born as Umberto Anastasio in Tropea, Italy, on 26 September 1902, one of nine brothers. Arriving in New York in 1919, Anastasia joined the waterfront trade union, the International Longshoremen's Association, where he quickly became shop steward. The docks were a breeding ground for the criminal classes and so it was perhaps inevitable that Anastasia would become involved in crime. (The character of Johnny Friendly – played by Lee J. Cobb – in *On the Waterfront* is based in part on Anastasia.) It was in his role as shop steward that Anastasia, who was nicknamed The Mad Hatter, committed his first murder.

Anastasia and a friend, Giuseppe "Joe" Fiorino, robbed James Fallon's jewellery shop on Myrtle Avenue, Brooklyn, of $95. George Tirello, another docker, was asked if he could find out who had robbed the jewellers. By asking the right questions and keeping his eyes open, Tirello discovered that the thieves were Anastasia and Fiorino. On 26 May 1920 he confronted them, but they turned on him, first with their fists and then both men pulled out guns and opened fire. Anastasia missed, but Fiorino pumped three bullets into Tirello. Three days later Fiorino was arrested, followed the next day by Anastasia.

On 26 May 1921, both men were found guilty of murder and sentenced to death in the electric chair in Sing Sing by Judge James C. van Siclen. However, gangster Frankie Yale (see box on right) decided to help out. He had a more than passing acquaintance with a friendly judge, Francis McQuade, who declared a mistrial on a

---

FRANKIE YALE

Born in Calabria, Italy in 1893 as Francesco Iole, he led New York's Five Points Gang. One of his foot soldiers was Al Capone, who later ordered his murder. On 1 July 1928, while driving down 44th Street in Brooklyn, Yale's car was forced off the road and when it crashed, was riddled with sub-machine-gun fire – it was New York's first tommy-gun killing.

---

technicality on 6 December 1921 and ordered a new trial. Justice McQuade was a silent partner in a Havana casino and numbered Lucky Luciano, Dutch Schultz, Meyer Lansky and the Mangano brothers as his friends. Anastasia walked free when four important witnesses were shot dead and a fifth confined to a mental asylum.

In April 1923, Anastasia was shot and a friend murdered during a bootlegging feud. That same year he was convicted of possession of a gun and sentenced to two years in prison.

Anastasia joined the gang lead first by Giuseppe "Joe the Boss" Masseria and then, when Giuseppe was murdered (by a four-man team on 15 April 1931 that included Anastasia), by Lucky Luciano and Frank Costello. Luciano rewarded Anastasia's loyalty by making him the head of Murder Inc.'s enforcement department. Anastasia's closest working colleague was Louis "Lepke" Buchalter and it is estimated that in a decade Murder Inc. killed about 500 people. However, Anastasia was never charged with murder – whenever a charge seemed likely, witnesses always disappeared or came down with a sudden case of amnesia.

Murder Inc.'s power began to decline in the early 1940s after the hit man, Abe Reles, was granted immunity from prosecution in return for his testimony, and their reputation as "untouchable" began to falter.

Before John Gotti became the "Dapper Don", Albert Anastasia was a sharp dresser.

However, Anastasia placed a bounty of $100,000 on Reles' head and on 12 November 1941, Reles accidentally fell from the sixth-floor balcony of his room at the Half Moon Hotel in Coney Island, where he was being guarded by the police. Anastasia became the sole head of Murder Inc. when Buchalter was executed for first-degree murder in March 1944. It is believed that Anastasia was a prime mover in a plan to free Lucky Luciano from his 30–50-year prison sentence by winning him a pardon for helping the war effort.

In 1951, Anastasia became the boss of the Mangano (later Gambino) crime family after Vincent Mangano went missing and his brother Philip was murdered. The Mangano crime family made their money on the docks – insisting that all dockers paid a fee to work and refusing to allow any ships to be unloaded unless the shipping companies paid a "tribute". Vincent Mangano, with his brother Philip by his side, headed the family from 1931 until he fell foul of Albert Anastasia. On 18 April 1951, Philip Mangano was in a betting shop, Joe the Bootblack's Shoe Shop on Sackett Street, Brooklyn, when he was told he was needed on Union Street. He left the illegal bookies and the next day was found murdered near Sheepshead Bay, Brooklyn, with three .45-calibre bullets in his head. Vincent vanished the same day. His body has never been found.

As a crime boss, Anastasia's brutality knew no bounds. In 1952, he ordered 24-year-old Arnold Schuster, a Brooklyn tailor's assistant, to be killed. Unfortunately for Schuster, Anastasia had seen him on television talking about his role as a lead witness in fugitive bank robber Willie Sutton's arrest. Anastasia is said to have shouted at his underlings, "I can't stand squealers! Hit that guy!" On 8 March, Arnold Schuster was found on the street where he lived, having been shot four times – once in each eye and twice in the groin. His killer was Frederick J. Tenuto, a career criminal who was on the FBI's "most wanted" list. Tenuto was spotted as he fled the murder scene and, fearful that he would lead the authorities to him,

Anastasia ordered Tenuto's own murder shortly afterwards. His body was never found.

Schuster's murder horrified other Mafia bosses because it brought more scrutiny on the organization and also broke a cardinal rule against killing outsiders. Luciano and Costello could not move against Anastasia as much as they would have liked to, because they needed his brutality in their power struggle with Vito Genovese, the head of a rival gang. Genovese began to canvass Anastasia's supporters to get them away from the Lord High Executioner. Carlo Gambino became an ally but still Genovese did not dare move against Anastasia and his real target, Costello (regarded by many as not being the rightful heir to the Luciano mantle; Genovese believed he should lead the family), because of the powerful Meyer Lansky, who would have to authorize any execution. It was not until Anastasia overstepped the mark and demanded a large slice of Lansky's Cuban gambling operation that Gambino agreed to support Genovese's plan to kill Anastasia. It was Anastasia's violent behaviour that finally caused Lansky to agree to his assassination.

One of Albert's brothers, Anthony "Tough Tony" Anastasio, also became involved in crime. He ran New York's docks with an iron fist. If he met with any dissent, he had only to utter the words "My brother Albert" for it to mysteriously vanish. He once berated a reporter on the New York World-Telegram and Sun who had written unfavourably of Albert, "How come you keep writing all those bad things about my brother Albert? He ain't killed no one in your family... yet." After his brother's murder, Tough Tony considered becoming a government informant but died of a heart attack on 1 March 1963 before the plan could be developed.

Date and Place of Assassination
25 October 1957, barber's shop in Park Sheraton Hotel (now the Park Central Hotel) at 870 Seventh Avenue at 56th Street, New York City.

The Event

On the morning of 25 October 1957, Anastasia was driven in his new Oldsmobile from his high-security home in Fort Lee, New Jersey, to the Park Sheraton Hotel in Manhattan. He went into the barber's, while his bodyguard, Anthony "Tough Tony" Coppola, parked the car in the underground car park. Rather than going to Anastasia's side, he took a walk. It is still a matter of conjecture whether Coppola was warned, but it seems likely that he was. The Lord High Executioner relaxed in his usual chair number four and chatted to the owner, Arthur Grasso. In chair number five was Vincent "Jimmy Jerome" Squillante, an associate of Anastasia. A doctor sat in the chair next to Squillante. At 10.10am, two masked men entered the hotel lobby and told the barber, Joseph Bocchino, to move out of the way before one of the men opened fire on Anastasia with a .38 calibre Colt pistol. One shot went into the back of Anastasia's head and lodged in the left side of his brain. Two more shots hit his left hand. Another bullet went into his back at a downward angle and penetrated a lung, a kidney and his spleen. The second assassin, equipped with .32 calibre Smith and Wesson long-barrel revolver, hit Anastasia's right hip and grazed the back of his neck. Anastasia crashed to the floor, dead.

Manicurist Jean Wineberger said the first killer was about 40 years old, 5 feet 10 inches–5 feet 11 inches (1.75–1.8 metres) tall, about 168 pounds (76 kilograms), had blond hair with a pompadour, a fair complexion and was right-handed. The second shooter, she said, was about 45 years old, 5 feet 7 inches (1.7 metres), stocky, medium complexion and may have been Italian or Jewish. Their mission complete, the two men tried to run into the street but the barber's door was locked, so they exited the way they came in, calmly walking through the hotel lobby. Police found one of the murder weapons discarded in the corridor leading from the barber's to the hotel lobby and one in the street two blocks away near a subway entrance.

The Assassins

The Anastasia murder remains officially unsolved. It is alleged that the killers were a three-man hit team (two killers and a lookout) selected by Joseph "Joe the Blonde" Biondo (died 1966), who became Carlo Gambino's underboss after the murder. Biondo is thought to have chosen Stephen Armone, drug dealer Arnold "Witty" Wittenberg and Stephen "Stevie Coogin" Grammauta, a convicted drug dealer and heroin smuggler.

The Aftermath

In 1959, the Manhattan District Attorney's office reviewed the case and mentioned that a subject had "identified Ralph Mafrici and Joseph Gioelli as the perpetrators of this crime". Conveniently, Gioelli was dead and Mafrici was in prison on an assault and robbery conviction. He was questioned but remained silent.

Despite professing his support, Carlo Gambino betrayed Genovese and told Luciano and Costello that he (Genovese) wanted them both dead. In concert with Meyer Lansky, Luciano and Costello, Gambino plotted Genovese's downfall. They engineered a drugs bust that saw him receive a life sentence.

Anastasia was buried in Section 39, Lot 38325 of Green-Wood Cemetery, 500 25th Street Brooklyn, New York 11232-1317.

The leader of the suspected three-man assassination team, Steve Armone, became a drug dealer at the end of the Prohibition era. He served 28 months in a federal penitentiary after being convicted in 1935. He died of natural causes in 1960. Witty Wittenberg died in 1978. Grammauta was convicted of trafficking heroin from Holland in 1965 and was sentenced to five years in prison. In the late 1990s, having kept a low profile after his release from prison, he became a *capo* (short for *caporegime*, meaning a high ranking member) in the Gambino family after its boss John Gotti (1940–2002) went to prison.

Reinhard Heydrich (1904–1942)

Ruthless and passionate, it was said that even Hitler was a little afraid of Reinhard Heydrich.

The Victim

One of Adolf Hitler's most enthusiastic henchmen, Reinhard Tristan Eugen Heydrich, described by Hitler as "the man with the iron heart", was born at 10.30am on 7 March 1904 at Marienstrasse 21 in Halle, the second child of three, and eldest son of the musician (Richard) Bruno Heydrich (born Leuben, Lommatzsch 23 February 1863, died 1938) and Elisabeth Anna Maria Amalia Kranz, whom he married in December 1897. Aged six months, little Reinhard fell seriously ill with encephalitis and fearing he would go to hell, his parents had him baptized a Catholic on 1 October 1904. Heydrich was a solitary child, ignored by his parents and bullied by his classmates.

By November 1918, Reinhard Heydrich was a passionate German and was horrified by his country's defeat in the First World War. Like many of his countrymen, he blamed the Jews, Communists and freemasons for Germany's defeat. Despite being two years underage, he joined the Freiwillige Landesjägerkorps (Voluntary Provincial Rifle Corps) in 1919 when Spartacists (Communist) terrorists occupied Halle. By 5 March the insurgency was over. Thirty Spartacists and seven soldiers died in the fighting. The following year another bloody uprising occurred in Halle and Heydrich was involved as a volunteer despatch messenger. It was at this time that Heydrich became *völkisch* (racially nationalist) and joined the 250,000-member Völkischer Schutz-und Trutzebund (Defensive and Offensive League), linked to the secretive Thule Gesellschaft (Thule Society), which was guided by Dietrich Eckart, Hitler's mentor. The Thule Gesellschaft had a swastika as its emblem and blamed the Jews for Germany's collapse.

On 30 March 1922, Heydrich joined the Reichsmarine at Kiel with a view to becoming an admiral. Under the Treaty of Versailles the German navy was severely depleted. On April Fool's Day 1924, Heydrich was promoted to senior midshipman and sent for officer training at the Mürwick Naval College near Flensburg. As at school, his contemporaries bullied Heydrich and belittled his high-pitched voice, his hooked nose and narrow eyes. They called him "The White Jew" and Heydrich responded by becoming exceptionally anti-Semitic. On 1 October 1926, he was promoted to lieutenant and then *oberleutnant*, the highest rank he would achieve before his dishonourable discharge on 30 April 1931 (after becoming involved in a minor sex scandal). He joined the National Sozialistische Deutsche Arbeiter Partei (National Socialist German Workers Party) on 1 June 1931 in Hamburg and the SS as Untersturmführer the following month on 14 July at a salary of 120 Reichsmarks.

On 1 December, Reichsführer-SS Heinrich Himmler promoted Heydrich to SS-Hauptsturmführer (captain). That same year, on Boxing Day, at the Evangelical Church of St Katherine at Grossenbrode on Fehmarn, he married Lina von Osten (born 14 June 1911, died Fehmarn 14 August 1985). Nazis forming a guard of honour gave the Hitler salute as the couple left the church. The Heydrichs had four children: Klaus (born 17 June 1933, killed 24 October 1943 in a road accident), Heider (born 28 December 1934), Silke (born 9 April 1939) and Marte (born posthumously on 23 July 1942).

JEWISH ANCESTRY?

Reinhard Heydrich was obsessed by the thought that he might have Jewish blood. There were regular rumours that his father's real name was Isidor Süss. In the 1916 edition of a reference work, *Musik-Lexikon*, the author Hugo Riemann referred to this "fact". Bruno Heydrich complained and it was deleted from subsequent editions. Perhaps the confusion arose because Heydrich's mother Ernestine Wilhelmine Lindner (1840–1923) married a locksmith's assistant named Gustav Robert Süss (1853–1931), three years after the death of her husband (and Bruno's father) Carl Julius Reinhold Heydrich (1837–1874). In fact, Gustave Süss was not Jewish but Evangelical-Lutheran.

HEINRICH HIMMLER

Born in Munich on 7 October 1900, Himmler was raised a devout Catholic. In 1928 he became a poultry farmer. On 6 January 1929 Hitler appointed him head of the SS. He set up the first concentration camp at Dachau and became supreme commander of the Volksturm, the People's Army, on 21 July 1944. However, he fell from favour in April 1945 when he made a clumsy attempt to contact the Allies. Hitler ordered his arrest. He attempted to flee following the German surrender but was captured. He killed himself with a suicide pill on 23 May 1945.

Heydrich began work in earnest rooting out informers and disloyal party members. He admired the work and organization of MI6 and took to signing his letters "C", in an apparent homage to the head of the British Secret Service.

In 1932 the old canard that Heydrich had "Jewish or coloured" blood surfaced and to rid himself of the "smear" which could end his career, he hired a genealogist to examine his ancestry (the genealogist found no evidence for Jewish heritage). Subsequently, many historians have examined Heydrich's ancestry and claim that Heydrich did not have Jewish blood (see box to left). However, there is a mystery that has yet to be explained. In 1810 his great-great-grandmother married Johann Gottfried *Heidrich*. Her name was Johanna Birnbaum and she was born in 1773 at Reichenbach and died in 1841 in Arnsdorf. Birnbaum is not necessarily of Jewish origin, but it opens an intriguing possibility. Heydrich's immediate boss Heinrich Himmler did believe that his deputy had Jewish blood.

By the time Hitler came to power on 30 January 1933, Heydrich was now head of Sicherheitsdienst, or SD, the secret police. With Himmler, Heydrich began arresting their political enemies. On 22 March the first concentration camp opened at Dachau. It would soon be full of opponents to the Nazi regime. On 11 April 1933 the SS took control of Dachau and, the next day, the first Jews were shot. Between 1933 and 1945 more than 206,000 people would be sent to Dachau. On 20 April 1934, Hitler's 45th birthday, Heydrich became Himmler's deputy at the Gestapo, while continuing as head of the SD. Heydrich was keen to show his worth to Hitler and, with the help of Joseph Goebbels, Hermann Goering and Himmler, persuaded him that there was a conspiracy against him. Between 29 June and 2 July 1934, 89 "enemies of the state" were murdered on Heydrich's orders including Ernst Röhm, the homosexual head of the SA (the secret service rivals to Heydrich's SD) and godfather to Heydrich's son. That month Heydrich was promoted to SS-Gruppenführer – he was just 30 years old.

On 26 June 1936, Hitler made Heydrich chief of the Sicherheitspolizei, the security police. Heydrich began to turn even more against his own background: he loathed freemasons (his father was a freemason), Jews (did he have Jewish blood?), and Catholics (his mother was a Catholic and he had been baptized into that religion). Away from home for long periods, he sought solace in the arms of women but according to a biographer he was so brutal in his attentions that ordinary women shunned him. He was a regular visitor to brothels where he indulged in bizarre sexual practices. He had no friends, only acquaintances that he used and discarded when they had served their purpose, and looked down on his colleagues who fraternized with lower ranks. Heydrich made it his business to know all the peccadilloes of the high-ranking Nazis from Reichsmarschall Goering's morphine addiction, to Himmler's stomach cramps, to Goebbels's infidelities, to what he believed to be the truth behind the death of Hitler's mistress Geli Raubal in 1931 (that she was murdered and Hitler was responsible).

In 1939, Heydrich joined the Luftwaffe and learned to fly Messerschmitts. His aerial ability was limited and his behaviour was often reckless; on more than one occasion, he wrecked the aeroplane. After one crash too many, Himmler banned Heydrich from the cockpit. In 1940, Heydrich was appointed head of the International Criminal Police Commission, the forerunner of Interpol. On 26 March 1941, Heydrich presented Goering with a document *The Solution of the Jewish Problem*, the prelude to the Final Solution. Bizarrely, although Heydrich was determined to exterminate the Jews, he did show mercy to some Semites. He was a keen and talented fencer and he arranged for the former German champion fencer, Paul Sommer, who was Jewish, to be given safe passage to America. He also insisted when war broke out that no member of the 1936 Polish Olympic fencing team be harmed.

In the summer of 1941, Heydrich summoned SS-Obersturmbannführer Adolf Eichmann, the Reichssicherheitshauptamt head of Jewish Affairs, and told him, "The Führer has ordered the physical destruction of the Jews." On 20 January 1942 at the Wannsee Conference in Berlin, Heydrich was chosen to administer the Final Solution. By that winter, more than 50,000 German Jews had been transported to ghettoes in Kaunas, Lodz, Minsk and Roga. On 24 September 1941, Hitler appointed Heydrich acting Reichs-Protektor

---

ADOLF EICHMANN

Born on 19 March 1906 at Solingen, Germany, Eichmann was nicknamed "the little Jew" by his classmates because of his dark complexion. He fled to Argentina at the end of the Second World War. He was captured by Mossad, the Israeli secret service, on 11 May 1960 and taken to Israel. Tried for war crimes between 11 April and 14 August 1961 in Jerusalem, he was sentenced to death on 15 December 1961. He was hanged at Ramle on 31 May 1962. He was 56 years old.

Reichs-Protektor Reinhard Heydrich (centre left) was a force to be feared. Cold and callous, he brooked no opposition.

of Bohemia and Moravia. Heydrich's predecessor Konstantin von Neurath (born at Klein Glattbach, Württemberg 2 February 1873, died at Enzweihingen 14 August 1956, two years after he was released from Spandau Prison) was "only" on sick leave, having been deemed not sufficiently strict with the Czechs. (He finally relinquished his post on 20 August 1943.)

On 19 November 1941, in the Wenceslas Chapel of the Prague Cathedral of St Vitus, Heydrich was shown the Bohemian crown jewels by the Czech president Emil Hacha. To the horror of all those present, Heydrich took the crown of Wenceslas and placed it on his own head. The crown carried with it a curse: "Whoever [shall] wear it without authority will die violently within a year, followed in death by his eldest son."

Life in Czechoslovakia was almost peaceful. The country escaped Allied air bombings and partisan resistance was almost non-existent – almost, but not quite. Reichs-Protektor von Neurath had been content to adopt a laissez-faire but firm attitude in his domain. Acting Reichs-Protektor Heydrich saw his appointment as an opportunity to impress Hitler and he had the Czech Prime Minister Alois Elias arrested, tried, convicted and sentenced to death within seven days. The reason given by Heydrich for the arrest was that Elias had been in touch with the Czechoslovak government in exile in London. In court Elias read out a statement thanking the Gestapo for their kind treatment of him and the fairness of his trial. He added that he was happy to die if it meant closer ties between Czechoslovakia and Germany were established. The sentence was not carried out. After the war, it was discovered that Elias had been threatened that if he did not make the public statement, 20,000 Czechs would be put to death.

As Heydrich's protectorate continued, the Czech resistance movement gathered momentum. In May 1942, Heydrich went on holiday to Paris. He spent part of the time preparing his next career move; he wanted to move to France, feeling that his work in Czechoslovakia was complete. He intended to use the methods he had used to quell Prague to similar effect in Paris. On 26 May, back in Prague, Heydrich held a concert at the Waldstein Palace in memory of his father who had died four years earlier. Heydrich believed that the people over whom he ruled respected him, if not actually loved him. A few hours before the concert, he told reporters, "I would not hesitate to respond with unheard-of violence if I should gain the feeling that the Reich is considered weak, and the loyal conciliation on my part is interpreted as weakness." When armaments minister Albert Speer visited Heydrich in the spring of 1942 he was amazed to learn that the Reichs-Protektor drove himself around Prague without bodyguards. When Speer protested, Heydrich replied, "Why should my Czechs shoot me?"

Date and Place of Assassination

27 May 1942, Lieben, Prague, Czechoslovakia.

The Event

At 10.15am on 27 May 1942, Jozef Gabcík waited nervously at the Klein-Holeschowitz tram stop in the Prague suburb of Lieben. Further up the road was Josef Valcik who, armed with a signalling shaving mirror, waited for the arrival of Reichs-Protektor Heydrich. Despite the warm weather, Gabcík carried a raincoat over his arm. Under it was a Mark II FF 209 sten gun. Across the road, Jan Kubic leant against a lamppost, two bombs hidden in his briefcase.

At 10.29am the number 3 tram approached and with it Heydrich's dark-green Mercedes 320 – registration number SS-3. In the car were Heydrich and a driver, SS-Oberscharführer Johannes Klein, and they were making their regular journey between Heydrich's home in Panenské Brezany and Prague Castle. The Mercedes stopped to allow passengers to get on and off the tram. From a distance of 3 metres (3 yards), Gabcík dropped his raincoat and pointed the gun at Heydrich and pulled the trigger. The weapon jammed. Heydrich stood up in the convertible and drew his pistol and aimed at Gabcík. He pulled the trigger but nothing happened – the gun was empty. Instead of driving off to safety, Klein put his foot on the brake. Kubic opened his briefcase and threw one of his bombs. It fell short and exploded by the rear right wheel. Splinters of metal and horsehair from the car's upholstery went into Heydrich's back. Gabcík threw away his sten gun and ran, pursued by Johannes Klein. The driver caught up with Gabcík in the butcher's, where the Czech pulled out a pistol and shot Klein in the leg, before

making good his escape. Kubic, who had also been wounded by his inept bomb throwing, fled the scene on his bicycle. The signaller, Valcik, also disappeared. Heydrich collapsed, bleeding from a small hole in his back.

At first no one went to help the fallen Reichs-Protektor. It was 11am before Heydrich was taken to the nearby Bulovka Hospital. When doctors operated, they discovered that Heydrich's spleen had been irreparably damaged. The first surgeon, Professor Walter Hollbaum, made too large an incision (above Heydrich's navel) and was quickly replaced by Professor Walter Dick. He made a cut in Heydrich's side and the spleen was removed. Heydrich's diaphragm was stitched and the wound was closed. Unfortunately, the original incision caused an infection in the stomach, which spread quickly. At 9am on 4 June 1942, seven days after the assassination attempt, Reichs-Protektor, SS-Obergruppenführer and General der Polizei Reinhard Heydrich died in Bulovka Hospital. He was 38.

The autopsy stated that death was due to septi-caemia. His body lay in state in the Hradshin Place, a giant Iron Cross behind it and black and white SS flags at half-mast. Thousands of Czechs filed by to pay their respects. Taken back to Germany, Heydrich was given a state funeral, the ceremony conducted mainly in the Mosaic Room of the New Reich Chancellery. The hall of the Chancellery was designed by the architect of the Third Reich, Albert Speer (1905–1982). Before its destruction, it was the scene of nine state funerals. Himmler paid tribute to Heydrich, although some felt that his eulogy was not as enthusiastic as it might have been and blamed this on the Reichsführer's belief that Heydrich had Jewish blood. Hitler then posthumously awarded Heydrich the highest stage of the German Order, the highest award in his gift. However, although Hitler praised Heydrich in public, in private he was furious at Heydrich's bravado in driving around Prague without bodyguards, calling it "a stupidity of no use to the nation". Heydrich was laid to rest at the Invaliden Cemetery, Scharnhorst Strasse, Berlin, Germany.

The Assassins

Three Czech partisans – Jozef Gabcík (born 8 April 1912), Josef Valcik and Jan Kubic (born 24 June 1913) – were responsible for Heydrich's assassination. They were trained by the elite British Special Operations Executive and the operation was codenamed Anthropoid by the Czech government in exile. Gabcík was a locksmith by trade while Kubic was a chimney builder. On 29 December 1941, the RAF had dropped Gabcík and Kubic over the wrong place near Prague. The Prague Resistance provided them with false ID papers.

The Aftermath

The Germans placed a monument adorned with Heydrich's bust on the site of the assassination. The memorial had a permanent SS guard until the Germans fled the city in 1945. In revenge for Heydrich's assassination, Hitler wanted to shoot 10,000 Czechs but was persuaded by Himmler to arrest 10,000 but only shoot the first hundred. One of the first to die was Alois Elias, the prime minister who had earlier escaped death. A Gestapo report claimed that the village of Lidice, near the mining town of Kladno, northwest of Prague, was hiding Czech partisans. The claim was false but on 10 June 1942 the Germans executed all of the village's 184 male inhabitants. They sent the rest of the villagers, 198 women and 105 children, to concentration camps; Ravensbrück and Lodz respectively. In the camps 55 of the women and 88 children perished. (Note that the numbers of the dead vary according to sources.) The village was torn down, dynamited and then levelled. After the war, some of the survivors built a new village called Lidice near the original site, near Prague, in what is now the Czech Republic. The original site now serves as a memorial to the sufferings of Czechoslovakia under German occupation. On 24 June 1942, the Gestapo shot all 33 inhabitants of the village of Lezaky after discovering a hidden Resistance transmitter.

Siegfried Heinz Heydrich, Rheinhard's younger brother, became a journalist and was publisher of the soldiers' newspaper *Der Panzerfaust*. After his brother's murder, he was given many of his brother's files. He read them and was horrified to discover the truth of the Final Solution. He began using his journalistic expertise to forge papers to help Jews escape to Scandinavia. In November 1944 his office came under investigation and believing that the authorities knew of his activities, he shot himself on 19 November in the train compartment that doubled as his office at the Front in east Prussia. In fact, his forgeries went unnoticed – the investigation was merely to discover why so much paper had gone missing.

The Czech government in exile, based in London and led by Eduard Benes, described Operation Anthropoid as a great success. However, the three assassins were betrayed by their comrade Karel Curda. Born on 10 October 1911 at Nová Hlína near Trebon, he was paid one million Reichsmark to become a Nazi informer. He was executed in Prague for treason on 29 April 1947.

Gabcík, Kubic and Valcik and four other partisans sought sanctuary in the Church of Saints Cyril and Methodius. At 2am on 18 June 1942, the church was surrounded by 800 Gestapo and SS troops. They began to storm the building at 4.15am but were kept at bay by three valiant partisans – Kubic, Adolf Opalka and Jaroslav Svarc – for almost 3 hours. By 7am, Opalka was dead and the other two badly wounded. Rather than surrender they shot themselves in the head, but were still alive when discovered and taken to an SS hospital. Both men died without regaining consciousness.

The Germans were unaware that four more partisans were hiding in the crypt until they found a suit that did not belong to Kubic, Opalka or Svarc. A long fight ensued and when the Germans finally got into the crypt they found the four men dead from self-inflicted gunshot wounds to the head. Over the next few weeks, 240 people who had helped the partisans were arrested and executed.

Thousands of Czechs died in the summer of 1942 in the reprisals that followed Heydrich's murder. A word was coined – Heydrichiade – to describe the terror.

Bugsy Siegel (1906–1947)

The Victim

Benjamin – no one called him "Bugsy" to his face if they had any sense – Siegel was born on 28 February 1906 in the Williamsburg district of Brooklyn, the second of five children of Max Siegel and Jennie Riechenthal. He grew up in the slums of New York's East Side.

Siegel was a villain from an early age – he joined a street gang on Lafayette Street on the Lower East Side and was soon stealing; he even started a protection racket charging local stallholders $5. In April 1918 Siegel, then just 12 years old, and a 13-year-old friend Herbie "The Marble" Kintisch robbed a loan office on West 48th Street. He met and befriended Meyer Lansky and the pair formed a gang of car thieves and ran illegal gambling dens. Bugsy was also said to be the gang's hit man and Lansky hired him out to other gangs.

Siegel began a semi-legitimate career as a taxi driver but used his position to work out rich pickings for robbery. He was probably the only New York cabbie to have business cards printed. On 3 January 1926, Siegel was arrested for raping a woman who had been a passenger in his cab. Under Lansky's persuasion, she decided not to testify. Four years later, Lansky and

---

MEYER LANSKY

Meyer Lansky was born on 28 August 1900 in Grodno, Poland as Maier Suchowljanksy. His family went to America, arriving at Ellis Island on 8 April 1911. He became close friends with Charles "Lucky" Luciano (see box on page 94) and Siegel after meeting them on 24 October 1918. In the 1920s Lansky and Siegel worked as bootleggers. Lansky rose to become one of the most powerful Mafioso in the 1940s and 50s. He allowed Luciano to nominally be the leader, fearing that a Jew as head of the organization would deter other Italian gangsters.

Siegel joined forces with Charles "Lucky" Luciano and Frank Costello, "the Prime Minister of the Underworld" (see box on page 94). Siegel began bootlegging in New York, New Jersey and Philadelphia.

In 1928 a turf war – the so-called Castellammarese War – began between Giuseppe "Joe the Boss" Masseria and Salvatore Maranzano. The war dragged on and some of those involved – particularly Luciano – called for a truce. The battle came to an end at Nouva Villa Tammaro, a restaurant on Coney Island, on 15 April 1931 when Vito Genovese, Siegel, Joe Adonis and Albert Anastasia (see pages 82–85) murdered Masseria as he ate linguine. Luciano told police that he had been in the men's room at the time of the assassination. Maranzano was named as the *capo di tutti* but realised that his lieutenants probably intended him to suffer a fate similar to Masseria and decided to act. However, before he had the chance, he, too, was assassinated at 230 Park Avenue on 10 September 1931 on Luciano's orders. The victors formed an organization called Murder Inc. (see box on page 82). In 1932, Siegel was arrested for gambling and bootlegging but received just a fine. In 1934 the Mafia and Murder Inc. joined forces. Lansky and Siegel formed a short-lived partnership with Dutch Schultz and killed rival loan shark Joseph C. Amberg in a Brooklyn garage on 30 September 1935. Three weeks later, on 23 October, Joseph's brother Louis "Pretty" Amberg and Dutch Schultz were murdered.

Two years later, Siegel went to California to set up gambling dens on the west coast. Siegel recruited Jewish gang boss Mickey Cohen as his lieutenant. Once he was established, Siegel sent for his wife and two daughters. He had married his childhood sweetheart, Estelle "Esta" Krakower (1911–1982), the sister of hit man Whitey Krakower, on 28 January 1929. Millicent Siegel was born in 1930 and her sister, Barbara, arrived in 1932. Siegel had

Sartorially elegant, Siegel's smooth demeanour hid a vicious killer who even murdered his brother-in-law.

innumerable extramarital affairs and among his most well-known mistresses were the actresses Ketti Gallian (1912–1972), Wendy Barrie (1912–1978) and Marie "The Body" MacDonald (1923–1965), and the Hollywood socialite Countess DiFrasso (née Dorothy Taylor). It was the countess and the actor George Raft (1895–1980), a long-time friend of Bugsy, who engineered Siegel's entry into Hollywood society.

CHARLES "LUCKY" LUCIANO

The founder of the Mafia in the United States was born Salvatore Lucania at Lercara Friddi, Sicily, on 11 November 1897. The family arrived in America in 1906 and ten years later, in June 1916, Luciano was sentenced to a year in prison for opium trafficking. During the Second World War, Luciano helped the authorities, although this was denied for political expediency. Luciano, who never became a US citizen, was deported to Italy on 10 February 1946.

FRANK COSTELLO

Born as Francesco Castiglia at Lauropoli, near Cosenza in Calabria, southern Italy, on 26 January 1891, he arrived in New York in 1895. By 1911 Costello had been arrested twice and twice freed on charges of assault and robbery. Costello became a bootlegger but was clever enough to create legitimate businesses, which he used to influence politicians. Costello was seen as a master criminal who ruled a vast empire and was duly nicknamed the Prime Minister of the Underworld. Nevertheless, the media could find little evidence to confirm such popular suspicion. In April 1954 Costello was convicted of income tax evasion and in May 1956 began serving an 11-month prison sentence. In 1957 Costello survived a gang assassination attempt inspired by Vito Genovese.

On 22 November 1939, Thanksgiving, Siegel, his brother-in-law Whitey Krakower, Frank Carbo and Harry Segal killed gangster Harry "Big Greenie" Greenberg who, short of money, had written a letter asking for cash but couched in such terms that it appeared a threat to go to the police if he did not receive $5,000. Murder Inc.'s acting boss, Emmanuel "Mendy" Weiss, ordered Greenberg's execution and he was shot as he sat in the front seat of his new yellow Ford convertible reading a newspaper. When four gangsters turned evidence, Siegel was arrested. To protect himself, Siegel murdered his brother-in-law as Krakower sat on his stoop on Delancey Street on the Lower East Side enjoying the summer sunshine on 31 July 1940.

On 16 August, Siegel, Carbo and Segal were indicted for Greenberg's murder. The case collapsed on 5 February 1942 when no witnesses could be found to the killing. In 1941, Siegel fell heavily for the Alabama-born good-time girl Virginia "Sugar" Hill (born Lipscomb, 26 August 1916) whom he bedded after a party at the Mocambo nightclub. The writer George Carpozi, Jr also links Hill romantically to Lucky Luciano, Joe Adonis, Frank Costello and other mob kingpins, as well as a number of Hollywood moguls.

Siegel later told friends that Hill was "the best piece of ass I ever had". When the film *Ball of Fire*, in which Hill had a bit part, premiered in December 1941, she turned up with Siegel on her arm. Their affair became so obvious that Esta Siegel divorced her husband in Reno, Nevada.

Date and Place of Assassination
20 June 1947, 810 North Linden Drive, Beverly Hills, California, USA. Virginia Hill rented the house and gave Siegel a key.

The Event
Legend has it that one day while driving through Las Vegas, then a sleepy town, Siegel had the idea to turn it into a gambling mecca. In 1941 Siegel moved to Vegas

EMMANUEL "MENDY" WEISS

Weiss went to the electric chair at Sing Sing on 4 March 1944, along with Louis "Lepke" Buchalter (born Manhattan 12 February 1897) and Louis Capone (born 1896), for the murder of Joseph Rosen, a sweetshop owner, eight years earlier on 13 September 1936.

and in 1945 he began work on what would become the Pink Flamingo Hotel & Casino. Flamingo was his nickname for Virginia Hill. Somewhat surprisingly, the contractors ripped off Siegel who had no experience in the construction business. Some would supply materials, steal them at night and then resell them to Siegel the next day. Costs mounted and Siegel became more and more angry. An honest building tycoon, Del Webb, became worried when Siegel arrived on the site and discovered more materials had gone missing. Siegel reassured him, "Don't worry, we only kill each other."

At a cost of $6 million, the 105-room Pink Flamingo Hotel & Casino finally opened on Boxing Day 1946. In fact, it was just the casino that opened that night; the rest of the building was still unfinished. That night the weather was terrible; the celebrities that Siegel wanted to add glamour to the place stayed away, some because of the bad weather and some because they had been advised not to be seen mixing with a gangster; the ornamental fountain outside that was supposed to have been seen from miles away did not work; and when the doors opened it was quickly apparent that there were more staff than customers. The night was a disaster and the Flamingo promptly suffered huge losses. Business was so bad that the casino had to close at the end of January 1947. Siegel promised that he would fix things and reopened the entire project on 1 March. The losses were not abated and it was discovered that Siegel had been less than honest with the building costs of the Flamingo. It was to be a fatal mistake. His death was ordered.

DUTCH SCHULTZ

Dutch Schultz was born on 6 August 1902 (his grave states he was born in 1901) at 1690 Second Avenue, off 89th Street, in the Bronx, as Arthur Flegenheimer. He began his crime career aged 17 when he was convicted of burglary and spent 15 months in borstal. In 1928 he became a partner in a Bronx bar during Prohibition and later became a bootlegger supplying booze to upper Manhattan and the Bronx. At one time he was a partner with Jack "Legs" Diamond, Edward "Fats" McCarthy, and Vincent and Peter Coll. On 25 January 1933 Schultz was indicted for income tax evasion but two trials failed to convict him. He was fatally shot by Charles "The Bug" Workman in the backroom of the Palace Chop House, a saloon in Newark, New Jersey, on 23 October and died in hospital at 8.35pm the next day. He was 33. Workman was paroled, aged 54, on 10 March 1964, after spending 22 years and 9 months in jail.

AMBERG BROTHERS

There were, in fact, four Amberg brothers – Joseph (born 1892), Louis (born 1899), Hymie "The Rat" (c. 1902–3 November 1926) and Oscar. Joseph and Louis (the nickname "Pretty" was ironic) were drug dealers and blackmailers and were credited with at least 20 murders each. Hymie killed himself while trying to break out of Manhattan's Tombs prison.

In the early hours of 20 June 1947, after a night out, Siegel picked up his friend Allen Smiley, the film director, and drove to Virginia Hill's home. After a few hours' sleep, the two men rose at noon and Siegel went for his weekly manicure at Harry Drucker's barbershop in Beverly Hills and then visited his lawyer. In the evening he and Smiley went out for a seafood dinner at Jack's restaurant in Ocean Park with Charles "Chick" Hill,

Virginia's 19-year-old brother, and Jerri Mason, a secretary, with whom he was having an affair. All four returned to Linden Drive and Hill and Mason went upstairs. Siegel and Smiley sat at opposite ends of the sofa in the living room. Siegel picked up the previous day's *Los Angeles Times* to read. At 10.45pm (the exact time of the murder varies with different sources; this is the time given on Siegel's death certificate) a mob hit man (reportedly one Eddie Cannizzaro, although this is unconfirmed and virtually nothing is known about him) opened up through the window with an M1 Carbine. Smiley dived to the floor. Seven rounds were fired and one of the .30 calibre bullets hit the bridge of Siegel's nose, blowing his left eyeball out of its socket and 14 feet (4 metres) across the room, where it was found intact. Despite the pictures, Siegel was not actually shot in the eye but in the cheek and lungs.

The Assassin
The killer of Bugsy Siegel is officially unknown. No one was ever charged with the murder.

The Aftermath
The mob continued its hold on America and Las Vegas in particular. Siegel's partners immediately assumed control of the Flamingo and turned it into a leading Las Vegas attraction. The Hilton Corporation bought the Flamingo in 1972 and, two years later in 1974, it became the Flamingo Hilton. On 14 December 1993, the last remaining part of the original building was bulldozed and a garden was constructed on the site. It features a plaque to Bugsy Siegel, the only place in Las Vegas that formally acknowledges the Mob.

The American authorities did not attempt to bring down Meyer Lansky until 1970. He fled to Israel and claimed Israeli citizenship. Despite ploughing millions of dollars into Israel, the government cancelled his passport on 18 May 1971 as an embarrassment. On 5 November 1972, he left Israel, arriving in Miami two days later. In July 1973, Lansky went on trial for income tax evasion but was acquitted. On 21 November 1974, the government gave up trying to prosecute the gangster. Lansky died in Mount Sinai Hospital, Miami Beach, on 15 January 1983.

Frank Costello survived an assassination attempt on 2 May 1957. His would-be killer was Vincent "The Chin" Gigante, a foot soldier of Vito Genovese. Costello spent his retirement fighting the attempts of the Immigration and Naturalization Service to deport him to Italy. He died in New York City on 18 February 1973.

Following his deportation on 9 February 1946, Lucky Luciano was accused of arranging a drugs supply to America but charges were never brought. His final years were spent under surveillance by the Italian police and the US Federal Bureau of Narcotics. On 26 January 1962, he died of a heart attack at Naples's Capodicino airport where he had gone to meet a scriptwriter with a view to turning his life into a film. Luciano's brothers, Bartolo and Joseph, brought his body back to America and buried it in the family vault at St John's Cemetery in Queens on 7 February 1962.

Virginia Hill was charged with income tax evasion in June 1954 but fled to Austria before she could be brought to trial. She committed suicide, aged 49, with a drugs overdose, on 24 March 1966 at Koppel, near Salzburg.

AS SEEN ON SCREEN

The film *Ocean's Eleven* (1960) which starred the Rat Pack – Frank Sinatra, Dean Martin, Sammy Davis, Jr etc., was filmed at the Flamingo. The Flamingo is at 3555 Las Vegas Boulevard South, Las Vegas, NV89109.

The character of Moe Greene in *The Godfather* (1972), who was shot in the eye, was based on Siegel.

Ronald Reagan (1911–2004)

The Victim

Ronald Wilson Reagan was born, weighing 10 pounds (4.5 kilograms), in a five-room rented flat above a bakery on Main Street, Tampico, Illinois on 6 February 1911, the second son of John Edward "Jack" Reagan (born Fulton, Illinois 13 July 1883, died West Hollywood, California 18 May 1941), an alcoholic shoe salesman, and his wife Nelle Clyde Wilson (born Fulton, Illinois 24 July 1885, died Santa Monica, California 25 July 1962), whom he married in a Roman Catholic ceremony at the Church of the Immaculate Conception in Fulton, Illinois on 8 November 1904. Reagan was nicknamed "Dutch" by his father, because Jack Reagan thought his son looked like "a fat, little Dutchman".

He was educated at Filas Willard School (February 1916–1918), Central School, Monmouth (1918–1919), Tampico Grade School (1919–December 1920), South Central Grammar School (December 1920–1923), South Dixon High School (1923–1927), North Dixon High School (1927–1928) and Eureka College, Illinois from September 1928 until he obtained a BA in sociology and economics on 7 June 1932. During the summers of 1926 until 1933 he worked as a lifeguard at Lowell Park riverside beach near Dixon, Illinois and saved 77 people from drowning. One man he rescued gave Reagan a $10 tip for retrieving his false teeth from the riverbed. The town even put up a plaque in his honour.

After a screen test in March 1937, Reagan signed a seven-year contract, at a salary of $200 a week, with Warner Bros and made his debut in *Love Is On The Air*

The cinematic cowboy left Hollywood to become the most powerful man in the world.

(opened on 12 November 1937) as Andy McLeod, a newsreader with a conscience. Reagan got the part because Ross Alexander, the actor originally cast, shot himself. In the 1940 film *Knute Rockne – All American* in which he played the terminally ill George Gipp, he uttered the words, "Someday, when things are tough maybe you can ask the boys to go out there and win just once for the Gipper", a phrase that he would regularly use in the White House.

On 14 April 1942 Reagan joined the army as a second lieutenant of cavalry but never saw active service because of poor eyesight. Before his demob with the rank of captain on 9 December 1945, he spent three years making training films. After the war he became active in politics having joined the board of the Screen Actors' Guild (SAG) in July 1941. On 17 November 1947, he became SAG's president and held the position for five terms until November 1952 when he was elected to a three-year term on the board. Further three-year terms followed in November 1955 and November 1958. In November 1959 he was again elected president, a position he held until his resignation on 6 June 1960. On 9 July 1960 he resigned from the SAG board.

In 1947 he had been a friendly witness before the House Un-American Activities Committee. During the 1940s, Reagan was an FBI informant, code-named T-10, and gave up the names of actors he believed were communists or had communist sympathies. In 1948 he campaigned for Democrat Harry S. Truman, but gradually moved to the right and in 1962 switched allegiance to the Republican Party. In 1964 he campaigned for the archconservative Senator Barry Goldwater (1909–1998) against incumbent President Lyndon Baines Johnson (1908–1973) but was on the losing side as the Texan won in a landslide on 3 November 1964 – 538 Electoral College votes to 52.

On 4 January 1966, Reagan announced his candidature for the governorship of California, promising to cut taxes and spending; he won the gubernatorial contest on 8 November 1966, beating the popular and experienced Democrat Pat Brown (1905–1996). Reagan was sworn in a few minutes past midnight on 2 January 1967. Jack Warner is said to have remarked,

"All wrong. Jimmy Stewart for governor, Reagan for best friend." Four years later, on 4 January 1971, he was sworn in for a second term having defeated Jesse Unruh.

In 1968 and 1976, Reagan tried for the Republican nomination for the presidency, but lost to Richard Nixon (Reagan came third with just 182 votes) and Gerald Ford (Reagan was only narrowly defeated – 1,187 votes to 1,070). Undeterred, Reagan stood again in 1980 and was adopted on 16 July 1980 in Detroit. The campaign was clumsy and many people registered anti-votes rather then actively voting for a candidate. Reagan spoke of renewing ties with Taiwan while his vice presidential nominee, George Bush, was in Peking trying to cultivate good relations. Reagan blamed trees not cars for the smog that crippled Los Angeles. At a later meeting, one wag tied a sign to a tree that read, "Chop me down before I kill again." He claimed that air pollution was under control, yet only a few days later his plane had to be diverted because LAX was closed due to smog.

On 13 November 1979, Reagan appeared on television and told interviewer Tom Brokaw that, even at 68, he would be younger than many of the leaders he would be dealing with. Brokaw mentioned Valery Giscard d'Estaing, then French president and 15 years Reagan's junior. "Who?" said Reagan. Brokaw repeated the name and Reagan admitted that "yes", he was a bit older than the Frenchman. Reporters were amazed at Reagan's ignorance, but his press secretary replied that the candidate had not heard Brokaw. Reporter Lou Cannon suggested, "We could run a correction. The good news is that Ronald Reagan knows who the president of France is. The bad news is that he can't hear." Reagan's flack said, "We'd rather you say he was too ignorant than too old." Reagan's people even stole President Jimmy Carter's briefing book, which meant that Reagan knew what the president's position was going to be on virtually every subject.

Regarded as a genial sort, Reagan used the charm and acting skills he had learnt in Hollywood to good effect in Washington.

Amazingly, the public didn't seem to mind that Reagan constantly engaged mouth before brain and on 4 November 1980 he beat President Carter in a land-slide, winning 489 Electoral College votes to 49. Reagan, then 69 years 349 days old – the oldest-elected president, was inaugurated on 20 January 1981 at 11.57am and gave a 20-minute speech calling for "an era of national renewal". The inauguration cost $8 milllion, then the most expensive in history. On 6 March 1981 Reagan held his second press confer-ence and the first in history in which the questioners' names were chosen from a jellybean jar. The event was boycotted by many of the major networks and the idea quickly abandoned.

Date and Place of Attempted Assassination

30 March 1981, Washington Hilton Hotel, Washington DC, USA.

The Event

John Hinckley arrived in Washington on Sunday 29 March 1981 via a Greyhound bus and checked into room 312 of the Park Central Hotel on 18th and G streets. The next day, his 70th in office, Reagan arrived at the Washington Hilton Hotel, a dozen blocks from the White House, at 1.45pm to address the American Federation of Labour and Congress of Industrial Organizations, more commonly known as the AFL-CIO. At 2.25pm

TV DRAMA

To see a dramatized version of very similar events, watch the episode entitled "In the Shadow of Two Gunmen" of the hit television show *The West Wing*, when President Jed Bartlet was shot. The episode was broadcast in America on 4 October 2000 and in Britain on 12 June 2001. *The West Wing*'s creator Aaron Sorkin stated in the DVD commentary (not available in the UK) for this episode that the manner in which Special Agent Ron Butterfield discovers President Bartlet was hit was inspired by the attempt on Reagan, where agents did not realise that the president had been shot until he was in the car. Unlike in real life, Bartlet was not the intended target. He was accidentally shot when white supremacists tried to kill Charlie Young, his black bagman, who was dating his youngest daughter, Zoey.

Reagan left the building by a side entrance on T Street and waved to the small crowd outside. As he waved, Hinckley stepped forward and fired a Rohm RG-14 .22 calibre blue steel pistol six times in three seconds. The six bullets were Devastors, designed to explode on impact, although thankfully none of them did. The first round struck White House press secretary James Brady in the head; the second hit 47-year-old DC policeman Thomas K. Delehanty in the back; the third missed its target and hit the window of a building across the road; the fourth hit Timothy J. McCarthy, 33, of the Secret Service in the abdomen as he courageously stood in front of Reagan; the fifth struck the bullet-proof glass of the presidential limousine and the sixth bounced off the side of the car and hit Reagan under his left arm. Agent Jerry Parr jumped on the president and pushed him to the ground while Agent Ray Shaddick pushed his colleague and the president into the car. Reagan winced in pain, "Jerry, you son of a bitch, I think you've broken one of my ribs." Parr told the driver, Agent Drew Unrue, to return to the White House and ran his hands over Reagan's body. The president then began coughing up blood and Parr screamed at Unrue, "Go to GW!" The limousine screeched away from the White House and towards George Washington University Hospital, which is five blocks away.

The car arrived at GW at 2.35pm and Reagan, ever the showman, walked into the hospital, but as soon as he was inside he collapsed. Parr and Shaddick carried him to Trauma Bay 5, where the medical staff cut off all the president's clothes. Reagan lay naked with blood pouring from his mouth, moaning that he could not breathe. A doctor cut a hole in Reagan's throat and put a breathing tube into his throat, but it did not help. Reagan's blood pressure fell to 78 and he passed out. The frothy blood in Reagan's mouth meant that a lung had collapsed. He came round to find a nurse holding his hand.

Nancy Reagan arrived at the hospital and Reagan supposedly said, "Honey, I forgot to duck." Vice President George Bush was in Texas and was recalled by Alexander Haig, the Secretary of State. At 3.24pm Reagan was taken into theatre for surgery to remove the bullet. Dr Benjamin Aaron, GW's chief of thoracic surgery, performed the operation. Dr Aaron found the bullet an inch below the president's heart. Reagan's chest cavity was filled with blood and he had lost half of the blood in his body. Dr Aaron immediately decided to operate to repair the damaged lung.

Back at the White House Al Haig announced to the press corps that he was in charge pending the return of the vice president. In fact, he was not. The 25th Amendment to the Constitution, ratified in 1967, allowed for the succession and the order was the vice president, the speaker of the house (then Tip O'Neill of Massachusetts), then the president *pro tempore* of the Senate (Strom Thurmond of South Carolina), then the secretary of state (Haig). The military command chain was the president, the vice president then the defence secretary (at the time Caspar Weinberger). At 6.20pm the surgery on Reagan was complete and ten minutes after that, Air Force Two landed at Andrews Air Force Base and taxied into a hangar so that no one, including snipers, could see George Bush disembark. Bush arrived in the situation room below the West Wing at 6.59pm. Reagan began to regain consciousness at 7.30pm.

The Would-be Assassin

John Warnock Hinckley, Jr was born in Ardmore, Oklahoma on 29 May 1955. Raised in Texas, he was educated at Highland Park High School and then Texas Tech University. In 1976 he moved to Los Angeles with a view to becoming a songwriter but his attempt came to nothing and he returned home. On 8 February of that same year, the film *Taxi Driver* (see box below) was released. Robert De Niro played mentally disturbed 26-year-old taxi driver Travis Bickle and 13-year-old Jodie Foster was the child prostitute Iris Steensma that Bickle tries to save from a life on the streets. When Bickle fails to woo a Senate aide, he plots to assassinate the senator. Hinckley saw the film several times and became obsessed with Jodie Foster.

When the actress moved to Yale, Hinckley also went to New Haven, Connecticut, where he began stalking her, putting poems under the door of her room and tele-

phoning her. Hinckley's advances were rebuffed. Hinckley was determined to get Foster to notice him and came up with some bizarre plans including hijacking a plane, killing himself in front of her and assassinating President Jimmy Carter. He trailed the president from state to state but was arrested in Nashville, Tennessee, on a gun charge. Back home, despite the fact that he underwent psychiatric treatment, he then began to stalk the newly-elected Reagan. An hour before he left to attempt to kill Reagan, he wrote a letter to Foster.

3/30/81
12.45PM

Dear Jodie,

There is a definite possibility that I will be killed in my attempt to get Reagan. It is for this very reason that I am writing you this letter now.

As you well know by now I love you very much. Over the past seven months I've left you dozens of poems, letters and love messages in the faint hope that you could develop an interest in me. Although we talked on the phone a couple of times I never had the nerve to simply approach you and introduce myself. Besides my shyness, I honestly did not wish to bother you with my constant presence. I know the many messages left at your door and in your mailbox were a nuisance, but I felt that it was the most painless way for me to express my love for you.

I feel very good about the fact that you at least know my name and know how I feel about you. And by hanging around your dormitory, I've come to realise that I'm the topic of more than a little conversation, however full of ridicule it may be. At least you know that I'll always love you.

TAXI DRIVER

The film was based in part on 21-year-old Arthur Bremer, who tried to assassinate Governor George Wallace (1919–1998) of Alabama on 15 May 1972. Wallace was paralysed by the event and Bremer was sentenced to 63 years in prison (later reduced to 53 on appeal). With good behaviour he could be released in 2015, although this seems unlikely due to his prison reports.

Jodie, I would abandon this idea of getting Reagan in a second if I could only win your heart and live out the rest of my life with you, whether it be in total obscurity or whatever.

I will admit to you that the reason I'm going ahead with this attempt now is because I just cannot wait any longer to impress you. I've got to do something now to make you understand, in no uncertain terms, that I am doing all of this for your sake! By sacrificing my freedom and possibly my life, I hope to change your mind about me. This letter is being written only an hour before I leave for the Hilton Hotel. Jodie, I'm asking you to please look into your heart and at least give me the chance, with this historical deed, to gain your respect and love.

I love you forever,
John Hinckley

The Aftermath

Reagan became the first president to survive the dreaded Zero Factor (see box on page 104). He left hospital on 11 April 1981. Reagan's presidency was an exceptionally right-wing one. On 1 March 1982, a member of Reagan's own party – Senator Bob Packwood from Oregon – criticized the president for passing off entirely fictional anecdotes as if they were real events. On 12 December 1983, before a meeting of the Congressional Medal of Honour Society, he told a story of airborne heroism in the Second World War that resulted in the posthumous award of a Congressional Medal of Honour. A search among all 434 recipients during the war failed to trace Reagan's story and a journalist reported that the tale was very similar to one that appeared in the 1944 film *Wing And A Prayer* and also the April 1944 issue of *Reader's Digest*.

On 5 April 1982 Reagan refused to back the UK task force as it sailed for the Falkland Islands to retake the dependency from the Argentine invaders. "We're friends of both sides," he said. Ten days later, he told an audience that "England was always very proud of the fact that the police did not have to carry guns … In England if a criminal carried a gun, even though he didn't use it, he was tried not for burglary or theft or whatever he was doing, he was tried for first-degree murder and hung if he was found guilty." The next day Larry Speakes, the White House press secretary, admitted that the president was talking rubbish. Incredibly, Reagan repeated the fiction on 21 March 1986. On 27 May 1983, the night before a world economic summit in Williamsburg, Reagan eschewed his briefing notes and instead watched *The Sound Of Music* on television.

On 29 June 1983, Reagan blamed poor student grades on the schools' efforts to comply with racial desegregation. He sought to destabilize governments he disagreed with and broke the law by sending aid to the Nicaraguan contras – rebels who were attempting to overthrow the government of Sandinista. Reagan clashed with the Senate, which disagreed with his policy. On 1 March 1985, Reagan called the contra leaders the "moral equivalent of our founding fathers", only to be rebuffed by historical novelist Howard Fast who said the comment was "an explosion of such incredible ignorance that … he is not fit for public office of any kind." Reagan despatched $155 million of aid – food and guns – to the contras. He denied that secret funds were being sent, "Nothing of that kind could take place without the knowledge of Congress." He sent aid to the Afghans fighting the Soviet troops and invaded Grenada on 25 October 1983 without informing the head of state (Queen Elizabeth II). Reagan claimed that it was "a rescue mission" rather than an invasion.

Despite all this he was re-elected on 6 November 1984 in yet another landslide, winning 525 Electoral College votes to the Democrat Walter Mondale's 13. It was the biggest number of Electoral College votes ever won. When some Democrats drew attention to Reagan's age, he came up with a nice response on 21 October 1984: "I will not make age an issue of this campaign. I'm not going to exploit for political purposes my opponent's youth and inexperience." Reagan's second inauguration, on 20 January 1985, took place in the foyer of the White House because it was too cold for the president outside. The inaugural parade was also cancelled, only the second time ever in history. (Andrew Jackson's in 1833 was the first.)

On 13 November 1986, Reagan admitted that his administration had been secretly selling arms to Iran in exchange for freeing the hostages. "Arms-for-hostages" contravened Reagan's public declaration of never dealing with terrorists. Later that month, it emerged that the Iranians had been overcharged for the weapons, and the profits – between $10 and $30 million – had been sent to the contras by members of the National Security Council (NSC). Reagan claimed not to know about the deals. A commission led by Senator John Tower was set up to investigate the misdemeanours. It discovered that Lieutenant-Colonel Oliver North had been leading a shadow government from inside the NSC and heavily criticized Reagan. When Rear Admiral John Poindexter, head of the NSC, testified before the Iran-Contra hearings on 15 July 1987 he said that he had made the decisions to send the money and kept Reagan in the dark. However, he added that if Reagan had known, which, of course, he didn't, he would have approved. In five days of testimony, Poindexter said, "I can't recall" or variations thereof 184 times.

During his candidature Reagan promised to resign at the first sign of senility, but on 20 February 1987 he told the Tower Commission that he did not remember if he had authorized materiel shipments. Despite claiming to save money, Reagan spent more on military expansion during peacetime than at any other time in American history. The country spent $148 million in 1980 and under Reagan more than $300 million.

Incredibly, Reagan believed that money spent on the armed forces did not add to the national deficit because it employed companies who hired American labourers who then "paid" the money back in taxes. During Reagan's presidency the national debt soared (as indeed it did during the presidency of George Bush. President Clinton balanced the budget). He also sponsored tax cuts for the wealthiest in society. Following his retirement, Reagan moved into a house at 666 St Cloud Road, Bel Air, bought for them by grateful friends. Superstitious Nancy Reagan changed the number to 668 in April 1987 before their move but city ordnance plans continued to refer to it as 666. It is believed that Reagan was diagnosed with the

US PRESIDENTIAL ASSASSINATION-ATTEMPT SURVIVORS

• Andrew Jackson: A mentally unbalanced house-painter called Richard Lawrence fired two pistols at him on 30 January 1835.

• Theodore Roosevelt: John Nepomuk Schrank shot Roosevelt on 14 October 1912 during his campaign for a third term.

• Franklin D. Roosevelt: He survived an attempt on 15 February 1933 by Giuseppe Zangara, whose bullet killed the mayor of Chicago instead.

• Harry S. Truman: Two Puerto Rican nationalists tried to kill him on 1 November 1950.

• Gerald Ford: He survived two assassination attempts in 1975. On 5 September Lynette "Squeaky" Fromme, a member of the Manson Family, aimed at Ford but a Secret Service agent put his hand over the gun stopping it from firing. Seventeen days later Sara Jane Moore, a former FBI informant, fired a single shot at Ford, missing him by 5 feet (1.5 metres) and hitting a taxi driver.

ZERO FACTOR

1840 William Henry Harrison

In 1809, William Henry Harrison, then territorial governor of the Indiana Territory at Vincennes, signed the Treaty of Fort Wayne, which bought more than 250,000 square acres of land from the Red Indians. A resistance movement had begun among the natives led by the Shawnee brothers Tecumseh and Tenskwatawa. Tecumseh asked Harrison to nullify the treaty and threatened violence if any whites tried to settle on the land. The result was Tecumseh's War in 1811, in which he won a major victory at Prophetstown. Harrison continued to win victories in the War of 1812. Tecumseh was killed at the Battle of the Thames on 5 October 1813.

Legend has it that Tecumseh placed a curse on Harrison, that he and every subsequent president elected in a year ending in zero would die in office.

On 3 March 1841, William Henry Harrison was inaugurated as the ninth US president. It was a bitterly cold day but Harrison insisted on delivering his inaugural address (at 8,445 words the longest ever; it took 2 hours to read out) without a coat. He caught a cold, which developed into pleurisy and pneumonia. Back in the White House, Harrison was unable to rest because of a busy schedule. His condition deteriorated and, at 12.30am on 4 April 1841, he died, having served the shortest term of any American president: 30 days, 11 hours and 30 minutes. The cause of death was right lower lobe pneumonia, jaundice and septicaemia. The curse of the "zero factor" had claimed its first victim.

1860 Abraham Lincoln

See pages 27–37.

1880 James Garfield

The second president to meet his end by an assassin's bullet, he also served the second shortest time in office. James Abram Garfield never actively sought the White House. He was more than happy to sit in Congress representing Ohio, but after 16 years in the lower house, he was elected to the Senate in 1880. However, before he could take his seat, Garfield found himself his party's nominee at the Republican National Convention. Reluctantly, he accepted the nomination and in the election in November 1880 he defeated General Winfield Scott Hancock by 214 electoral votes to 155.

Garfield was inaugurated as the 20th president on 4 March 1881 and spent much of the next few months being accosted by people wanting jobs. Bizarrely, in those days the president was responsible for the majority of the hirings in his administration since everyone – from cabinet to clerks – was summarily sacked when the previous incumbent left office. One of the people turned down for a job was a mentally unbalanced 37-year-old religious fanatic called Charles Julius Guiteau. Somehow he believed that he had been responsible for Garfield's election and thought that an appointment as consul general in Paris would be a fitting reward for his efforts. He wrote a meandering letter to Garfield seeking his just desert and then travelled to Washington, DC.

Security at the White House was almost non-existent and Guiteau got to see the president. He handed him another copy of his letter with "Paris consulship" on the cover. Guiteau became convinced that Garfield was deliberately blocking his appointment. He began to stalk the new chief executive. At 9.30am on 2 July 1881, Guiteau seized his opportunity and shot Garfield as he walked through the Sixth Street Station of the Baltimore and Potomac Railroad. One bullet went through the president's shoulder and exited his back, while a second lodged in his chest. A policeman grabbed Guiteau, while the crowd wanted to lynch him. Garfield was taken to the White House to recover.

The president seemed to recover and was taken to Elberon, New Jersey to recuperate further. On 19 September 1881 at 10.35pm Garfield died of a massive heart attack, exactly two months after his 50th birthday. It is generally believed that if the medical attention he received had been competent, Garfield would have survived the assassination attempt. Guiteau's lawyers entered a plea of insanity but it was rejected and he was hanged on 30 June 1882 at the Washington Asylum and Jail. As he went to the gallows he recited a poem he had written while awaiting execution. It was called "I am Going to the Lordy."

1900 William McKinley

See pages 38–41.

1920 Warren Harding

Harding was a dark horse candidate when he became the Republican nominee for the presidency in 1920. He ran on a promise to "Return to Normalcy", a term Harding coined to reflect three trends of his time: renewed isolation following the First World War, nativism (a policy of discriminating between native-born Americans and immigrants) and rejection of government interference. The campaign also turned dirty when a rumour spread that Harding's great-great-grandfather was black. The 1920 presidential election was the first in which women were enfranchised.

After his inauguration in 1921 Harding appointed many of his old friends – the Ohio Gang – to positions of power. Some of the Ohio Gang used their positions for their own preferment. The biggest scandal was the Teapot Dome Affair – which lingered after Harding's death – in which the secretary of the interior, Albert Fall, was convicted of accepting bribes and no interest loans for leasing oil fields to business colleagues. In 1931, he became the first cabinet member to be sent to prison. Other Harding associates also fell foul of the law, causing him to comment, "My God, this is a hell of a job! I have no trouble with my enemies, but my damn friends, my God-damned friends … they're the ones that keep me walking the floor nights!" On 20 June 1923, Harding began a "meet the people" tour. Travelling to San Francisco, he caught pneumonia. At 7.35pm on 2 August 1923, Warren Gamaliel Harding died aged 57 from a cerebral haemorrhage.

1940 Franklin D Roosevelt

The only man to be elected to the presidency four times (1932, 1936, 1940 and 1944), FDR was the 48th governor of New York before he became the 32nd president. The country was in the grip of the Great Depression when Roosevelt was elected and he launched the New Deal to combat the tide of misery caused by unemployment and poverty. Roosevelt used the wireless to deliver "fireside chats" to the people to let them know what measures he was taking.

History could have been very different had the assassination attempt on Roosevelt's life by Giuseppe Zangara on 15 February 1933 succeeded. It did not and Roosevelt was re-elected by a landslide in 1936 winning every state except Maine and Vermont. In 1940, he carried 38 of the 48 states. Roosevelt was elected for the fourth and final time in 1944. He was only 62 but had been ill for some time (it is now thought that he suffered from Guillian-Barré syndrome rather than polio). With Harry S. Truman as his vice presidential running mate, Roosevelt carried 36 states against the New York governor Thomas Dewey. On 12 April 1945, Roosevelt awoke with a headache, caused by a cerebral haemorrhage. He died that day.

1960 John F. Kennedy

See pages 107–128

degenerative Alzheimer's disease while he was still in office but that the diagnosis was covered up until November 1994.

Reagan died at 1.09pm aged 93 at his home on 5 June 2004. His wife and son Ron and daughter Patti were at his bedside. Son Michael arrived shortly afterwards. Reagan was the longest-lived American president beating John Adams (90) and Herbert Hoover (also 90).

John Hinckley was charged with attempting to kill the president and 12 other charges of assault and illegal possession of a firearm. In his wallet Hinckley had the following items: $129, a Texas driver's licence, a Colorado identity card, a picture of Jodie Foster (from *Esquire*) dressed up as a co-ed and holding a basketball, four more pictures of Jodie Foster, a card on which was printed the Second Amendment ("the right to bear arms") and a photo of Hinckley's nephew. In his hotel room was a letter to Jodie Foster, a 1981 John Lennon calendar, two suitcases, an empty box of Devastator bullets, a box of normal (non-exploding) bullets, a variety of pills, including Valium, Surmontil, and Drixoral, a Band-Aid® box containing a hijacking note ("This plane has been hijacked! I have a bomb…"), *The Catcher in the Rye* by J.D. Salinger, *The Skyjacker* by David Hubbard, *Welcome to Xanadu* by Nathaniel Benchley, *The Fox is Crazy Too* by Eliot Asinof, *Romeo and Juliet*, *The Fan* by Bob Randall, *Taxi Driver*, 38 pages of Hinckley's own writings, an army fatigue jacket, several wool lumberjack shirts and a postcard with a picture of Ronald and Nancy Reagan and a note to Jodie Foster asking "You are a virgin, aren't you?" on its other side.

On 21 June 1982, after a seven-week trial, Hinckley was found not guilty by reason of insanity but sent to St Elizabeth's Hospital, an asylum. On 17 December 2003, Judge Paul Friedman decided that Hinckley no longer posed a serious danger to himself or others and approved unsupervised visits to his parents in the Washington DC area. At the time of writing he is still confined to St Elizabeth's.

Jodie Foster has only ever once spoken publicly of Hinckley's fascination with her and has subsequently ended interviews if his name has been mentioned.

James Brady became an advocate of gun control and with his wife, Sarah, founded the Brady Campaign to Prevent Gun Violence. On 30 November 1993 the Brady Handgun Violence Prevention Act was passed.

Policeman Thomas Delehanty, a native of Pittsburgh, Pennsylvania, who had been on the force for 17 years, made a full recovery from his injuries and later retired on a full disability pension.

Secret service agent Tim McCarthy, who took a bullet for Reagan, was awarded the National Collegiate Athletic Association Award of Valor in 1982 in recognition of his bravery that day. He received 50,000 get-well cards including one from John Hinckley's parents. Ironically, Agent McCarthy should not even have been on duty that day. The team was an agent short and McCarthy and a colleague tossed a coin. McCarthy lost. He spent eight years on the presidential protection division and 14 years as a criminal investigator in Chicago until his retirement in October 1993. In May 1994 he became chief of police of Orland Park in Illinois and unsuccessfully ran for Illinois Secretary of State on the Democrat ticket in 1998. He is married with three children.

John F. Kennedy (1917–1963)

The Victim

The 35th president of the United States – the youngest elected president, the first Roman Catholic president, the first president born in the twentieth century, the first whose inauguration was shown in colour on television – John Fitzgerald Kennedy was born at 83 Beals Street, the family home in lower middle-class Brookline, Norfolk County, Massachusetts, at 3 pm on 29 May 1917. He was the second son of Joseph Patrick Kennedy, a business-man who made much of his vast fortune as a bootlegger and served as American ambassador to the Court of St James's, and Rose Elizabeth Fitzgerald. On 19 June 1917, the new baby was baptized at St Aidan's church in Brookline. Joseph and Rose had seven more children, making a total of nine Kennedy siblings.

In February 1920, Jack (as John was sometimes called) fell victim to a scarlet fever epidemic that was sweeping Boston. Jack was a sickly child and chicken pox, ear infections, colds and mumps followed. In September 1930, Jack enrolled at Canterbury Prep, a Catholic boarding school, at 101 Aspetuck Avenue in New Milford, Connecticut. The following year, in April 1931, he left Canterbury after being struck by appendicitis.On Friday 2 October 1931, he joined big brother Joe at the boarding school Choate

Despite his year-round tan (thanks to a sunlamp), President Kennedy was in a state of almost constant poor health.

Academy at 333 Christian Street, Wallingford, Connecticut 06492. In June 1934, JFK underwent tests at the Mayo Clinic in Minnesota for colitis. On 23 September 1935, after less than a week at the London School of Economics (he left after suffering jaundice), he

The president and first lady arrive in Texas aboard Air Force One, November 1963.

enrolled at Princeton University. Three months later, in January 1936, he was hospitalized for possible leukaemia at Peter Bent Brigham Hospital in Boston, having left Princeton on 12 December 1935.

On 5 September 1936 he went to Harvard. JFK and his close friend Lem Billings spent the summer of 1937 travelling around Europe. In December 1937, his father, Joe Kennedy, was appointed American ambassador to the Court of St James's. John graduated *cum laude* from Harvard on 21 June 1940. Two months later, his thesis, *Why England Slept*, was published. The following month, he enrolled at Stanford University.

In December 1940, JFK was treated for gonorrhoea at the Lahey Clinic.

On 27 October 1941, he joined the Office of Naval Intelligence in Washington DC where he began an affair with a beauty queen called Inga Arvad. On 1 October 1942, Kennedy began the eight-week training course towards becoming a patrol-torpedo (PT) boat commander. On completion of his training he was made commander of PT101. He was subsequently appointed commander of the 24-metre (80-foot) long, 38-ton, plywood torpedo boat PT109 at 11am on 25 April 1943. One author described the boat as "a grimy, battle-scarred, rat-ridden, cockroach-infested veteran of the Guadalcanal campaign". At 2am on Monday 2 August 1943, the *Amagiri*, a Japanese destroyer captained by Lieutenant-Commander Kouhei Hanami, deliberately rammed and bisected PT109 in the Blackett Strait between Kolombangara and Arundel in the Solomon Islands, killing two of the 13-man crew. JFK was awarded the Navy and Marine Corps Medal for helping to rescue his surviving crew. The incident would later be made into a film starring Cliff Robertson as JFK. Years later JFK was asked how he became a war hero and replied, "It was involuntary. They sank my boat."

On 31 May 1944, Kennedy was hospitalized in Chelsea, Massachusetts with back problems. Meanwhile, Joe, John's elder brother, was the apple of

his father's eye and Ambassador Kennedy determined to get his son into the White House. On 12 August 1944 his dreams were shattered: Joe was killed when his aeroplane exploded over a mile-wide area of New Delight Woods near Blythburgh, Suffolk, England, in a mission code-named Anvil. The father's ambitions were transferred to his second son. "I got Jack into politics. I was the one. I told him Joe was dead and that it was therefore his responsibility to run for Congress. Jack didn't want to," recalled Ambassador Kennedy. His son responded, "It was like being drafted. My father wanted his eldest son in politics. 'Wanted' isn't the right word. He demanded it, you know my father."

From April until July of 1945, after his demob from the navy, JFK worked as a journalist reporting on the British general election and the conference in San Francisco that led to the formation of the United Nations. The next year, his political career began in earnest when he was elected to Congress for the eleventh Boston district on 5 November 1946, winning 69,093 votes to Lester Bowen's 26,007. JFK took his seat in Congress on 3 January 1947. In October 1947,

JFK was diagnosed with Addison's disease, an autoimmune disorder, while on a trip to London and was given the last rites. On his return to the States, he was treated with cortisone injections and told that he had probably no more than 15 years left to live. On 2 November 1948 and 7 November 1950, he was re-elected to Congress.

On 4 November 1952 he was elected senator for Massachusetts, beating the incumbent Henry Cabot Lodge, Jr, who had held the seat since 1936, by 70,000 votes. JFK was so youthful looking that a policeman once stopped him from using a phone in the Senate with the words, "Sorry mister, these are reserved for the senators." On 12 September 1953, the handsome young senator married wealthy socialite Jacqueline Lee Bouvier at St Mary's Church, Newport, Rhode Island.

On 21 October 1954 JFK underwent an operation on his back that almost killed him. His backbone was broken and reset and he lapsed into a coma. Again, a priest administered the last rites. On 11 February 1955, he again almost died on the operating table while undergoing another surgery on his back. During his recuperation, Kennedy wrote *Profiles in Courage*, a book that would win him a Pulitzer Prize on 6 May 1957. Published on 1 January 1956, the book – a study of heroic US senators – has been controversial because most scholars believe that Kennedy did not actually write the book and that the real author was Kennedy speechwriter and "research associate" Theodore Sorenson. Journalist Drew Pearson said on television, "Jack Kennedy is … the only man in history that I know who won a Pulitzer Prize on a book which was ghost-written for him."

On 17 August 1956 JFK failed in his bid to become the Democratic nominee for vice president, losing to Senator Estes Kefauver of Tennessee by just 38 votes. Six days later, Jackie Kennedy gave birth to a premature stillborn daughter (some sources state that the baby was called Arabella but this is speculation). Just over a year later, on 27 November 1957, Caroline Bouvier

Kennedy was born at Lying-in-Hospital, Cornell University Medical Center, New York.

In 1958, reporters teased Kennedy at a Gridiron Club dinner by staging a skit featuring the senator singing *Just Send the Bill to Daddy* (to the tune of *My Heart Belongs to Daddy*). JFK took the teasing in good heart and in his speech after joked, "I have just received the following wire from my generous daddy: 'Dear Jack. Don't buy a single vote more than necessary. I'll be damned if I'm going to pay for a landslide.'" On 4 November 1958, JFK was re-elected to the Senate beating the unknown Vincent J. Celeste by 874,608 votes. Youngest brother Teddy was nominally the campaign manager. On 2 January 1960, JFK announced his candidature for the presidency.

On 5 April 1960, he won the Wisconsin Democratic primary followed by the West Virginia primary on 11 May. At the 33rd Democratic party convention, held on 11–15 July 1960, at the Los Angeles Memorial Sports Arena and the Coliseum in Los Angeles, JFK was nominated to be the party's candidate for the presidency. Lyndon B. Johnson was nominated as his running mate. On 26 September 1960, he took part in the first ever televised presidential debate with his Republican

---

JACQUELINE LEE BOUVIER

Born at Southampton Hospital, Long Island, New York, six weeks late, on 28 July 1929, she was the daughter of John Vernou "Black Jack" Bouvier, III and was debutante of the year 1947–1948. Jackie was a photographer for the *Washington Times-Journal* when she met JFK, the charismatic senator from Massachusetts, at a dinner party thrown by George and Martha Bartlett at Georgetown, Washington DC, in May 1951. He proposed in the middle of May 1953 just before she left for London to cover the coronation of the Queen Elizabeth II.

opponent Vice President Richard M. Nixon. Seventy million Americans tuned in to watch the first of four verbal gladiatorial battles. It was broadcast from Studio One of WBBM TV at 630 North McClurg Court, Chicago, Illinois (a plaque in the lobby commemorates the historical event). Nixon, in an ill-fitting shirt, perspired under the hot lights and looked shifty with a five o'clock shadow, unlike the tanned Kennedy who was declared the winner by the television audience. However, those who listened on the wireless thought Nixon had won or the debate had been a draw.

On 8 November 1960, Kennedy narrowly beat Nixon to become president. Kennedy received 34,227,096 votes to Nixon's 34,107,646. He won 303 Electoral College votes and 22 states to Nixon's 219 votes and 26 states. Despite pleas by President Eisenhower and other leading Republicans, Vice President Nixon decided not to demand a recount in Texas and Illinois even though voter fraud was suspected in both states.

On 25 November, John Fitzgerald Kennedy, Jr was born at Georgetown University Hospital, Washington DC. At noon on Friday 20 January 1961, JFK took the oath of office administered by Chief Justice Warren and gave one of the great political speeches (comprising a total of 1,355 words) including such memorable phrases as:

Let every nation know, whether it wishes us well or ill, that we shall pay any price, bear any burden, meet any hardship, support any friend, oppose any foe to assure the survival and the success of liberty ... If a free society cannot help the many who are poor, it cannot save the few who are rich ... Let us never negotiate out of fear. But let us never fear to negotiate ... In the long history of the world, only a few generations have been granted the role of defending freedom in its hour of maximum danger. I do not shrink from this responsibility – I welcome it. I do not believe that any of us would exchange places with any other people or any other generation. The energy, the faith, the devotion which we bring to this endeavour will light our country and all who serve it – and the glow from that fire can truly light the world. And so, my fellow Americans: ask not what your country can do for you – ask what you can do for your country. My fellow citizens of the world: ask not what America will do for you, but what together we can do for the freedom of man.

Five days later, the president hosted the first live television press conference and five days after that he delivered his first State of the Union address. On 2 February, he asked Congress to raise the minimum wage to $1.15 an hour and increase social security from $33 to $43. On 1 March 1961, JFK created the Peace Corps and with his desire to keep things within the family, he appointed his brother-in-law, Sargent Shriver, as director on 4 March. JFK's was a presidency begun amid much optimism. Then on 17 April 1961, it began to unravel.

Around 1,400 Cuban exiles, trained and equipped by the CIA, attempted to retake their country from Fidel Castro, landing at Bahia de Cochinos (Bay of Pigs). The event was a disaster – 114 Cubans were killed and 1,189 captured – and JFK, who had withdrawn American military aid at the last moment, much to the fury of right-wing elements within the CIA, publicly took the blame. He said to aide Ted Sorenson, "How could I have been so far off base? All my life I've known not to depend on experts. How could I have been so stupid to let them go ahead?"

In May of that year "freedom riders" – black and white people – rode together on buses to show up the racism and bigotry that was endemic in the southern states. On 20 May, JFK ordered Bobby Kennedy, the Attorney General, to "take all necessary steps" after freedom riders – including John Seigenthaler, the president's personal representative – were attacked in Montgomery, Alabama. The Attorney General ordered 400 US marshals to the capital of Alabama to deal with the troublemakers. On 25 May 1961, the president spoke to Congress and promised "before this decade is out [to] land a man on the moon and return him safely to earth." On 19 December 1961, Ambassador Kennedy was stricken by a stroke that left him unable to speak in the last eight years of his life.

On 27 February 1962, FBI chief J. Edgar Hoover warned Bobby Kennedy and presidential aide Kenny O'Donnell that the president was having an affair with Judith Exner (Frank Sinatra introduced them on 7 February 1960 at the Sands Hotel in Las Vegas) who was also sharing her favours with Sam Giancana, the Mafia boss.

On 11 April 1962, Kennedy denounced the rise in the cost of steel and two days later the price hike was cut. A month later, on 19 May, the actress Marilyn Monroe performed the sexiest ever version of *Happy Birthday* for the soon-to-be 45-year-old Kennedy at Madison Square Garden at 50th Street and Eighth Avenue. (The first lady was horse riding in Virginia instead of attending the celebration. Jackie played the part of loyal wife to perfection but rarely spent time at the White House. She preferred to be in Virginia or in Europe with a coterie of male friends. Her frequent absences allowed her husband to indulge his taste for extra-marital sex, which although known to the press went unreported in the media.) Despite the oft-repeated rumours, there was no orgy with the president and the actress at the Carlyle Hotel following the event. Monroe took her former father-in-law Isadore Miller, her date for the evening, home to Brooklyn, and then she went back to her own apartment.

On 14 October 1962, a U2 spy plane photographed Soviet missiles in Cuba prompting President Kennedy to call for a naval blockade of the island. On 24 October,

two Soviet ships turned away instead of breaching the 805-kilometre (500-mile) exclusion zone around the island. Three days later, a U2 was shot down over Cuba and Soviet premier, Nikita Khrushchev, demanded that the United States withdraw its Jupiter missiles from Turkey. On the same day, Attorney General Kennedy told the Soviet ambassador Anatoly Dobrynin that America would remove its weaponry but only in secret and only after the crisis was over, a plan Khrushchev agreed to the following day. The blockade of Cuba was lifted on 21 November 1962. In his memoirs, smuggled out of the Soviet Union and published in the West after he was deposed, Khrushchev called Kennedy "a real states-man" and believed the two of them could have brought about world peace. On 11 September 1971, less than a year after his book was published, Khrushchev died of a heart attack.

On 26 June 1963, on a visit to the walled city of West Berlin, President Kennedy announced, "Ich bin ein Berliner" at the city hall. The following day, he flew to Ireland where he met some distant relatives. On Wednesday 24 July 1963, a delegation from the American Legion visited the White House and met the president in the Rose Garden. Among them was a 16-year-old boy from Arkansas named Bill Clinton.

At 12.52pm on 7 August 1963, Jackie Kennedy gave birth to their fourth child, a boy named Patrick Bouvier, at Otis Air Force Base in Massachusetts, but the infant died two days later in Boston. On 30 August 1963, the hotline to Moscow was installed. In October, Kennedy agreed to withdraw 1,000 troops from Vietnam (where American troops had been stationed after the defeat of France in 1954) by the end of the year. In November 1963, facing a battle for re-election, a need to raise campaign funds and to mend fences with local Democrats, Kennedy and Vice President Johnson decided to take a trip to Texas. They had won the state by just 46,233 votes, having lost Dallas, and Johnson's vacated Senate seat had been taken by Republican John Tower.

Date and Place of Assassination

22 November 1963, Dealey Plaza, Dallas, Texas, USA.

The Event

The most talked about, the most written about, assassination of all time has a simple core of truth. More than one thousand books have been published about the events in Dealey Plaza that sunny November day. All kinds of hypotheses as to what really happened have been suggested from the plausible to the utterly bizarre and far-fetched.

On 21 November 1963, Kennedy left for a three-day visit to Texas. That day a map of the presidential route was published in both Dallas newspapers and two days earlier the motorcade route had also been published in the *Dallas Times Herald*. The scheduled route was: left turn from the south end of Love Field to West Mockingbird Lane, right on Lemmon Avenue, right at the "Y" on Turtle Creek Boulevard, straight on Cedar Springs Road, left on North Harwood Street, right on Main Street, right on Houston Street, sharp left on Elm Street, through Triple Underpass, right turn up the ramp to North Stemmons Freeway, to Dallas Trade Mart at 2100 North Stemmons.

On the morning of Friday 22 November, the president landed in a rainy Fort Worth and addressed the Fort Worth Chamber of Commerce. The next step on the itinerary was Dallas. Air Force One, the presidential Boeing 707, arrived at Love Field, 8008 Cedar Springs Road, Dallas, at 11.38am. The sun now shone on the young president and his glamorous wife. At 11.47am, the motorcade left for an 18-kilometre (11-mile) journey through downtown Dallas to the Merchandise Mart where he was to address a lunch group of 2,600 people. Kennedy was to denounce those who had decried his peace talks with Nikita Khrushchev. En route, cheering crowds greeted the president. The motorcade stopped twice so President Kennedy could shake hands with some Catholic nuns and then some schoolchildren.

22 NOVEMBER 1963 – A TIMELINE

12.07am – Air Force One landed at Fort Worth

12.50am – President Kennedy arrived at the Hotel Texas in Fort Worth

7.23am – Lee Harvey Oswald left for work at the Texas School Book Depository

7.55am – Oswald arrived at the Texas School Book Depository

8.01am – Dallas policeman JD Tippit began his patrol

8.45am – The president left his hotel in Fort Worth

8.53am – President Kennedy told an appreciative crowd that Mrs Kennedy was "organizing herself. It takes longer, but, of course, she looks better than we do when she does it."

9.05am – The president attended a breakfast sponsored by the Fort Worth Chamber of Commerce

9.25am – Mrs Kennedy arrived in a pink suit and pill-box hat

10am – Dallas police blocked all traffic in Dealey Plaza

10.10am – The president and the first lady returned to their suite

10.30am – The president stated that it would be easy to kill him with a rifle from a tall building

11.03am – The aeroplane containing much of the cabinet took off from Honolulu

11.38am – President and Mrs Kennedy landed at Love Field in Dallas, Texas, aboard Air Force One

11.45am – Lee Harvey Oswald stayed on the sixth floor of the Texas School Book Depository while his co-workers went to the second floor for lunch

11.47am – The motorcade left Love Field for Dallas

11.55am – Oswald assembled his rifle and created a "sniper's nest"

12.29pm – The presidential limousine entered Dealey Plaza

12.30pm – President Kennedy shot by Lee Harvey Oswald

12.31pm – Oswald stopped in the lunchroom by Patrolman Marrion L. Baker but the superintendent of the building, Roy Truly, vouched for Oswald

12.33pm – Lee Harvey Oswald left the Texas School Book Depository

12.36pm – The president arrived at Parkland Memorial Hospital

12.39pm – Local radio station KLIF became the first to announce that shots had been fired at the motorcade. Newsreader Gary Delaune interrupted *I Have A Boyfriend* by The Chiffons to break the news

12.40pm – Oswald boarded a bus to make his escape

12.44pm – Oswald left the bus when it became caught in traffic

12.45pm – J. Edgar Hoover rang Attorney General Kennedy to tell him of the shooting

12.48pm – Oswald hailed a cab and told the driver to take him to 500 North Beckley Avenue

12.54pm – Oswald left the cab at 700 North Beckley Avenue and walked the rest of the way to 1026, his room

1pm – President Kennedy pronounced dead at Parkland Hospital by William Kemp Clark, its senior neurosurgeon

1.05pm – Attorney General Kennedy told of the president's death

1.13pm – Vice President Johnson informed of the president's death

1.15pm – JD Tippit shot dead by Oswald

1.22pm – A Dallas detective discovered Oswald's Italian-made 1938 Mannlicher-Carcano, 6.5-millimetre rifle

1.33pm – Acting White House press secretary Malcolm Kilduff made the official announcement of President Kennedy's death

1.40pm – The president's body wrapped in a sheet, and then placed inside a satin-lined coffin. Mrs Kennedy placed her wedding ring on her husband's finger

1.50pm – Lee Harvey Oswald arrested inside the Texas Theater cinema

2pm – All three television networks broke off from regular programming to report on the Dallas tragedy

2.08pm – The president's body removed from Parkland by the Secret Service despite the protests of the hospital staff

2.30pm – Oswald questioned by Dallas police

2.38pm – President Kennedy's death announced on television as Vice President Johnson sworn into office

2.47pm – Air Force One took off for Washington DC

3.01pm – FBI Director J. Edgar Hoover wrote a memo to his assistant directors: "I called the Attorney General at his home and told him I thought we had the man who killed the president down in Dallas, at the present time."

7.05pm – Lee Harvey Oswald charged with "murder with malice" in the killing of policeman JD Tippit

8pm – The autopsy on President Kennedy began at Bethesda Naval Hospital

11.36pm – Oswald charged with the murder of President Kennedy (there being no crime of assassination at that time)

At 12.29pm, the motorcade entered Dealey Plaza and travelling at about 12 miles (19 kilometres) per hour, approached the Texas School Book Depository at 411 Elm Street. The cars then turned 120 degrees directly in front of the depository, just 65 feet (20 metres) away. The motorcade moved down Elm Street and Nellie Connally, the governor's wife, said, "Mr President, you certainly can't say that Dallas doesn't love you." Senator Ralph Yarborough, a political rival of Vice President Johnson with whom he had been forced to travel, was not so sure. At street level, crowds yelled and screamed their appreciation of the Kennedys, but Senator Yarborough's eyes were constantly drawn to the office blocks that looked down on the route. In the windows stood unhappy-looking businessmen, hatred for the president in their eyes. The senator was relieved as the buildings gave way to the open spaces of Dealey Plaza. He thought that they were now safe.

One man had other ideas. At 12.30pm, Lee Harvey Oswald shot President Kennedy from the sixth floor window of the depository with a 6.5 x 52mm Italian Mannlicher-Carcano M91/38 bolt-action rifle with a six-round magazine. The first bullet hit the president's upper back, penetrating his neck and exiting his throat before entering Texas governor John B. Connally's back, chest and right wrist. Nellie Connally cried out, "My God, they are going to kill us all!" She saved her husband's life. Holding him firmly, she blocked the hole in his body. A second bullet missed. As the motorcade passed the John Neely Bryan north pergola concrete structure, a third shot rang out and hit Kennedy in the head smothering the inside of the car and a nearby motorcycle policeman with blood and brain matter. The first lady shouted, "Jack! Jack! They've killed my husband! I have his brains in my hands!" Mrs Kennedy later recalled for *Life* magazine: "His last expression was so neat; he had his hand out, I could see a piece of his skull coming off, it was flesh coloured not white. He was holding out his hand – and I can see this perfectly clean piece detaching itself from his head; then he slumped in my lap."

Special Agent Clint Hill of the Secret Service (see box on left), travelling in the car behind, ran and jumped onto the back of the presidential limousine (registration number GG300) where Mrs Kennedy had scrambled (she later had no recollection of this), to try and retrieve a piece of the president's skull. Agent Hill pushed the first lady back into the car and held on as the car sped to Parkland Memorial Hospital at 5201 Harry Hines Boulevard. Mrs Kennedy recalled, "These big Texas interns kept saying 'Mrs Kennedy, you come with us.' They wanted to take me away from him. Dave Powers came running to me; my legs, my hands were covered with his brains. When Dave saw this, he burst out

SPECIAL AGENT CLINT HILL

Special Agent Hill (born in 1932) was assigned the role of protecting Mrs Kennedy. He retired early from the Secret Service in 1975. In the autumn of that year Mike Wallace interviewed him on *60 Minutes*. As he spoke, Hill began to cry but insisted the interview continue. He said that he has wished he had reacted a split second earlier then the bullet that killed the president would have hit him. Wallace asked, "And that would have been all right with you?" to which Hill responded, "That would have been fine with me." Wallace asked, "But you couldn't. You got there in less than two seconds, Clint … you surely don't have any sense of guilt about that?" "Yes, I certainly do," said Hill. "I have a great deal of guilt about that. Had I tented in a different direction, I'd have made it. It's my fault … If I had reacted just a little bit quicker, and I could have, I guess. And I'll live with that to my grave." Hill's life was dramatized by Clint Eastwood in the film *In the Line of Fire* (released on 27 August 1993).

THE PRESIDENTIAL MOTORCADE IN DALLAS

The lead car, an unmarked white Ford:
Dallas Police Chief Jesse Curry (driver)
Secret Service Agent Winston Lawson (right front)
Sheriff Bill Decker (left rear)
Agent Forrest Sorrels (right rear)

The second car, SS 100 X, a 1961 Lincoln Continental:
Agent Bill Greer (driver)
Agent Roy Kellerman (right front)
Nellie Connally (left middle)
Texas Governor John Connally (right middle)
First Lady Jacqueline Kennedy (left rear)
President John F. Kennedy (right rear)

The third car, Halfback, a convertible:
Agent Sam Kinney (driver)
Agent Emory Roberts (right front, agent in charge of the vehicle)
Agent Clint Hill (left front running board)
Agent Bill McIntyre (left rear running board)
Agent John Ready (right front running board)
Agent Paul Landis (right rear running board)
Presidential aide Kenny O'Donnell (left middle)
Presidential aide David Powers (right middle)
Agent George Hickey (left rear)
Agent Glen Bennett (right rear)

The fourth car, Lincoln four-door convertible:
State highway patrol officer Hurchel Jacks (driver)
Agent Rufus Youngblood (right front)
Senator Ralph Yarborough (left rear)
Lady Bird Johnson (centre rear)
Vice President Lyndon B. Johnson (right rear)

The fifth car, Varsity, a hardtop:
A Texas state policeman (driver)
Vice Presidential aide Cliff Carter (front middle)
Agent Jerry Kivett (right front),
Agent Woody Taylor (left rear)
Agent Lem Johns (right rear)

The sixth car, press pool car (on loan from the telephone company):
Telephone company employee (driver)
Malcolm Kilduff, White House assistant press secretary (right front)
Merriman Smith, UPI (middle front)
Jack Bell, AP (left rear)
Robert Baskin, *The Dallas Morning News* (middle rear)
Bob Clark, ABC (right rear)

The seventh car, press car:
Bob Jackson, *The Dallas Times Herald*
Tom Dillard, *The Dallas Morning News*
Mal Couch, WFAA-TV

weeping. From [the forehead down Jack] was so beautiful. I'd tried to hold the top of his head down; maybe I could keep it in … I knew he was dead. When they carried Jack in, Hill threw his coat over Jack's head."

The president was taken to trauma room number one where the medical staff worked on their hopeless task. Malcolm Perry, the surgeon trying to revive the president, asked Jackie to leave the room but she refused. Mrs Kennedy said in a later interview, "There was a sheet over Jack, his foot was sticking out of the sheet, whiter than the sheet. I took his foot and kissed it. Then I pulled back the sheet. His mouth was so beautiful, his eyes were open. They found his hand under the sheet and I held his hand all the time the priest was saying extreme unction." George Gregory Burkley, JFK's personal doctor, arrived at Parkland five minutes after

As the motorcade approached Dealey Plaza, the crowds on the ground cheered but the businessmen in their office blocks glowered at the procession.

the president. Dr Burkley saw both the head wound and a wound to the back, and determined the head wound was the cause of death. Dr Burkley signed the death certificate. At 1pm, President Kennedy was officially pronounced dead. "We never had any hope of saving his life," one doctor said.

The Assassin

Lee Harvey Oswald was born on 18 October 1939 at Slidell, Louisiana, the third son of Marguerite Claverie (born New Orleans 19 July 1907, died 1981 of cancer). His insurance salesman father, Robert Edward Lee Oswald, Sr had died before Lee was born, on 19 August 1939 of a heart attack. Lee was raised with his brother Robert, Jr (born 7 April 1934) and half-brother John Pic (born 17 January 1932, from his mother's first marriage to Edward John Pic, Jr at Gulfport, Mississippi on 8 August 1929). Oswald's childhood was anything but stable. His mother was in turns dismissive and suffocating. By the time he was 18, he had lived in 22 different homes and attended a dozen schools. On 3 January 1942, the elder boys were sent to the Bethlehem

Children's Home but young Lee was not permitted to go because of his age, so he spent time with his aunt Lillian Murret. On Boxing Day, Oswald finally joined his brothers in the home.

The following year, Marguerite met and began a relationship with Edwin A. Ekdahl, an electrician. On 29 January 1944, his mother removed Oswald from the home and they moved to Dallas. In June, the two elder boys rejoined the family. In February 1945, Marguerite Oswald tried to send John and Robert back to Bethlehem but the home refused to take them. She married Edwin A. Ekdahl on 5 May 1945. Four months later, she put John and Robert into the Chamberlain-Hunt Military Academy in Mississippi. On 31 October 1945, Lee Oswald entered Benbrook Elementary, the first of the dozen schools he would attend. On 8

February 1946, Oswald entered Harris Hospital in Fort Worth for a mastoidectomy. In the summer, Oswald's mother and stepfather separated and she moved to Covington, Louisiana. Ekdahl made efforts to win his wife back and on 23 January 1947 they got back together and moved to Eighth Street in Fort Worth. Four days later, Oswald enrolled at Lily B. Clayton Elementary School. In the summer, Marguerite discovered that Ekdahl was having an affair and threw him out. On 19 March 1948, Oswald moved to George C. Clark Elementary School. Four days later, Ekdahl filed for divorce. It was granted on 24 June and Marguerite went back to the name Oswald. The following month, Lee threatened his brother John with a knife.

In September 1949, Oswald joined Ridgelea West Elementary School where he stayed for three years. In January 1950, John Pic joined the Coast Guard and in July 1952 Robert enrolled in the Marine Corps. The following month, Oswald and his mother moved to New York where they stayed with John Pic and his wife on East 92nd Street until Oswald threatened his sister-in-law with a knife. In September the Oswalds moved to Sheridan Avenue in the Bronx, and Lee enrolled at Public School 117, but often truanted. The next move was to East 179th Street. On 16 April, Oswald was sent to Youth House, a borstal, where he underwent a three-week psychological evaluation. Dr Renatus Hartogs said Oswald had a "vivid fantasy life, turning around the topics of omnipotence and power, through which he tries to compensate for his present shortcomings and frustrations," adding that the boy had a "personality pattern disturbance with schizoid features and passive-aggressive tendencies". On 7 May, he was placed on probation. On 14 September, he joined Public School 44.

In January 1954, the Oswalds moved to New Orleans. On 13 January, he entered Beauregard Junior High School. In school tests in October, Oswald performed well in reading but poorly in mathematics. It was around this time that Oswald became a committed

> **SECRET SERVICE CODENAMES – NOVEMBER 1963**
>
> Lancer – President John F. Kennedy
> Lace – Jacqueline Kennedy
> Lyric – Caroline Kennedy
> Lark – John F. Kennedy, Jr
>
> Volunteer – Vice President Lyndon B. Johnson
> Victoria – Lady Bird Johnson
> Velvet – Lynda Bird Johnson
> Venus – Lucy Baines Johnson
>
> Castle – The White House
> Angel – Air Force One
> Cabin – Kennedy compound at Hyannis Port, Massachusetts
> Calico – Pentagon
> Cork – FBI headquarters
> Volcano – The vice president's home in Texas
>
> Wand – Kenny O'Donnell
> Willow – Evelyn Lincoln
> Wayside – Pierre Salinger
> Warrior – Malcolm Kilduff
> Freedom – Dean Rusk
>
> Dazzle – Clint Hill
> Digest – Roy Kellerman
> Dusty – Emory Roberts
> Dagger – Rufus Youngblood

Marxist. He wrote in his diary, "I was looking for a key to my environment, and then I discovered socialist literature. I had to dig for my books in the back dusty shelves of libraries." It was on 27 July 1955 that Oswald joined the Civil Air Patrol, a civilian division of the United States Army Air Force where, the conspiracy theorists have it, he met Captain David Ferrie (see box on page

118). There is no substantive evidence that the two men knew each other.

On 8 September, Lee enrolled at Warren Easton High School. The following month, on 7 October, Oswald left school and attempted to join the marines but was turned down. On 10 November 1955, he began work as a messenger boy at Gerald F. Tujague Inc. In January 1956, he landed a job as an office boy at J.R. Michels Inc. His professional career was as peripatetic as his schooling and the following month he began work at Pfisterer Dental Laboratory. In July, Marguerite, Lee and Robert moved to Collinswood Street in Fort Worth. In September, he entered Arlington Heights High School but left on 28 July. On 24 October, he enlisted in the US Marine Corps and two days later reported for duty in San Diego. In his assessment tests on 30 July, his score was two points below average. On 21 December, he scored a 212 (Sharpshooter) on a marksmanship test

---

CAPTAIN DAVID FERRIE

David William Ferrie was born in Cleveland, Ohio on 28 March 1918 and, according to Jim Garrison (see page 123), was involved in the assassination of Kennedy. Ferrie contemplated becoming a Roman Catholic priest but became involved with the Civil Air Patrol. He became a pilot but was sacked after being arrested on a morals charge. In 1962, Ferrie began working with Guy Banister as a private investigator for lawyer G. Wray Gill on behalf of his client, the gangster Carlos Marcello, whom the government wanted to deport to Guatemala. Marcello escaped an immigration fraud charge on 22 November 1963. After the assassination, the FBI questioned Ferrie but they did not find any information linking him to the murder. On 22 February 1967, Ferrie was found dead in his apartment. The cause of death is unknown.

---

with a M-1 rifle. (In May 1959, Oswald took another test and scored 191, which was a point over the minimum for ranking as a marksman).

On 18 January 1957, he reported to Camp Pendleton, California, and was assigned to the A Company of the 1st Battalion, 2nd Infantry Training Regiment. On 1 May, he was promoted to Private 1st Class and two days later received a security clearance listed as "Confidential." On 9 July, he reported for duty with the Marine Corps Air Station at El Toro, California, and was assigned to the 4th Replacement Battalion. On 12 September, Oswald joined Marine Air Control Squadron Number One, Marine Air Group 11, 1st Marine Aircraft Wing, based in Atsugi, Japan. On 27 October, he accidentally shot himself in the elbow with a Derringer and was hospitalized at Yokosuka until 15 November.

On 11 April 1958, Oswald was court-martialled for the first time for illegal possession of a firearm. On 27 June, Oswald was again court-martialled, this time for attacking a sergeant who he blamed for getting him court-martialled the first time. Oswald was demoted and sent to the glasshouse (army prison). On 13 August, he was released. In Taiwan, Oswald suffered a nervous breakdown and was sent back to Japan. On 15 November, he returned to San Francisco. On 9 March 1959, Oswald was promoted to Private 1st Class again. On 11 September, Oswald was demobbed from the marines and on 20 September left for the Soviet Union arriving in Moscow on 16 October. He registered at the Hotel Berlin, and met an Intourist guide called Rima Shirokova. On 21 October, with his visa about to expire, Oswald tried to commit suicide by slashing his left wrist in the bath and was placed in a psychiatric ward at the Botkin Hospital. Ten days later, Oswald attempted to renounce his American citizenship. On 4 January 1960, he was sent to Minsk in Belarus where he started work at the Gorizont (Horizon) Electronics Factory, a huge factory that manufactured radios and televisions along with military and space electronic components. On

13 September, he was given an "undesirable discharge" from the Marine Corps.

In early 1961, Oswald began to think about a return to America. He wrote, "I am starting to reconsider my desire about staying. The work is drab, the money I get has nowhere to be spent. No nightclubs or bowling alleys, no places of recreation except the trade union dances. I have had enough." On 17 March he met Marina Prusakova, a member of the Komsomol (the communist youth movement) and the niece of a lieutenant-colonel in the Ministerstvo Vnutrennikh Del (Ministry of Internal Affairs). They began a relationship and on 20 April 1961 he proposed. Ten days later, they were married. On 15 February 1962 his daughter, June Lee, was born.

On 1 June, the Oswalds left for America, arriving in Hoboken, New Jersey on the 13 June. The next day, they flew to Fort Worth and moved in with Robert Oswald. On 26 June, the FBI interviewed Oswald about his time in the USSR and his reasons for returning to the USA. On 14 July, the Oswalds moved in with Marguerite at 1501 West 7th Street in Fort Worth. On 10 August, they moved to 2703 Mercedes Street in Fort Worth. On 16 August, the FBI interviewed Oswald for a second time. On 12 October, he began work at the graphic arts firm Jaggars-Chiles-Stovall. The Oswalds separated for a short while. On 28 January 1963, Oswald ordered a .38 calibre Smith and Wesson revolver in the post. On 2 March 1963, the Oswalds – by this time back together again – moved to 214 West Neely Street in Oak Cliff. Ten days later, Oswald ordered a rifle from Klein's Sporting Goods in Chicago, Illinois. On 25 March, the weapons arrived. Six days later, Marina took the infamous pictures of Oswald posing with the weaponry in the back garden at West Neely Street. On 1 April, Oswald was sacked from Jaggars-Chiles-Stovall.

On 10 April 1963, Oswald tried to assassinate Major General Edwin Walker (see box on right). The soldier had been sitting at his desk in his dining room filling in his

---

MAJOR GENERAL EDWIN WALKER

Born on 10 November 1909 at Center Point, Texas, Major General Edwin Anderson Walker, a bachelor, was a fervent anti-communist, segregationist and member of the right-wing John Birch Society. Walker was commanding officer of the 24th Infantry Division in West Germany until President Kennedy sacked him for distributing right-wing literature to his troops. In a fit of pique, Walker resigned from the service and returned to Texas. Walker was one of six candidates in the Democratic gubernatorial primary in 1962 but lost to John Connally, who went on to win the race. Walker, then 66, was arrested on 23 June 1976 after being accused of fondling an undercover policeman in a public lavatory in a Dallas park. On 16 March 1977, he was arrested again in Dallas for public lewdness. He pleaded no contest and was fined $1,000. He died on 31 October 1993.

The identity of Walker's would-be assassin was not discovered until after the assassination of the president when a note and pictures of Walker were found in Oswald's house. The bullet that was fired at Walker was too badly damaged to run conclusive ballistics studies on it. However, neutron activation tests later proved that it was from the same cartridge maker as the two bullets that hit the president.

---

federal income tax returns when Oswald fired one shot at him. It hit the wooden window frame, saving Walker's life. He was hit in the forearm by bullet fragments. A fortnight later, Oswald left for New Orleans and roomed with his aunt Lillian Murret.

On 10 May, he started work at the Reily Coffee Company and moved into a new home at 4905 Magazine Street. In New Orleans Oswald became involved in the Fair Play for Cuba Committee. On

3 June, he rented a post office box using the name Alek James Hidell. The next month, on 19 July, he was again sacked for incompetence. At the end of September, Oswald moved to Mexico arriving in Mexico City at 10am on 27 September. An hour and a half later, he went to the Cuban embassy to apply for a visa to visit the Caribbean island. He was told that he would need a Russian visa as well and one was not forthcoming. Furious, Oswald returned to America on 3 October at 1.35am and at 2.20pm he arrived in Dallas. He used the alias O. H. Lee to avoid questioning by the FBI. On 16 October, he began work filling book orders at the Texas School Book Depository. Four days later, Marina gave birth to another daughter, Audrey Marina Rachel. At this time, Oswald stayed in a bed and breakfast at 1026 North Beckley Avenue during the week and returned at weekends to Marina who was staying with a friend in Irving, about 15 miles (24 kilometres) from downtown Dallas. On 21 November, Oswald asked a work colleague to give him a lift to Irving because he wanted to collect some curtain rods. He returned to Dallas with a long paper bag. On 22 November, Oswald rose at 6.30am and left for work at the Texas School Book Depository at 7.23am. At 11.45am, Oswald stayed on the sixth floor when everyone else went down to the second floor for lunch.

The Aftermath

In November 1963, there was no federal law against assassinating a United States president, which meant that the murder should have been investigated by the Texas authorities under the auspices of the Texas coroner. However, just after 2pm, Secret Service agents, brandishing their weapons, removed the slain president's body from Parkland Hospital ignoring the protests of the medical staff.

Within 90 seconds of the shots being fired and the president being taken away, Dallas police had surrounded the Texas School Book Depository. The first policeman inside the building was Marrion L. Baker, accompanied by Roy Truly, the superintendent. The building was virtually empty. In the second floor canteen, Baker and Truly came across a young man buying a Coca-Cola® from a vending machine. Truly vouched for him to the policeman and Lee Harvey Oswald was allowed to leave the scene of the crime.

Vice President Johnson took the oath of office administered by United States District Court Judge Sarah Tilghman Hughes (then the district judge of the North District of Texas, she remains the only woman ever to administer the oath of office to a president) at 2.38pm on board Air Force One just before it departed Love Field. Mrs Kennedy was still wearing her blood-stained pink suit, having refused to change. The plane then flew back to Andrews Air Force Base carrying the new and the previous president. It landed two and a half hours later and as the Attorney General ran onto the plane, Jackie pushed past Lyndon Johnson to go to him, an act that the new president did not forget. President Kennedy's body was taken to Bethesda Naval Hospital where an autopsy was performed.

At 1.15pm Lee Harvey Oswald shot Dallas policeman JD Tippit. Half an hour earlier, Tippit, on beat number 78, was told to report to central Oak Cliff. At 12.54pm he radioed his base to inform them he had arrived at the new location. He was on the lookout for a suspect whose description had been broadcast on the police radio. At 1.11pm, Tippit was driving his patrol car east on East 10th Street in Oak Cliff. Almost 100 feet (30.5 metres) past the junction of 10th Street and Patton Avenue, Tippit stopped his car by Lee Harvey Oswald. The two men spoke and then Tippit opened the door and began to walk to the front of his car. When he reached the front wheel, Oswald pulled a gun and shot Tippit three times in the chest. Tippit collapsed to the floor, whereupon Oswald walked up to the stricken policeman and shot him in the head. There were 12 witnesses to the murder.

A state funeral was arranged for the slain president. His assassin was laid to rest the same day.

Oswald walked briskly from the scene and into the Hardy Shoe Store (now a bridal shop) at 213 West Jefferson Avenue. Oswald left the shoe shop, followed by shop manager Johnny Calvin Brewer, and went into the Texas Theater, a cinema at 231 West Jefferson Avenue, where, at 1.50pm, police arrested him after Mr Brewer pointed him out. Policeman M. N. McDonald approached Oswald who said, "Well, it's all over now" but as McDonald tried to arrest him, Oswald hit the policeman and pulled a gun. A struggle ensued before Oswald was subdued and taken into custody. That night, both President Johnson and Attorney General Kennedy rang Mrs Tippit to offer their condolences. Jackie Kennedy later wrote her a sympathetic letter. The plight touched the nation and the American public donated $647,579, including $25,000 (of the $150,000) Abraham Zapruder (see box below) made from selling his 26.6 second, 466-frame film of the assassination to *Life* magazine.

JD Tippit was buried on 25 November at Laurel Land Memorial Park, Dallas. In January 1964, the slain police-man was posthumously awarded the Medal of Valor from the National Police Hall of Fame and also received the Police Medal of Honor, the Police Cross, and the Citizens Traffic Commission Award of Heroism.

Police found three spent cartridges and a rifle by a window of the Texas School Book Depository where Oswald worked. At 11.36pm on 22 November, Oswald was charged with the murder of President Kennedy.

John F. Kennedy was the sixth president to lie in state in the Capitol Rotunda. The others were Lincoln, Garfield, McKinley, Harding and Taft. President Kennedy's coffin was placed on the same catafalque that had been used for Abraham Lincoln, 98 years earlier. John F. Kennedy was buried with full military honours in Arlington National Cemetery on 25 November 1963, his son's third birthday. Dignitaries from 102 countries attended the event including Prince Philip, Haile Selassie and Charles de Gaulle.

At around 12.05am on Saturday 23 November, Lee Harvey Oswald appeared before the press in the basement of City Hall at 2001 Commerce Street in Dallas. He denied all knowledge of the killing. At 1.30am, he was formally arraigned with the murder of the president. At 10.25am, the police again began to question Oswald. At 3.30pm, Oswald received a visit from his brother, Robert. At 4.35pm he appeared at the number

UNIQUE FOOTAGE

Abraham Zapruder was born at Kovel in the Ukraine on 15 May 1905. He emigrated to the United States in 1920 and lived in Brooklyn until 1941, when he relocated to Dallas. In 1959, he founded his own clothing company. He filmed the assassination on his 414 PD 8-mm Bell & Howell Zoomatic Director Series movie camera. He suffered from vertigo and had to be helped by his receptionist, Marilyn Sitzman (born 14 December 1939, died Dallas 11 August 1993). The film was shown on television for the first time in March 1975 on *Good Night America* hosted by Geraldo Rivera. The camera used by Zapruder is now housed in the US National Archives. Zapruder died in Dallas on 30 August 1970 of a malignant brain tumour.

The Dallas police mugshot of Lee Harvey Oswald, taken the day after he killed Kennedy and the day before his own death at the hands of Dallas nightclub owner Jack Ruby.

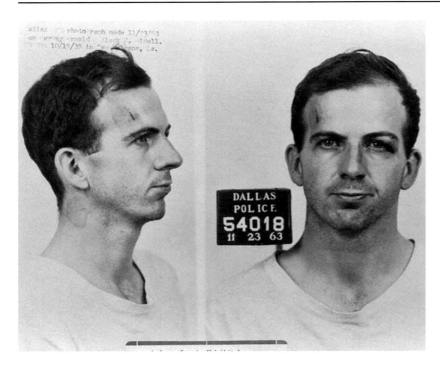

two spot in a line-up alongside W. E. Perry (under number one), Richard L. Clark (three) and Don Ables (four), and was identified as Officer Tippit's killer by witness Helen Markham. At 6pm, he faced more questions. At 9.30am the next day, preparations were made to transport Oswald from his fifth-floor cell to the local jail. At 11.15am the journey began.

Six minutes later, as the handcuffed Lee Harvey Oswald was being led to a waiting vehicle, Jack Ruby, a local nightclub owner, shot him in the stomach, shouting, "You killed the president, you rat." The assassination was watched live on television by millions. Oswald died without regaining consciousness. At 1.07pm, Oswald was pronounced dead at Parkland Hospital where his victim, the president, had been taken two days earlier.

On 29 November 1963, President Johnson asked Chief Justice Earl Warren, who had administered the oath of office to Kennedy, to head a commission to discover the truth behind the assassination under executive order 11130. On 9 December 1963, the FBI told the commission that Oswald had fired all three shots, with the first and third hitting the president and the second Governor Connally. The Warren Commission published its report on 24 September 1964 and said that there had been no evidence of a domestic or foreign conspiracy, that Oswald was the lone gunman and that one shot had missed but the other two had hit their targets including one bullet that hit both the president and the governor. This became known to conspiracy theorists as the "magic bullet theory" because of its supposed ability to enter the president, leave, make a right then a left turn in mid-air before going into Connally. The theorists are wrong. If the governor had been sitting immediately in front of the president and at the same height, then there might be some credibility to the magic bullet theory. In fact, he was sitting below JFK and further into the car. Additionally, he was turning as the bullet hit him. In a recent poll, 80 per cent of Americans said that they did not believe the findings of the Warren Commission.

Mrs Kennedy gave an interview to *Life* magazine but the article, which was published on 6 December 1963, focused mainly on Kennedy's love of the musical *Camelot*. It was not until after the death of Mrs Kennedy that the notes taken by reporter Theodore White were released.

There are innumerable theories as to who "really" shot John F. Kennedy at Dealey Plaza that November day. Most Americans and many others around the world do not believe that a lone, deranged gunman murdered the president, even though the evidence points to exactly that conclusion. The conspiracy madness began less than a month after John F. Kennedy's death. On 19 December 1963, *The Guardian*, a left-wing national weekly, published a 10,000-word article by a lawyer called Mark Lane (born at New York 24 February 1927). The feature opened the floodgates for a deluge of conspiracy theories that shows no sign of abating more than 40 years after the event. The mainstream American media ignored Lane's article and *The Guardian* published it as a standalone pamphlet. It sold in its thousands.

On 14 January 1964, Marguerite Oswald hired Lane to represent her son *pro bono* before the Warren Commission. Mrs Oswald believed that her son was a spy for America and had been "set up to take the blame for the assassination". The commission refused to let Lane represent the Oswald family. Marguerite Oswald sacked Lane on 1 April 1964. When Lane testified before the commission, he insisted it was not done *in camera*, the only time this occurred. "We had very, very little trouble of any kind," recalled Earl Warren, "except for one fellow by the name of Mark Lane. And he was the only one that treated the commission with contempt."

Former *Dallas Morning News* reporter Hugh Aynesworth declared that Lane "almost single-handedly invented the lucrative JFK conspiracy industry". Lane was certainly the most voluble of the conspiracy theorists and even the KGB donated $2,000 through an intermediary to his funds, which financed a trip to Europe in 1964 for Lane to spread his message. (A KGB defector revealed the donation in 1992. There is no suggestion that Lane was aware of the original source of the money.) In 1966, Lane published a best-selling book called *Rush to Judgment* that stayed on the *New York Times* best-seller lists for 17 weeks. However, even some left-wingers were embarrassed by the distortions and outright fabrications in the work by Lane, who later went on to represent James Earl Ray, the assassin of Martin Luther King, and Jim Jones's People's Temple in Guyana. Harold Weisberg was a critic of the Warren Commission but he told the left-wing publication *Mother Jones*, "I only wish [that Lane] would steal from others, but he has this urge to invent his own stuff." In the book, Lane adopted a scattergun approach to the

GARRISON'S SUSPECTS

William Guy Banister was born at Monroe, Louisiana on 7 March 1900. After university, he joined the Monroe Police Department and then in 1934 joined the FBI. Banister's work impressed J. Edgar Hoover who promoted him to run the bureau in Butte, Montana. He retired in 1954. He served in the Lousiana force for two years before being sacked, whereupon he established his own private detective agency, Guy Banister Associates. The firm's office was based at 531 Lafayette Street. In the same building but accessed by a different street, 544 Camp Street, had been (October 1961 to February 1962) the offices of the Cuban Revolutionary Council, an anti-Castro group. On 9 August 1963, Lee Harvey Oswald distributed Fair Play for Cuba leaflets. On this most flimsy of evidence and the word of a man beaten up by Banister, Garrison became convinced that there had been a right-wing plot to kill Kennedy.

Carlos Jose Bringuier was born in Cuba on 22 June 1934. He studied law at the University of Havana, qualifying as a lawyer in 1957. Anti-Castro, he emigrated to America in February 1961. In New Orleans, he became publicity director for the Directorio Revolucionario Estudiantil. Bringuier and two other Cubans, Celso Macario Hernandez and Miguel Mariano Cruz, became embroiled in a confrontation with Oswald as he handed out his pro-Castro literature on 9 August 1963.

Clay Laverne Shaw was born on 17 March 1913. He was demobbed from the army in 1946 having been presented with medals not only by the United States but also by France and Belgium. After the war, Shaw became a successful businessman and altruist co-founding the International Trade Mart. He died on 14 August 1974 of lung cancer.

assassination throwing out so many non-sequiturs that one never knows what is true but irrelevant and what is merely false. For example, he spent 11 pages writing about a barmaid who worked for Jack Ruby two years before the assassination. Lane also ignored the role of Johnny Calvin Brewer who was responsible for Oswald's arrest. In fact, he does not even refer to Oswald's capture. Lane also quotes selectively to suit his purpose. During his testimony Jack Ruby tells Earl Warren, "All I want to do is tell the truth and that is all." End of Lane quote. What Lane omitted are the next four words spoken by Ruby, "There was no conspiracy."

In 1963, New Orleans district attorney Earing Carothers "Jim" Garrison opened an investigation into the murdered president. Garrison stood 6 feet 7 inches (1 metre 98 centimetres) tall, weighed more than 17 stone (108 kilograms) and was known locally as "The Jolly Green Giant". He was discharged from the army during the Korean War for psychiatric reasons and joined the FBI, but left after just four months. Garrison made a name for himself after being elected district attorney by leading armed raids on brothels on Bourbon Street. He was, however, no stranger to the ladies of the night himself. In March 1962, Garrison was invited to the White House but instead of taking his wife, he took his girl-friend of the moment, an air hostess called Judy Chambers. The couple hit the nightspots of Washington the night before the meeting, overslept and missed see-ing the president. He did wake up in time for a meeting at 1.30pm at the Justice Department with Bobby Kennedy though. Garrison was convinced that a group of right-wing activists, including David Ferrie, fellow pri-vate investigator William Guy Banister, Carlos Jose Bringuier and Clay Shaw, were involved in a conspiracy with the CIA to kill John F. Kennedy. Garrison alleged that the murder was to wreck Kennedy's efforts to find peace in Cuba and Vietnam. Banister died of a heart attack on 6 June 1964 rather inconveniently for Garrison who then made David Ferrie his chief suspect.

However, before Ferrie could be arrested he was found dead in his apartment.

On 22 March 1967, Garrison indicted Clay Shaw "with David W. Ferrie, Lee Harvey Oswald and others" for the murder of John F. Kennedy. Shaw denied knowing Ferrie and Oswald and insisted he had not "conspired with anyone at any time or at any place to murder our late and esteemed president". In Garrison's fecund mind there were, in fact, seven assassins at Dealey Plaza, none of them Oswald who was, as he claimed, a patsy. On *The Tonight Show with Johnny Carson* on 31 January 1968, Garrison told the television audience that "elements" of the CIA had been involved in the murder of Kennedy. However, at the trial Garrison produced no evidence of CIA involvement or indeed anything linking Shaw, Oswald or Ferrie to the CIA. The trial began on 29 January 1969 and lasted for 34 days before the jury returned a verdict of "not guilty" in less than an hour on 1 March. In his diary, Shaw had written, "Aside from any questions of guilt or innocence, anyone who knows me knows that I would have better sense than to plot with two nuts like [Oswald and Ferrie]." In 1988, Garrison published a book, *On the Trail of the Assassins*. Film director Oliver Stone read the book (three times, he says) and bought the rights to it for $250,000. Stone gave the thoroughly discredited Garrison kudos with the entertaining but historically inaccurate $40million film *JFK* (released on 20 December 1991) which starred

---

JFK – THE MOVIE

The film had an all-star cast including Tommy Lee Jones, Kevin Bacon, Gary Oldman, Jack Lemmon, Laurie Metcalf, Sissy Spacek, Joe Pesci, John Candy, Walter Matthau, Sally Kirkland, Donald Sutherland, Edward Asner, Lolita Davidovich and Jim Garrison – who in a cheeky piece of casting played Earl Warren.

Kevin Costner as Garrison. Senator Arlen Spector, a junior counsel on the Warren Commission, said, "Stone's film has done more than any single effort to distort history and the commission's work."

Jack Ruby, Lee Harvey Oswald's assassin, was born Jacob Rubenstein, probably on 25 March 1911 at Chicago, Illinois. The Warren Commission reported, "There is much confusion about his exact birth date. School records report it as 23 June, 25 April, 13 March and, possibly, 3 March 1911. Other early official records list his date of birth as 21 April and 26 April 1911. During his adult life the date Ruby used most frequently was 25 March 1911. His driver's licence, seized following his arrest, and his statements to the FBI on 24 November 1963, listed this date. However, the police arrest report for 24 November gave his birth date as 19 March 1911. Since the recording of births was not required in Chicago prior to 1915, Ruby's birth may never have been officially recorded."

Jacob was the fifth of nine children of Joseph Rubenstein (born Sokolów Podlaski, Poland 1871, died in Chicago 1958), a womanizing, alcoholic carpenter, and Fannie Turek Rutkowski (born Warsaw, Poland 1876, died 1944 of a heart attack and pneumonia) who suffered from a mental disease and was sectioned in 1937. The Rubinstein children grew up in abject poverty. On 6 June 1922, Jacob was sent to the Institute for Juvenile Research by the Jewish Social Service Bureau because he played truant. On leaving school, young Jacob, known as Sparky, a nickname he liked, began drifting, wanting to make something of himself but without the means or talent to achieve very much. For a time he worked as a ticket tout. From 1937 until 1940 he worked as a trade unionist for Local 20467 of the Scrap Iron and Junk Handlers' Union, which later became part of the International Brotherhood of Teamsters. On 8 December 1939, the union's president Leon Cooke was shot, dying a month later. Rubenstein was implicated but later cleared of any involvement in the murder. He took Leon as his middle name in honour of Cooke.

He was called up to the air force on 21 May 1943. Following demob as a private first class, on 21 February 1946, he returned to Chicago and sold novelties with his brothers, Earl and Sam. In 1947, after his brothers bought his share of the business for more than $14,000, he moved to Dallas, Texas to help his sister, Eva Grant, with the running of the Singapore Supper Club. On 30 December 1947, he officially changed his name to Jack L. Ruby. In the third largest city of the Lone Star State, he became the owner of the Carousel Club, a sleazy strip club on Commerce Street. Patrons and strippers remembered his mercurial nature. He also spent much time cultivating police contacts.

Despite his best efforts to ingratiate himself with the police, Ruby was arrested on a number of occasions between 1949 and 24 November 1963, usually for minor offences. He was accused of fondling the breasts of teenage girls and claimed, "I'm just breaking them in to come to work for me". A more bizarre charge concerned Ruby's dog, Sheba. He often referred to the animal as his wife and the Society for the Prevention of Cruelty to Animals became concerned that Ruby was taking his appellation for the animal slightly too literally. Although as a nightclub owner he mixed with underworld figures, the FBI admitted that he did not have the contacts to be a useful informer. It is an opinion backed up by many who knew Ruby. Dallas reporter Tony Zoppi said that Ruby "couldn't keep a secret for five minutes … Jack was one of the most talkative guys you would ever meet. He'd be the worst fellow in the world to be part of a conspiracy, because he just plain talked too much."

At 11.17am on 24 November 1963, Ruby was at the Western Union building opposite City Hall where Oswald was being held. Ruby was wiring some money to one of his strippers. He walked into the basement of City Hall, which was packed with 70 policemen and reporters. At 11.21am, Oswald appeared handcuffed to Detective James R. Leavelle. Ruby pulled a snub-nosed Colt Cobra .38 and shot Oswald fatally. Taken into custody, Ruby said that he had killed Oswald to save the first lady from the pain of a trial. He told Assistant D. A. Bill Alexander, "Well, you guys couldn't do it. Someone had to do it. That son of a bitch killed my president."

He was indicted with the murder on 26 November 1963. A defence lawyer said that Ruby had serious psychiatric problems. Ruby was tried for Oswald's murder, found guilty on 14 March 1964 and sentenced to death. The death sentence puzzled many because the usual sentence for a gunshot murder was eight years in prison. On 5 October 1966, the Texas Court of Criminal Appeals overturned the sentence and the judge also agreed to a change of venue to ensure a fair trial. A new trial was scheduled for February 1967 in Wichita Falls, Texas. However, on 9 December 1966, Ruby fell ill with pneumonia and was taken to Parkland Memorial Hospital, where both Kennedy and Oswald had also been taken. Doctors discovered that Ruby was in the advanced stages of liver, lung and brain cancer. Jack Ruby, the man who killed the man who killed John F. Kennedy, died of a pulmonary embolism and bronchiolar lung cancer at Parkland Memorial Hospital, Dallas on 3 January 1967. He never married. He is buried in Westlawn Cemetery, Chicago.

Jackie Kennedy dedicated her life immediately following her husband's death to ensuring his legacy was kept alive and to creating the idea of Camelot. On 11 December 1963, Congress voted to give her a staff and office for one year at a cost of no more than $50,000 plus money for funeral costs. She was also granted the presidential widow's pension of $10,000 per annum – payable until remarriage or death. Further, she was given free postage for life. Mrs Kennedy and her children were given Secret Service protection for two years, later increased to four. In 1968, following the assassination of her brother-in-law Robert Kennedy (see pages 147–158), Secret Service protection was extended to all presidential widows till death or remarriage and for presidential children until they reached the age of 16.

In the chapel of the Little Virgin on the island of Skorpios, Greece, on 20 October 1968, Jackie married the Greek shipping tycoon Aristotle Socrates Onassis in a Greek Orthodox ceremony. She was the second presidential widow to remarry (the first being Grover Cleveland's widow). Onassis died in Paris on 15 March 1975. On 22 September of that year she began work as a consulting editor at the publishing house Viking. She resigned from the company in 1977. In February 1978, she became a book editor working for Doubleday at 245 Park Avenue in New York. Her salary was $15,000 a year. She did not remarry but she began seeing Maurice Tempelsman in 1975 and in 1982 he moved in with her. She died of Non-Hodgkin's lymphoma at her 1040 Fifth Avenue, New York home at 10.15pm on 19 May 1994.

Caroline Kennedy married the designer Edwin Arthur Schlossberg on his 42nd birthday, 19 July 1986. The couple has three children: Rose Kennedy (born New York 25 June 1988), Tatiana Celia Kennedy (born New York 5 May 1990), and John Bouvier Kennedy (born New York 19 January 1993).

John F. Kennedy, Jr broke hearts worldwide when on his third birthday he saluted his father's coffin. He graduated from Brown University on 6 June 1983. He became one of America's most eligible bachelors and was linked to a variety of glamorous women including the singer Madonna, and the actresses Sarah Jessica Parker and Darryl Hannah. On 7 September 1995, he founded the unsuccessful political magazine George. On 21 September 1996, at Cumberland Island, Georgia, he married Carolyn Bessette, a publicist for the fashion designer Calvin Klein.

Three years later, on Friday 16 July 1999, John set off in his Piper Saratoga to fly to the wedding of his cousin, Rory. The plan was to take off at 7.15pm so they would land at Martha's Vineyard at 8.30pm as night was falling. Flying with him would be his wife and sister-in-law, Lauren Gail Bessette, but they were late getting to Essex County Airport in Fairfield, New

Jersey. The day before, John had had a cast removed from a broken ankle and his leg was still sore. The plane took off at 8.38pm – 12 minutes after sundown. During the early part of the flight, the plane narrowly missed hitting an American Airlines jet. At 9.18pm the visibility had dropped to zero. On board the plane was an autopilot that could have flown the flight for him but no one had told him of this facility. At 9.34pm, he began a descent but a whiteout enveloped the plane and John did not know where he was or indeed if he was flying upside down. He flew 300 feet (92 metres) up to try and get above the haze. At 9.40pm, he began another descent but the plane accelerated and it was soon heading towards the sea at 5,000 feet (1,500 metres) per minute. As an inexperienced pilot, John did the worse thing possible – he tried to pull the nose up when he should have straightened the wings and then pulled up. The plane began to rotate clockwise in what aviators call a "graveyard spiral". As the plane plummeted towards the sea at 99 feet (30 metres) per second, it would still have been possible to recover but John was inexperienced. The three passengers were forced into their seats by the G-force as the plane hurtled towards the Atlantic. They were killed instantly when the plane smacked into the water. John F. Kennedy, Jr was 38 years old. His wife was 33 and his sister-in-law was 34. Their bodies were recovered on 21 July 1999. The next day, the ashes of the three were scattered at sea.

Edward Kennedy is still senator for Massachusetts, the seat he inherited from his elder brother, the president, in November 1962. Kennedy is currently the second-longest serving member of the Senate, after Robert Byrd of West Virginia. Senator Kennedy survived an aeroplane crash in 1964 that killed two people. Then, on 18 July 1969, there was a party to thank the "Boiler Room Girls", a group of young women, for their help in Bobby Kennedy's presidential campaign. Despite the subsequent stories, they were not goodtime girls providing sexual favours for the men present. Senator Kennedy offered one, Mary Jo Kopechne, a lift home after she complained of feeling unwell. Kennedy, having had too much to drink, mistook the speed he was driving and the car ran off Chappaquiddick Bridge into the water. The senator made seven or eight attempts to rescue his passenger but was beaten back by the strong current. Mary Jo's corpse was found the next day. The senator pleaded guilty to a charge of leaving the scene of an accident after causing injury and was sentenced to two months in jail, which was suspended. After refusing to run in 1972 and 1976, he ran for president in 1980 against the incumbent Jimmy Carter, the leader of his own party. He was not chosen and President Carter went on to lose against Ronald Reagan. In 2004, Edward Kennedy supported his colleague John Kerry, the junior senator from Massachusetts, in his unsuccessful bid for the White House. Senator Kennedy has been twice married.

Lyndon B. Johnson was elected president in his own right on 3 November 1964, beating Barry Goldwater, but did not stand in 1968. He died at San Antonio, Texas on 22 January 1973.

Idlewild Airport in New York was renamed John F. Kennedy International Airport on 24 December 1963.

The Warren Commission's report was published on 24 September 1964. Of its members: Earl Warren died on 9 July 1974 in Georgetown University Hospital in Washington, DC; Senator Richard B. Russell (Democrat/Georgia) was in the Senate from 1933 until his death on 21 January 1971; Senator John Sherman Cooper (Republican/Kentucky) said, "Now, people have said that somebody told them that they saw somebody on the railroad bank or saw somebody going over the bank, but no one has ever been able to show any cartridges, any rifle, any pistol, no one has ever found anything other than the evidence about Oswald." He retired from the Senate in 1973 and died on 21 February 1991;

Representative Hale Boggs (Democrat/Louisiana) disappeared on 16 October 1972 while flying in a twin engine Cessna 310 over Alaska; Congressman Gerald Ford (Republican/Michigan) replaced Richard Nixon as president in August 1974 but lost to Jimmy Carter two years later. President Ford died on Boxing Day 2006; Allen Dulles had resigned after eight years in charge of the CIA in September 1961 after the Bay of Pigs fiasco; he died of pneumonia on 29 January 1969. John J. McCloy was a banker and adviser to John F. Kennedy, Lyndon Johnson, Richard Nixon, Jimmy Carter and Ronald Reagan; he died on 11 March 1989.

On 14 May 1965, Queen Elizabeth II dedicated a memorial to President Kennedy at Runnymede in Surrey, England. The memorial consists of a Portland stone memorial tablet inscribed with the words, "This acre of English ground was given to the United States of America by the people of Britain in memory of John F. Kennedy/Born 29 May 1917/President of the United States 1961–1963/Died by an assassin's hand 22 November 1963/Let every Nation know, whether it wishes us well or ill, that we shall pay any price, bear any burden, meet any hardship, support any friend or oppose any foe, in order to assure the survival and success of liberty, 1961/From the inaugural address of President Kennedy 21 January 1961."

In 1965, Marina Oswald married Kenneth J. Porter, a Dallas carpenter. Their son, Mark, was born in 1966. The couple divorced in 1974 but continued to live together.

At 6.30am on Sunday 4 October 1981, Lee Harvey Oswald's body was exhumed from Rose Hill Burial Park in Fort Worth, Texas. British author Michael Eddowes had become convinced that it was not Oswald who had returned to America from the Soviet Union but an impostor. In 1975, Eddowes self-published a book called *Khrushchev Killed Kennedy*. It was the first time Eddowes had gone public with his view about the Soviet impostor. The following year, he wrote another book on the asssssination *Nov. 22, How They Killed Kennedy*. Two years later, he began his campaign to have Oswald exhumed. It succeeded when he persuaded Oswald's widow to join his campaign, against the wishes of Robert Oswald. At 10am the examination began and it was discovered that water had done much damage to the corpse. The remains were examined for identification and at 3pm a doctor announced, "The findings of the team are as follows: We independently and as a team have concluded beyond any doubt, and I mean beyond any doubt, that the individual buried under the name of Lee Harvey Oswald in Rose Hill Cemetery is in fact Lee Harvey Oswald." Eddowes took his defeat graciously. He said, "Though surprised, I am in no way disappointed in the apparent disproving of my evidence of imposture. Rather, I have accomplished my objective in obtaining the exhumation and I am glad for those who have steadfastly maintained the contrary for whatever reason."

MICHAEL EDDOWES

Michael Henry Eddowes was born in Derby, England, on 8 October 1903 and became a successful lawyer. He was also a restaurateur and car designer. In addition to his book on the Kennedy assassination, he wrote one claiming that Timothy Evans was innocent of the Rillington Place murders. So interested was Eddowes in the case that he actually bought 10 Rillington Place. In 1962, after a car crash, Eddowes visited society osteopath Stephen Ward for treatment for a bad back. He said, "The Ward consulting rooms were an espionage centre. I realised I was on to something terrifying." Eddowes became convinced that Ward and Russian spy Eugene Ivanov conspired to bring about the downfall of war minister John Profumo. Michael Eddowes died in late December 1993.

Indira Gandhi (1917–1984)

The Victim

Indira Priyadarshini Gandhi was born on 19 November 1917 at Allahabad, Uttar Pradesh, India, the only child of Jawaharlal Nehru (1889–1964), India's first prime minister, and Kamala (c. 1899–1936), daughter of Atal Kaul, a businessman of Delhi. During her childhood both her parents and other family members spent time in prison for their nationalist views. She was educated in many different establishments at home and abroad and she ended up at Somerville College, Oxford. She was by no means an intellectual, had an inability to maintain close relationships with people outside her family and a tendency to blame others for difficulties. In 1941, she returned to India and threw herself into the nationalist movement.

On 16 March 1942 she married, against her father's wishes, Feroze Gandhi (born 12 August 1912), a friend of her mother's. They had two sons: Rajiv, born on 20 August 1944 and Sanjay, born two years later on 14 December 1946, but the couple were soon estranged.

In September 1942, Indira Gandhi was arrested by the British authorities for fomenting revolt and detained without charge for 243 days before her release on 13 May 1943. During Lord Mountbatten's poorly organized Partition of India in the summer of 1947, she helped in refugee camps. Four years later, during the country's first

Indira Gandhi's father begat a political dynasty that is still influential in India today.

general election, Gandhi managed the campaigns of both her father and her husband, who was standing in the constituency of Rae Bareilly. Feroze Gandhi was opposed to corruption and his investigation into the nationalized insurance industry resulted in the resignation of one of his father-in-law's ministers. In 1959, Mrs Gandhi was elected president of the Indian National Congress, while her father was prime minister. Her husband Feroze died on 8 September 1960 from a heart attack.

On 27 May 1964 her father, who had served four terms in office, died, and Lal Bahadur Shastri succeeded him. Urged by the new premier, Gandhi stood for election and when she was elected he found her a seat in the cabinet as Minister for Information and Broadcasting. At 1.32am on 11 January 1966, Shastri unexpectedly died of a heart attack as he concluded the peace treaty in Tashkent in the Indo-Pakistan War, which had begun in August 1965. On 19 January, Gandhi beat Morarji Desai by 355 votes to 169 to become the fifth prime minister of India and the first woman to hold that position. Her election was due in no small part to her gender – she was seen by the Syndicate, a powerful group of regional power brokers, as someone who would be malleable, unlike Desai.

She took office on 24 January, replacing the caretaker Gulzarilal Nanda (who had also been caretaker after her father's death). In the disastrous 1967 general election, the Congress failed for the first time to win a two-thirds majority in parliament, and lost power in half of the Indian states. Two years later, she defied the Syndicate when she lobbied for a non-party member to become president of India. She was expelled from the Congress. She became head of a rival Congress, which eventually became her party, called the Indian National Congress (Indira), or, for short, the Congress (I). Her party triumphed at the 1971 general election as they did in the March 1972 state elections. The victories allowed her to stamp her imprimatur on politics and on the country.

On 16 December 1971, India defeated the Pakistan army in east Pakistan, and thereby brought independence to the new state of Bangladesh. Despite her election success Gandhi never felt secure in her mandate. Elections to party positions in the Indian National Congress were stopped, and her closest advisors made all-important party appointments and decisions. Increasingly, Gandhi took decisions independently of the cabinet, in consultation only with a shifting clique of high-level bureaucrats personally loyal to her, and her younger son, Sanjay. On 12 June 1975, the High Court of Allahabad declared Gandhi's 1971 election invalid on the grounds of corrupt practices. This constituted election fraud, and the court ordered her to be removed from her seat in parliament and banned from running in elections for six years. Since the prime minister must be a member of either the Lok Sabha (lower house) or the Rajya Sabha (upper house), this decision had the effect of removing her from office.

As Gandhi appealed, the opposition parties rallied and called for her resignation. Gandhi advised President Fakhruddin Ali Ahmed to declare a state of emergency, which he did on 26 June 1975. Complete press censorship was imposed and the laws under which Gandhi's election was declared invalid were themselves invalidated. Gandhi also strengthened the powers of the prime minister and extended the terms of the national parliament and of the state legislatures, as well as nullifying habeas corpus. Gandhi appointed her son, Sanjay, to recruit thousands of young people to rally to her cause. Many were thugs who intimidated opponents. Simultaneously, thousands of political activists were arrested and tortured. Sanjay ordered the clearing of slums around Delhi's Jama Masjid, which left hundreds of thousands of people homeless and thousands killed. As part of Sanjay's family planning campaign, thousands of men were forcibly sterilized.

In January 1977, Gandhi released nearly all political prisoners and called elections. She was defeated by the rival Janata Party and Morarji Desai became prime minister on 24 March 1977. The party stayed in power until 14 January 1980, although it split in July 1979 over in-fighting. Attempts to arrest and convict Indira and Sanjay Gandhi failed. In fact, the Gandhis won public sympathy over the way the Janata Party went after them and on 14 January 1980 Mrs Gandhi was returned to power. Local elections were called and Congress (I) was returned in most states.

On 23 June 1980, the first tragedy struck the family when Sanjay, the heir apparent, was killed in an aeroplane crash. During the next four years Gandhi ruled without resorting to the extreme measures of her pre-

vious administration. She did attempt to consolidate her power, however, which led to turmoil in the northeast, in Kashmir and in Punjab. In 1983, tensions rose between India and Pakistan. Sikhs in Punjab demanded autonomy and on 3 June 1984 Gandhi launched Operation Bluestar. Troops were sent into the Golden Temple at Amritsar, the holiest site of the Sikh religion, to quell an uprising and to capture Jarnail Singh Bhindranwale, the Sikh leader, who was demanding an independent homeland for Sikhs. Rather than being

RAJIV GANDHI

The Victim: The elder son of Indira and Feroze Gandhi, Rajiv Ratna Gandhi initially had no interest in politics and worked as a pilot. His mother persuaded him to become involved after the death of his brother. In December 1984, he led his mother's party to a landslide in the general election. In November 1989 he lost power.

Date and Place of Assassination: 21 May 1991, Sriperumbudur, Tamil Nadu, India.

The Event: Campaigning during mid-term elections for the Sriperumbudur Lok Sabha Congress candidate, Maragatham Chandrasekhar, in Tamil Nadu, he was driven to Sriperumbudur, accompanied by a foreign journalist who was interviewing him in the car. When he reached the venue, Gandhi got out of the car and began to walk towards the dais where he would deliver his speech. Along the way, fans, children and party workers greeted him. At 10.10pm, a young woman approached him and bent down to touch his feet. As she did so, she detonated a RDX (Research Department Explosive; about ten thousand 2-millimetre steel balls were embedded in the bomb) explosive-laden belt tucked below her dress. Gandhi and 16

others around the scene were killed. A local photographer, who also died in the blast but whose camera was found intact afterwards, caught the event on film.

The Assassin: Thenmuli Rajaratnam may have been born in 1974 (her date of birth has not been officially confirmed), making her just 17 years old when she murdered Rajiv Gandhi. She was also known as Dhanu. It is believed that she was a member of the Tamil Tigers. In 1987, Gandhi had sent peacekeeping troops to Sri Lanka and her supporters later claimed that Indian soldiers had raped her. Others suggest that the claim is nothing more than a smokescreen to garner sympathy for the Tamil Tigers.

The Aftermath: It appears that Gandhi had tried to stop her touching his feet as his face bore the impact of the blast. Seven years later in 1998, an Indian court convicted 26 people in the conspiracy to assassinate Gandhi. Upon appeal, only four of the conspirators were executed. Rajiv Gandhi's Italian-born widow Sonia became the leader of the Congress (I) party in 1998, and led the party to victory in the 2004 elections. His son, Rahul, has entered the family business and is a member of parliament.

captured, he was killed by Indian troops on 6 June. Deaths have been estimated at 1,000 including 100 soldiers. Sikhs were outraged and one killed a senior army officer while another hijacked an aeroplane. "Mrs Gandhi made a fatal mistake," said a Sikh leader in exile. "Every man who thinks himself as a Sikh can never forget that she has signed her own death warrant." Gandhi's Sikh bodyguards were relieved of their duties but she insisted that they be reinstated believing it sent out a positive message. Bhindranwale remains a controversial figure in history – some seeing him as a martyr, others as a terrorist and extremist.

Date and Place of Assassination

31 October 1984, 1 Safdarjung Road, New Delhi, India.

The Event

On the morning of 31 October, Indira Gandhi was due to be interviewed by the actor Peter Ustinov at her office, so she walked from her official residence in Safdarjung Road, New Delhi. As she passed a gate she greeted two of her Sikh bodyguards Satwant Singh and Beant Singh. They responded by opening fire with their semi-automatic machine pistols. Her other guards opened fire killing Beant Singh and wounding Satwant Singh. Mrs Gandhi died on her way to hospital, in her official car, but was not declared dead until many hours later. She was taken to the All India Institute of Medical Sciences, where doctors operated on her and reportedly removed 31 bullets from her body.

The Assassins

The murderers were her Sikh bodyguards Satwant Singh and Beant Singh. Beant Singh was born in the Punjab village of Maloya in 1950. He joined the police in 1975 and was posted to New Delhi in 1980. He was soon recognized and appointed to Indira Gandhi's personal protection squad. He travelled abroad with her and even had the same blood group, O negative, so was available for blood transfusions if necessary. He was killed at the scene of the assassination.

Satwant Singh was born in 1963 and joined the Delhi Police in 1982. He was arrested at the scene. A third Sikh, Kehar Singh, the uncle of Beant Singh, was later arrested for conspiracy in the assassination. The three men had planned the murder at Kehar Singh's New Delhi home. On 30 October 1984, Beant Singh asked a colleague if he could swap places on the next day's protection rota. He took his place on the gate on the path that linked the prime minister's home and office. Satwant Singh was already assigned but was due to be positioned on an outer perimeter position. He told a colleague that he had a bad stomach and had to be near a lavatory so he, too, arranged to be near the gate. Satwant Singh and Kehar Singh were sentenced to death and hanged in Tihar jail in Delhi on 6 January 1989.

The Aftermath

After her death, anti-Sikh pogroms engulfed New Delhi and spread across India, killing thousands and leaving tens of thousands homeless. The conflict in the Punjab lasted for a decade after the army attack.

Indira Gandhi's body was cremated on 3 November near her father's and son's cremation sites at Raj Ghat in Delhi and her ashes were scattered from a plane over the Himalayan mountains by her surviving son, Rajiv.

Sanjay Gandhi's widow, Maneka, who was estranged from Indira Gandhi after Sanjay's death, has also entered politics and is a member of the main opposition BJP party, as is her son, Varun.

HH Pope John Paul II (1920–2005)

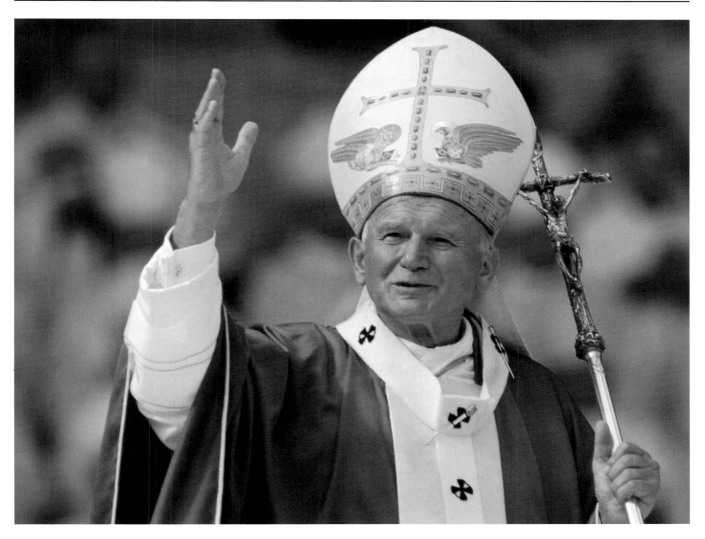

Although he did not expect to be made pontiff, John Paul II became one of history's most beloved popes.

The Victim

The 264th and first non-Italian pope since Adrian VI in 1522, Karol Józef Wojtyla was born on 18 May 1920 on the first floor at 7 Koscielna Street, Wadowice, Poland, the second son of Karol Wojtyla, a retired army lieutenant, and Emilia Kaczorowska. (An elder brother, Edmund, known as Mundek and a doctor, died of scarlet fever contracted from a patient at the age of 26 in 1932. There was an elder sister, Olga, who died in infancy before Karol was born.) The future pope was baptised on 20 June 1920. When he was four years old, Karol became an altar boy. His mother died in 1929, during childbirth.

At the age of 11, Karol was recognized as the cleverest boy in his school and also, unsurprisingly, the most well-behaved. He met the Archbishop of Kraków, Cardinal Adam Saphieha, who, spotting his intelligence, asked if young Karol intended to become a priest. The boy said that he didn't and that his interests lay in literature and the theatre. In 1938 he went to the Jagiellonian University where he appeared in plays. Unlike his fellow students who spent their time drinking, carousing and trying to bed women, the future Pope spent his time on his studies. On 1 September 1939, Germany invaded Poland, and Karol and his father fled eastwards from Kraków with thousands of other Poles, but they were forced to return to the city. In November, 184 of the academic staff at Kraków were arrested and the institution closed after 575 years. Karol found a job as a messenger for a restaurant.

From the autumn of 1940, Karol worked for almost four years as a manual labourer in a limestone quarry. His father died in 1941 of a heart attack. In 1942, Karol entered the underground seminary run by Cardinal Sapieha. B'nai B'rith and other authorities have testified that Karol helped Jews find refuge from the Nazis. On 29 February 1944, on the way home from the quarry, a German truck knocked him down. He spent a fortnight in hospital, suffering from severe concussion, numerous cuts and a shoulder injury. On 1 August 1944, the Warsaw uprising began and the Gestapo swept the city of Kraków on 6 August, "Black Sunday", rounding up young men to avoid a similar uprising there. Karol escaped by hiding behind a door as the Gestapo searched his house. He took sanctuary at the archbishop's residence, where he stayed until after the war.

On the night of 17 January 1945, the Germans abandoned Kraków. The Archbishop of Kraków ordained Karol Wojtyla priest on 1 November 1946. He then travelled to Rome to begin doctoral studies in the Pontifical Athenaeum of St Thomas Aquinas. He lived for two years in Rome in the Belgian College alongside 21 student priests and seminarians. Returning to Poland in the summer of 1948, his first pastoral assignment was as auxiliary priest to the village of Niegowic, 15 miles (24 kilometres) from Kraków. In March 1949, he became auxiliary priest to St Florian in Kraków. Both churches proudly display their affiliation with Father Karol to this day.

In 1953, the Primate of Poland, Cardinal Stefan Wyszynski, was placed under house arrest – the heavy hand of Stalinism made it difficult for priests who did not follow the official state line. It was not until 1955, two years after Stalin's death, that restrictions began to slowly ease. On 5 August 1958, while on a fortnight's holiday, Father Karol received a letter ordering him to report immediately to Cardinal Wyszynski in Warsaw. When he arrived, he was told of his appointment as auxiliary bishop of Kraków. He was consecrated a bishop by Archbishop Baziak on the feast of St Wenceslaus, 28 September 1958, in Wawel Cathedral in Kraków. At 38, he was the youngest bishop in Poland.

In 1960, Bishop Karol published an influential book *Love and Responsibility*, a defence of the traditional church teachings on sex and marriage. On 15 June 1962, Archbishop Eugeniusz Baziak died and a month later, on 16 July, Bishop Karol was elected as Vicar Capitular, or temporary administrator, of the Archdiocese until an archbishop could be appointed. On 5 October 1962, Bishop Karol left for Rome to take part in the Second Vatican Council under Pope John XXIII. On 30 December 1963, Pope Paul VI appointed him as the Metropolitan Archbishop of Kraków. In 1967, Archbishop Karol was instrumental in formulating the encyclical *Humanae Vitae*, which forbids abortion and artificial birth control. That year on 26 June, Pope Paul VI made him a cardinal.

On 6 August 1978, Pope Paul VI died and Cardinal Karol travelled to Rome to help elect the new pontiff. On the first ballot on the third day of the conclave the princes of the church elected Cardinal Albino Luciani, the patriarch of Venice who became Pope John Paul I, the Smiling Pope. Cardinal Karol received seven votes. Papa Luciani was only 65 when elected and so was expected to rule for many years. On 28 September 1978, after just 33 days as pope, the new pontiff was discovered dead in the papal apartments. Since his death there have been constant rumours that the Holy Father was murdered, rather than dying of natural causes. The Vatican did not help matters by dissembling.

In October, the cardinals returned to Rome for the second time in two months. It was believed that the two favourites to become the next pope were Giuseppe Siri, the Archbishop of Genoa, and Giovanni Benelli, the Archbishop of Florence and a close associate of Pope John Paul I. England and Wales's Cardinal Basil Hume was also spoken of as a possible pontiff. On the late afternoon of Saturday 14 October, 111 cardinals filed into the conclave and at 4.46pm the doors of the Sistine Chapel were closed and locked. Just after 9am the next morning, the cardinals began their deliberations. The winner would need a majority of two-thirds of the votes plus one – 75 in all. In early ballots, Benelli came within nine votes of victory, but the Italians realised that it was unlikely there would be another Italian pontiff. One critic described Cardinal Siri as "an archconservative's archconservative".

At midday, the thousands gathered in St Peter's Square watched for the smoke that would either hail a new papacy or that the cardinals were undecided. The smoke began and at first it appeared white to herald a new Pope but then quickly turned black. The first two ballots had not produced a clear result. In the evening the smoke again began to pour out of the Vatican chimney – it was still black. On 16 October, Cardinal Wojtyla won the fifth ballot and then the sixth by a larger majority, but not enough for the papacy. The seventh ballot was held in the early evening and although Cardinal Wojtyla again won, he still did not have enough votes. It took an eighth ballot for victory – the cardinal took 90 of the votes, 81 per cent of the princes of the church had voted for him. Once again, the Vatican chimney began spewing smoke but this time it was white. The crowd outside went wild and awaited the news of the name by which the new Pope would rule over the world's one billion Catholics. The news was brought by Cardinal Pericle Felici who said in Latin, "I announce to you a great joy. We have a Pope. Carolum Cardinalem Wojtyla who has taken the name of John Paul."

The next day the new Pope celebrated Mass together with the College of Cardinals in the Sistine Chapel. After the Mass, he delivered his first Urbi et Orbi message, broadcast worldwide via radio. On 22 October, Cardinal Karol was inaugurated as Pope John Paul II. It was a bitterly cold day. Donald Coggan became the first Archbishop of Canterbury to attend a papal inauguration since the split from Rome in the sixteenth century. An estimated one billion people watched the ceremony on television. The reign of John Paul II officially began at 10.18am. The celebratory Mass lasted 3 hours and 10 minutes, during which time John Paul and several of the congregation cried. The Holy Father's homily was interrupted by applause 47 times. He spoke in Italian, Polish, French, English, German, Spanish, Portuguese, Russian, Lithuanian, Czech and Ukrainian. During the Mass, the wind dropped and a warm sun broke through the clouds.

An early biographer wrote presciently, "John Paul still retains the compulsive need to touch people which was characteristic of his days in Kraków. He hates to sit aloof on the gestatorial chair preferring to plunge into crowds, an action that gives his security men nightmares."

Date and Place of Attempted Assassination

13 May 1981, St Peter's Square, Rome, Italy.

The Event

In the first three years of his papacy, John Paul II had become one of the most beloved statesmen of the twentieth century. Little did he know that a Turkish man was intent on assassinating him. In August 1980, Mehmet Ali Agca left Sofia in Bulgaria and began travelling across the Mediterranean region using a variety of aliases and forged travel documents. He left Milan and arrived in Rome via train on 10 May 1981. In the Italian capital, Agca met three accomplices – a fellow Turk and two Bulgarians, with the operation commanded by Zilo Vassilev, the Bulgarian military attaché in Italy.

On 13 May 1981, Agca and a back-up gunman, Oral Çelik, sat in St Peter's Square writing postcards and waiting for the Holy Father to arrive. They planned to shoot Papa Wojtyla, set off a small bomb and in the ensuing confusion escape to the Bulgarian embassy. The Pope appeared in a white open-topped jeep among a crowd of 20,000 pilgrims. As John Paul passed, Agca fired several shots before the crowd grabbed him. Four bullets hit the Pope, two of them lodging in his lower intestine, the others hitting his left hand and right arm.

A SECOND ASSASSINATION ATTEMPT

Date and Place of Attempted Assassination: 12 May 1982, Fatima, Portugal.

The Event: The Pope was in Fatima when an ultra-conservative Spanish priest named Juan María Fernández y Krohn tried to stab him with a bayonet. The papal bodyguards overwhelmed him.

The Would-be Assassin: Juan María Fernández y Krohn was born in Spain in 1950. He was ordained in 1978. He joined the Society of Saint Pius X in 1979 but was expelled the same year. He claimed that John Paul was "an agent of Moscow" and he (Krohn) opposed the reforms of the Second Vatican Council. After the attempt, he was sent to prison for six years but was released and deported after only three and moved to Belgium where he became a lawyer. He gained a reputation when he smacked a judge and handed out anti-Semitic literature in the Brussels Palace of Justice. In 1996, he was arrested in Spain for arson when he tried to burn down an office of Herri Batasuna, a Basque separatist organization. Four years later, in July 2000, he was in trouble again when he broke into the Belgian Royal Palace, intent on killing King Albert II. He received a five-year sentence.

Two bystanders were also hit. Çelik panicked and fled without setting off his bomb or opening fire. The Holy Father was taken to the Agostino Gemelli University Polyclinic, where he underwent emergency surgery and an extensive blood transfusion.

The Would-be Assassin

Mehmet Ali Agca was born at Hekimhan, Malatya, Turkey on 9 January 1958. He quickly fell foul of the law, joining gangs in his hometown, and he later became a smuggler. He was a member of the ultra-nationalist terror group the Grey Wolves. On 1 February 1979, on orders from the Grey Wolves, he murdered Abdi Ipekçi, the editor of the moderate left-wing newspaper *Milliyet*. He escaped a life sentence after only six months in prison with help from the Grey Wolves, and ran away to Bulgaria.

The Aftermath

In July 1981, Agca was sentenced to life imprisonment in Italy. In November 1982, Sergei Ivanov Antonov, a Bulgarian working in Rome for Balkan Air, was arrested, based on Agca's testimony. He was accused of being the Bulgarian agent who masterminded the plot. In 1986, after a three-year trial, he was found "not guilty" through lack of evidence. The Bulgarian Secret Service has consistently denied being involved in the plot to murder the Pope and claimed that Agca's story was a classic piece of disinformation planted by the Italian Secret Service, the terror group the Grey Wolves and the CIA.

The Italian newspaper *Corriere della Sera* has reported that it has seen documentary proof that the assassination attempt was ordered by the KGB and assigned to Bulgarian and East German agents with the Stasi. On 25 September 1991, the former CIA analyst Melvin A. Goodman revealed that his colleagues, following orders from above, had falsified their analysis in order to support the accusation. He told the US Senate intelligence committee "the CIA hadn't any proof" concerning the alleged "Bulgarian connection". In March

A brief taste of freedom: Mehmet Ali Agca is released from Kartal prison in Istanbul in January 2006, only to be recalled eight days later.

2006, an investigation by the Italian senator Paolo Guzzanti also claimed "leaders of the former Soviet Union were behind the assassination attempt". Both Russia and Bulgaria condemned the report.

John Paul's previous fitness no doubt saved his life and as his recovery continued apace he began to give speeches from the window of the hospital, much to the delight of the pilgrims. The Holy Father forgave Mehmet Ali Agca and on 27 December 1983, he and Agca met and spoke privately at the prison where Agca was being held. The Pope said, "What we talked about will have to remain a secret between him and me. I spoke to him as a brother whom I have pardoned and who has my complete trust." Almost 22 years later, in early February

2005, during the Pope's final illness, Agca sent a letter to John Paul wishing him well.

In June 2000, at the Pope's request, Agca was pardoned by President Carlo Azeglio Ciampi and extradited to Turkey. He was then jailed for the murder of left-wing journalist Abdi Ipekçi in 1979 and two bank robberies carried out in the 1970s. In November 2004, a Turkish court said that Agca would not be eligible for parole until 2010. On 12 January 2006, he was released only for him to be recalled to prison eight days later when the Turkish Supreme Court declared that time spent in Italian jails did not count towards his Turkish sentence.

John Paul made 104 pastoral visits outside Italy and 146 within Italy. As Bishop of Rome, he visited 317 of the city's 333 parishes. During his papacy he celebrated 147 beatification ceremonies – during which he proclaimed 1,338 blesseds and 51 canonizations for a total of 482 saints. He made St Thérèse de Lisieux of the Child Jesus a Doctor of the Church. As Pope he considerably expanded the College of Cardinals, creating 231 cardinals (plus one in pectore) in nine consistories. He also called six full meetings of the College of Cardinals, organized 15 Assemblies of the Synod of Bishops – six Ordinary General Assemblies (1980, 1983, 1987, 1990, 1994 and 2001), one Extraordinary General Assembly (1985) and eight Special Assemblies (1980, 1991, 1994, 1995, 1997, 1998 (2) and 1999). His most important documents include 14 encyclicals, 15 apostolic exhortations, 11 apostolic constitutions and 45 apostolic letters.

Karol Wojtyla was the youngest man to be elected Pope since Pope Pius IX in 1846 and he still enjoyed many of the pursuits he had enjoyed as a young priest in Poland. However, after the assassination attempt in 1981, and a number of cancer scares, the Holy Father's health began to decline. He had a tumour removed from his colon in 1992, dislocated his shoulder in 1993, broke his femur in 1994 and had his appendix removed in 1996. In 2001 he was diagnosed with Parkinson's disease, a diagnosis confirmed publicly by the Vatican in 2003.

On 1 February 2005, Papa Wojtyla was taken to the Agostino Gemelli University Polyclinic in Rome suffering from acute inflammation of the larynx and laryngospasm, brought on by a bout of influenza. He missed the Ash Wednesday ceremonies in St Peter's on 9 February for the first time in his 26-year papacy, and returned to the Vatican on 10 February. Exactly two weeks later, the Pope had difficulty breathing and was taken back to the Agostino Gemelli University Polyclinic where he underwent a tracheotomy. Doctors advised the Holy Father not to speak, but he conversed with aides who visited him in his tenth floor suite of the Gemelli on Tuesday 1 March. Cardinal Ratzinger (later Pope Benedict XVI) told journalists: "The Pope spoke to me in German and Italian. He was completely lucid. I brought the Holy Father greetings from the plenary of the congregation for the divine cult, which is meeting at this moment in the Vatican. The Holy Father will be working on material, which I gave him today. I am happy to see him fully lucid and mentally capable of saying the essential matters with his own voice. We usually speak in German. The details are unimportant – he spoke of essential matters."

On 13 March the Pope returned to the Vatican. The following Sunday – Palm Sunday – the Pope was unable to officiate at the Mass, the first time in his papacy that this had happened. On 27 March, Easter Day, the Pope appeared at his window in the Vatican for a short time. Angelo Sodano read the Urbi et Orbi message while the Pope blessed the people with his own hand. He tried to speak but he could not. On 31 March, Papa Wojtyla developed a "very high fever caused by a urinary tract infection". According to his wishes he was not taken to hospital. Later that day, His Holiness was given the Anointing of the Sick (last rites) of the Roman Catholic Church. The next day, he took a turn for the worse as his heart and kidneys failed. The Holy Father died at 9.37pm on 2 April 2005 – he was 46 days short of his 85th birthday. His death certificate listed septic shock and heart failure as primary causes.

His Holiness Pope John Paul II's funeral was held on 8 April. Joseph, Cardinal Ratzinger, by virtue of his office as Dean of the College of Cardinals, offered the Requiem Mass. After being sealed in three caskets, the Holy Father was buried beneath St Peter's Basilica in the tomb vacated by Pope John XXIII, who was moved by Pope John Paul II for beatification.

On 9 May 2005, Pope Benedict XVI, John Paul II's successor, waived the five year waiting period for a cause for beatification to be opened. Cardinal Camillo Ruini, vicar general for the diocese of Rome, officially opened the cause on 28 June 2005. Karol Wojtyla, John Paul the Great, is on the way to sainthood.

Malcolm X (1925–1965)

The Victim

Malcolm X was born as Malcolm Little on 19 May 1925 at University Hospital, Omaha, Nebraska, the fourth child and third son of Louise Helen Norton and the one-eyed Earl Little, an itinerant Baptist lay preacher, supporter of Marcus Garvey, and a member of the Universal Negro Improvement Association. (Three of Earl's brothers died violently at the hands of white men, and one of his uncles was lynched.) Louise Little was born at La Digue, St Andrew, Grenada in 1897; her father was white, which meant that Malcolm Little was light-skinned with reddish hair. (In his autobiography, X claimed that his mother had been threatened by the Ku Klux Klan while she was pregnant with him in December 1924.) The Littles were married on 10 May 1919. The family moved to Milwaukee, Wisconsin in 1926, and then to East Lansing, Michigan. On Monday 28 September 1931, Earl Little died after being run over by a streetcar. His death was ruled a suicide but family and friends believed that he had been murdered by the white supremacist group Black Legion. Although Earl Little had two insurance policies, only one paid out because of the suicide. In December 1938, Louise Little was declared legally insane and committed to the State Mental Hospital at Kalamazoo, Michigan, where she stayed until 1963. The children were sent to different foster homes.

Despite the upset at home, Little graduated from junior high school at the top of his class. He left school after a teacher he admired told him that it was pointless studying to be a lawyer because it was "no realistic goal for a nigger". Little became a delinquent and was sent to borstal. In 1941, he left Michigan to live in Boston, Massachusetts, with his half-sister, Ella Collins. In Boston he worked on the New Haven Railroad but also became involved in more criminal behaviour such as drug dealing and running numbers.

In 1943, he moved to New York City where he found work as a shoe-shiner at a Lindy Hop nightclub. He avoided being conscripted into the army by acting mad. Doctors said that he was "mentally disqualified for military service". Nicknamed "Detroit Red", he fell further into crime and on 29 November 1944, at Boston, he was convicted of stealing a fur coat and sentenced to three months. On 12 January 1946 he was arrested at Milton, Massachusetts. He had broken into a jewellers to take back a watch he had stolen and then taken in for repairs. Two days later, he was arrested for carrying a gun and on 16 January he was charged with grand larceny and breaking and entering. Convicted on 27 February, he was sentenced to eight to ten years in Massachusetts State Prison in Charlestown. In February 1948, Little was transferred to Concord Reformatory, an experimental prison, in Norfolk, Massachusetts.

While at Concord, he made great use of the prison library. At the urging of his brother Reginald, Little became attracted to the Temple of Islam (later the Nation of Islam), a Muslim organization that referred to white people as "devils". On 7 August 1952, he was paroled and went to meet Elijah Muhammad (see box below) in

---

ELIJAH MUHAMMED

Born as Robert Poole at Sandersville, Georgia, on 7 October 1897, he was a leader of the Nation of Islam. He changed his name to Elijah Muhammed in 1931 and believed that the black man was the "original man". Whites, he claimed, were a hybrid created by Yacub, a mad black scientist. They would rule the earth for 6,000 years, after which time there would be a battle that the black man would win. On 25 February 1975, Muhammed died in Chicago and was succeeded by the fifth of his six sons, Wallace Deen Muhammad. After Wallace disbanded the Nation of Islam and led many of its members into the fold of Sunni Islam, the Nation of Islam was reformed by Louis Farrakhan in 1978.

Chicago. It was after this meeting that he took to calling himself Malcolm X. In March 1953, X came under scrutiny by the FBI. Two months later, in May 1953, the bureau's investigation decided that X had an "asocial personality with paranoid trends (pre-psychotic paranoid schizophrenia)". That year, he moved to Chicago to stay with Elijah Muhammad but was soon back in Boston as minister of the Nation of Islam's Temple Number Eleven.

By 1954, Malcolm X had become minister of New York Temple Number Seven on Lenox Avenue in Harlem, and he later helped establish Islamic temples in other cities. X worked hard to recruit new followers in the 1950s and 60s, some estimates place a figure of 30,000 members in 1963, up from 500 in 1952 (a rise of 5,900 per cent). One new member was the boxer Cassius Clay who joined the Nation of Islam in 1964 and became Cassius X until Elijah Muhammad changed the name to Muhammad Ali. (Ali later left the Nation of Islam and joined the mainstream religion.)

From 1959, X began to appear on television as spokesman for the Nation of Islam, until then a little known group. On 14 January 1958, X married Betty Jean Sanders in Lansing, Michigan (they subsequently had six daughters). Two years later, in September 1960, X met Fidel Castro, the Cuban dictator, when he travelled to the United States to address the United Nations General Assembly.

In the spring of 1963, X began to collaborate with the journalist Alex Haley on the book that would become *The Autobiography of Malcolm X*. In the book, X explained his split from Elijah Muhammad because of the latter's affairs with young secretaries and his illegitimate children. In August 1963, X criticized Martin Luther King's March on Washington, unable to comprehend why blacks were enthused at a protest "run by whites in front of a statue of a president who has been dead for a hundred years and who didn't like us when he was alive". Three months later, he was equally critical when commenting on the assassination of President Kennedy. His outbursts led to widespread public outcry and he was banned from public speaking for 90 days by Elijah Muhammad.

On 8 March 1964, X announced that he had left the Nation of Islam and four days later founded Muslim Mosque, Inc. He converted to Sunni Islam and on 13 April left America on a pilgrimage to Mecca. On 20 April, during his visit, he said that seeing Muslims of all colours worshipping together made him reject the opinion that all whites were devils. That month he gave a speech entitled "The Ballot or the Bullet", in which he said he "realise[d] that it is best for [black people] to first see that we have the same problem, a common problem – a problem that will make you catch hell whether you're a Baptist, or a Methodist, or a Muslim, or a nationalist". He also travelled to Egypt, Lebanon, Nigeria, Ghana, Senegal and Morocco. After he returned to America on 21 May, X announced that he had adopted a Muslim name, el-Hajj Malik el-Shabazz, and that he was forming a new political group, the Organization of Afro-American Unity.

At the founding rally on 28 June 1964, X said, "The time for you and me to allow ourselves to be brutalized non-violently has passed. Be non-violent only with those who are non-violent to you. And when you can bring me a non-violent racist, bring me a non-violent segregationist, then I'll get non-violent. But don't teach me to be non-violent until you teach some of those crackers to be non-violent." On 9 July, he again left the United States for Africa. On 17 July 1964, X addressed the Organization of African Unity's first ordinary assembly of heads of state and governments in Cairo, Egypt, as a representative of the Organization of Afro-American Unity. He returned to America on 24 November 1964. On 3 December 1964, he took part in a debate at the Oxford Union.

In 1965, he gave an interview in which he stated:

I realised racism isn't just a black and white problem. It's brought bloodbaths to about every

Malcolm X realised that he had been wrong to demonize white people.

nation on earth at one time or another. Brother, remember the time that white college girl came into the restaurant – the one who wanted to help the Muslims and the whites get together – and I told her there wasn't a ghost of a chance and she went away crying? Well, I've lived to regret that incident. In many parts of the African continent I saw white students helping black people. Something like this kills a lot of argument. I did many things as a [black] Muslim that I'm sorry for now. I was a zombie then – like all [black] Muslims – I was hypnotized, pointed in a certain direction and told to march. Well, I guess a man's entitled to make a fool of himself if he's ready to pay the cost. It cost me 12 years. That was a bad scene, brother. The sickness and madness of those days – I'm glad to be free of them.

The Nation of Islam regarded X as a traitor and tried to evict him from his home in Queens, New York. The organization claimed that they had paid for the building. On Sunday 14 February 1965, the house was firebombed.

Date and Place of Assassination

21 February 1965, Audubon Ballroom, Broadway and 165th Street, New York, USA.

The Event

As tensions increased between X and the Nation of Islam, he was scheduled to speak at a meeting at the Audubon Ballroom in Washington Heights, New York City on the first day of National Brotherhood Week. He had just got onto the stage at 3.10pm and began his speech before a crowd of 400, when a man in the audience shouted, "Get your hand outta my pocket! Don't be messin' with my pockets!" As bodyguards moved in to quell the disturbance, X called out "Cool it there". A man rushed forward with a sawn-off shotgun and shot X in the chest. Two more men rushed the stage and fired pistols at X who was hit by 16 bullets. The 39-year-old was pronounced dead on arrival at 3.30pm at New York's Columbia Presbyterian Hospital.

The Assassins

Three men were charged with the murder and convicted. Thomas Hagan aka Thomas Hayer aka Talmadge Hayer was born in 1942 and, at the time of the killing, was living at 347 Marshall Street, in Paterson, New Jersey. A member of the Nation of Islam, in 1961 he was arrested for disorderly conduct and two years later was again in trouble for the possession of stolen guns. Hayer confessed in a court hearing on 30 April 1966 to firing the shotgun but alleged that the two other accused, Norman 3X Butler and Thomas 15X Johnson, were innocent. Instead, he said that Leon David and Wilbur McKinley were his accomplices.

Norman 3X Butler aka Muhammad Abd Al-Aziz has always maintained his innocence of murdering Malcolm X. He was paroled in 1985, still a member of the Nation of Islam. In 1998 he was made the head of Mosque Number Seven in Harlem (a different one to the mosque run by X).

Thomas 15X Johnson, like Butler, claims that he is not guilty of killing Malcolm X. He was paroled in 1987 and calls himself Khalil Islam.

The Aftermath

On Saturday 27 February 1965 more than 1,500 people attended Malcolm X's funeral in Harlem at the Faith Temple Church of God in Christ (now Child's Memorial Temple Church of God in Christ). X was buried at the Ferncliff Cemetery in Hartsdale, New York.

In 1994, X's widow Betty Shabazz spoke publicly for the first time against the Nation of Islam and blamed it for her husband's death, even going so far as to claim that its current leader, Louis Farrakhan, was behind the assassination, an allegation vigorously denied by Farrakhan.

On 12 January 1995, Qubilah Shabazz, Malcolm X's second child, was arrested and indicted at Minneapolis for trying to hire an assassin to murder Farrakhan in retaliation for the murder of her father. The assassin, Michael K. Fitzpatrick, was revealed to be a government informant who was paid $45,000. Farrakhan spoke up for Qubilah and, four months later, Betty Shabazz and Farrakhan shook hands on the stage of the Apollo in Harlem at a fundraiser to pay for Qubilah's defence. Betty Shabazz reciprocated by giving a speech at Farrakhan's Million Man March in October of the same year.

Qubilah Shabazz was ordered to undergo psychological counselling and treatment for drug and alcohol abuse for two years. Her son, Malcolm, then 12, was sent to live with his grandmother in Yonkers, New York. On 1 June 1997, the boy set the apartment ablaze and Betty Shabazz suffered burns to 80 per cent of her body. She spent three weeks in intensive care at the Jacobi Medical Center in the Bronx before she died on 23 June aged 61. A wake was held at the Unity Funeral Home in Harlem (the same place her husband's wake had been held 32 years before). She was buried next to her husband.

Malcolm Shabazz, described as psychotic and schizophrenic at his trial, was sentenced to 18 months in juvenile detention for manslaughter in August 1997. In January 2002, he and another 17-year-old, Thomas Carter-Love, beat up and robbed a teenager of $100 in Middletown, New York. He was sentenced to three years in prison on 29 August 2002. Released in September 2005 on parole, he was returned to prison in January 2006 for a parole violation and released again in May 2006. On 3 August of that year, he was arrested for smashing the window of a Dunkin' Donuts shop at 850 Bronx River Road in Yonkers. On 21 November, he pleaded guilty to fourth-degree criminal mischief.

The Audubon Ballroom was demolished in 1992 and the Audubon Business and Technology Center, part of Columbia University, was built on the site. A museum dedicated to Malcolm X and Betty Shabazz opened inside the building in 2005.

Ross McWhirter (1925–1975)

The Victim

Alan Ross McWhirter (known as Ross McWhirter) was born at Giffnock, 10 Branscombe Gardens, Winchmore Hill, north London at 8pm on 12 August 1925, the third and youngest son and the younger twin son (there were no daughters) of William Allan McWhirter, and his wife, Margaret (Bunty) Moffat Williamson (1900–1972). (William Allan McWhirter was known as "Squire." He was born in Glasgow on 14 September 1888, became the first man to edit three national newspapers – *Sunday Pictorial*, *Sunday Despatch* and *Daily Mail* – and later became the managing director of Northcliffe Newspapers and Associated Newspapers. He died in 1955.) Ross's twin, Norris Dewar, was born 20 minutes earlier. An elder son, Kennedy Graeme, had been born on 22 October 1923.

Record breaking twins: Norris (left) and Ross (right) McWhirter, photographed in 1968 with their best-selling book.

Although Ross McWhirter was known primarily for co-founding and co-editing *The Guinness Book of Records*, there was much more to him – he was a superb athlete, a tenacious litigant and would-be MP. All three boys were educated at Marlborough College. The only time the twins were separated in their adult lives was when they served in the Royal Navy during the Second World War. The only time they met during service was when their respective ships struck each other in Valetta, Malta on 24 August 1946.

In January 1947, the twins returned to Trinity College, Oxford, to resume reading jurisprudence (Ross) and economics (Norris). At Oxford, they both belonged to the same record-setting athletics relay team. As the slightly faster of the two, Norris also competed abroad. After graduating from Oxford, the twins moved back to their parents' home. One of their friends commented, "They had minds like Japanese calculators. They talked to each other in a code that only they fully comprehended. One would start a sentence and the other would finish it up. When you called them on the phone you never could really be sure which one you were talking to. I remember that Norris once had to make a quick trip to Paris and couldn't find his own passport, so he just took Ross's. Nobody noticed the difference."

On 2 March 1951, Ross and Norris established McWhirter Twins Ltd, an agency at 15 Great James Street, Holborn, London, to provide facts, figures and features to the press, publishers and advertisers. From 1951, Norris worked as a freelance writer on athletics and Ross covered rugby and tennis for the *Star* (not the *Daily Star*, but a London evening newspaper) until that paper closed in October 1960.

In 1951, the twins also published their first book *Get to Your Marks*, on the history of athletics. Two fellow athletic writers said that it was "distinguished by a degree of precision and thoroughness which no athletics historian had achieved before". On 25 February 1954, the McWhirters became the only company directors in the country to insist on their names being put on the local government electoral register after the county court accepted that the words "does not entitle" have a different meaning from "disentitle". Later that same year, in October, Ross sued the National Union of Journalists, of which he was an involuntary closed shop member, after a fellow member, J. L. Manning, the chairman of the London Central Branch, libelled Norris. The case went against the union, along with damages and costs.

On Saturday 10 November 1951 Sir Hugh Beaver, the managing director of the Guinness Brewery, had been on a day's shoot in Ireland by the River Slaney when he aimed at and missed a golden plover. Back at the staff house, known as Bodiam, he wondered what the fastest game bird was but was infuriated and perplexed to find that none of the expensive encyclopaedias in his library could furnish the answer. Three years later, on 12 September 1954, the twins were invited to a lunch at Park Royal, Guinness's headquarters, where they were "interviewed" for the job of compiling a book that would settle arguments in the 81,400 pubs in the country. The job was theirs when Norris happened to mention that Turkish was the language with the fewest irregular verbs – just one, *imek*, to be (there are around 180 irregular verbs in English). The twins set to work and, on 27 August 1955, a slim, 198-page volume entitled *The Guinness Book of Records* was published. It cost 5 shillings.

Two years later, on 18 May 1957, Ross married Rosemary Joy Hamilton at Christ Church, Old Southgate, Waterfall Lane. They had two sons: Iain (born at 50 Village Road, Enfield, Middlesex 17 January 1959) and James (born at the same address in July 1960). In the general election of 16 October 1964, in which Harold Wilson swept to power, Ross stood as Conservative candidate for Edmonton. He lost to the sitting Labour MP Austen Albu (who had held the seat since 1948 and would hold it until February 1974). Ross polled 19,245 votes, 38.9 per cent of those cast, to Albu's 24,373, a majority of 5,128, or 10.3 per cent.

On 1 March 1966, it was announced that all 30 secondary schools in Enfield were to be grouped into 16 comprehensives. Ross brought four High Court actions in 43 days to challenge the plan and won injunctions against Enfield council and the secretary of state, who was forced to go back to parliament for new powers. The *Daily Mirror* carried a leader, which rejoiced, "Liberty still has its vigilant defenders". On 9 May 1968, local government elections were held in the 32 London boroughs. Six months later, Ross took on the Home Office to challenge the miscounting of votes in Enfield. Having lost in the Crown Court on 1 August, he defeated the Home Office in the High Court on 5 November to win an order signed by the Lord Chief Justice requiring a unique recount of votes, which proved him right. The following year, on 20 October, he took James Callaghan, the Home Secretary, to court for not giving effect to the recommendations of the boundary commissions to redistribute parliamentary seats.

During a Labour Party political broadcast on 8 May 1970, the Independent Television Authority acted illegally by allowing three subliminal flashes to be aired on both BBC and ITV. Ross's original application was thrown out of the High Court because he had no status, or *locus standi*, but Ross pointed out that as a licence payer, he had the maximum possible *locus standi*. He went to the Court of Appeal where Lord Denning accepted the plea that the licence gave him the maximum possible *locus*. The authority took the unusual step of giving a written undertaking that no further subliminal messages would be transmitted. Three years later, on Sunday 14 January 1973, ITV advertised that on the following Tuesday it would broadcast a documentary about the painter Andy Warhol that was described as "offensive". Since this was contrary to the Television Act 1964, Ross again sued and succeeded in getting the programme delayed until members of the Independent Broadcasting Authority could watch "to satisfy themselves" that the programme was not "offensive to public feeling". In the meantime, Ross had been battling the government led by Ted Heath and their determination to enter the Common Market. Ross claimed that by signing the treaty of accession, Heath was putting the queen in breach of her coronation oath to govern her peoples "according to their respective laws and customs". On 30 June 1972, the judges exercised their discretion not to make a declaration. On 15 December 1972, Norris and Ross began appearing on the BBC1 television show *Record Breakers* (the show ran for 29 years). His last litigation was against the ferry *Eagle* and the National Union of Seamen, which on 17 October 1975 had impounded around 40 vehicles at Southampton in a dispute over redundancy notices. Ross went to court and won his case in just nine minutes. The cars were unloaded.

Date and Place of Assassination

27 November 1975, 50 Village Road, Enfield, Middlesex, England.

The Event

In 1974, IRA bombers plagued England, particularly London. There had been 40 attacks in a year, including the pub bombings in Guildford (5 October 1974 in the Horse and Groom at 8.50pm killing four soldiers, one civilian and injuring 57 others and at 9.25pm in the nearby Seven Stars pub causing injuries to only eight people, mainly staff, because the manager had cleared the pub after the Horse and Groom explosion), Woolwich (on 7 November 1974 a 6-pound (2.7 kilogram) bomb packed with bolts exploded in the King's Arms, injuring 26 people including five soldiers) and the accidental murder of cancer specialist Gordon Hamilton-Fairey in Campden Hill Square on the morning of 23 October 1975 (the car bomb was intended for his next-door neighbour, the Tory MP Sir Hugh Fraser). Ross decided to shame the Home Secretary and his advisors into taking action. McWhirter offered £50,000 to anyone who could give information that would lead to the capture of the bombers.

Three weeks later, on 27 November, Ross and his wife, Rosemary, were intending to go to the theatre with some friends. Mrs McWhirter drove off to fill her blue Ford Granada with petrol. As she returned home at 6.50pm, two men ambushed her and took her car keys. She ran to her front door to get help from her husband and rang the doorbell. As he opened the door, she pushed past him into the hallway and he stood outlined in the doorframe. An IRA gunman shot him in the body and then again in the head. Mrs McWhirter was later told that the shot to the body would not alone have been fatal. Ross McWhirter was pronounced dead on arrival at Chase Farm Hospital, Enfield. He was buried in an unmarked grave at Southgate Cemetery in north London.

The Assassins

The gang members were Hugh Doherty, the brother of Sinn Féin vice president Pat Doherty, Eddie Butler, Harry Duggan and Martin O'Connell.

The Aftermath

On Saturday 6 December 1975, the four IRA terrorists responsible for the bombing campaign and Ross McWhirter's assassination burst into the council flat home of John Matthews, 54, and his wife Sheila, 53. Earlier that evening the Irishmen had sprayed the front of Scott's Restaurant, Oyster Terrace and Bar, 20 Mount Street, Mayfair, west London with machine-gun fire from their stolen car. (They had thrown a bomb through the window on 12 November and were furious because Scott's refused to close.) That night, 6,000 policemen were on duty on the lookout for the terrorists. Two plain-clothes officers spotted four men acting suspiciously and gave chase. The four men shot at the unarmed officers (who did not even have a truncheon between them) and ran into the flats near Dorset Square.

Thus began the Balcombe Street siege that was to last for six days. Detective Chief Superintendent Peter Imbert, a future Metropolitan Police force commissioner, oversaw the police operation. For six long days the siege continued. At 2.54pm on 12 December, shortly after Mrs Matthews's negotiated release, police sent in hot sausages, Brussels sprouts and potatoes, peaches and cream, the first food the terrorists had eaten since the siege began. At 4.15pm, the terrorists agreed to surrender. One by one they left the flat with their hands in the air. The siege had lasted 138 hours. The gang members, Hugh Doherty, aged 27, Eddie Butler, 28, Harry Duggan, 25, and Martin O'Connell, 22, were given 47 life sentences at the Old Bailey in February 1977. All four men were released on 14 April 1999 under the Good Friday Agreement and were greeted as heroes by Martin McGuinness and Gerry Adams who referred to them as "our Nelson Mandelas".

On the initiative of his friends, the Ross McWhirter Foundation was established with £100,000 subscribed by admirers. It sought to advance Ross McWhirter's qualities of "good citizenship … personal initiative and leadership, and personal courage as an example to others".

Norris McWhirter continued to edit *The Guinness Book of Records* alone until his retirement on 31 March 1986. He left *Record Breakers* in 1995 and was ousted from his role as consultant editor of the *Guinness Book of Records* in 1996. He went on to compile *Norris McWhirter's Book of Millennium Records*, published on 21 October 1999. He died at the age of 78 on Monday 19 April 2004, after suffering a heart attack while playing tennis at his Wiltshire home.

Robert F. Kennedy (1925–1968)

The Victim

Robert Francis Kennedy was born at 131 Naples Road in Brookline, Massachusetts, on 20 November 1925, the seventh child and third son of Joseph Patrick Kennedy and Rose Elizabeth Fitzgerald Kennedy (they had a total of nine children). Among so many boisterous children, he struggled to impress. He taught himself to swim as a toddler by throwing himself into the Nantucket Sound, but he was not especially clever or athletic like his elder brothers, Joe and Jack (JFK, see pages 107–128).

Mutual hatred: J. Edgar Hoover, the FBI chief, and Bobby Kennedy detested one another.

He was the most devoutly Catholic of the Kennedy boys.

In September 1942 he enrolled at Milton Academy in Massachusetts, his seventh school in around a decade (including establishments in New York and London when his father was Ambassador to the Court of St James's). In October 1943, he joined the naval reserve. He matriculated at Harvard in March 1944 and formally graduated from Milton Academy in June. On 1 February 1946, he joined the US Navy and served on the USS Joseph P. Kennedy Jr, the ship named for his eldest brother. He was demobbed on 30 May 1946 and, four months later, Bobby returned to Harvard University, graduating in March 1948.

Bobby's future wife, Ethel Skakel, was born on 11 April 1928 at the Lying-In Hospital in Chicago, Illinois. In September 1945, she enrolled in Manhattanville College in New York City. Her best friend and roommate was Jean Kennedy, Bobby's little sister. She met Bobby during a skiing trip to Mont-Tremblant, Quebec, Canada, during the winter of 1945, when he was seeing her elder sister, Patricia. She was interested in his brother, Jack. Eventually the relationship between Bobby and Patricia ended and Ethel and Bobby began dating. She campaigned for John F. Kennedy in 1946, and wrote her college thesis on his book *Why England Slept*. Bobby and Ethel became engaged in February 1950 and on Saturday 17 June 1950, they married before 1,500 guests at St Mary's Catholic Church in Greenwich, Connecticut. They had 11 children, one born posthumously to her father.

In September 1948, he enrolled at the University of Virginia Law School and was admitted to the Massachusetts Bar Association on graduation (he was 56th in a class of 124) in 1951. That year he entered the government as an attorney in the Department of Justice. On 6 June 1952, he became manager of his brother John's campaign for the US Senate, despite knowing little or nothing about Massachusetts politics. Kennedy worked relentlessly from 8am to midnight to ensure a successful campaign outcome. In 1953, he became a counsel for the Senate Permanent Subcommittee on Investigations. After seven months, he resigned on 29 July 1953 after an argument with the committee chairman, Senator Joseph McCarthy. On 23 February 1954, he rejoined the committee, at first as minority counsel and then as majority chief counsel under new chairman Senator John McClellan. In January 1957, Kennedy came to public attention as chief counsel for the Senate committee that investigated improper labour and management activities. He revealed the criminal links of

BOBBY THE FATHER

Long-time Kennedy friend Lem Billings said, "Bobby was much more openly loving with his children than Joseph Kennedy had been. He touched them all the time. It seems like a small thing, but in the Kennedy family it wasn't. Mr Kennedy never touched them when they were young. Jack was the same way – didn't touch and didn't want to be touched." The children were Kathleen Hartington (born Greenwich, Connecticut 4 July 1951), she was lieutenant governor of Maryland from 1995–2003; Joseph Patrick III (born Brighton, Massachusetts 24 September 1952), in 1986 he was elected to the US House of Representatives from Massachusetts, from the district formerly represented by his uncle, John F. Kennedy (from 1947–1953). He served until 1999; Robert Francis, Jr (born 17 January 1954), he is an environmental lawyer; David Anthony (born Washington DC 15 June 1955, died of an overdose of cocaine, Demerol and Mellaril in Room 107 of the Brazilian Court Hotel, Palm Beach, Florida 25 April 1984); (Mary) Courtney (born Boston, Massachusetts 9 September 1956), she is a lawyer, a human rights advocate and married Paul Hill, one of the Guildford Four, although they are now separated; Michael LeMoyne (born 27 February 1958, died in a skiing accident in Aspen, Colorado 31 December 1997); (Mary) Kerry (born Washington DC 8 September 1959), she is a lawyer, a human rights advocate and the founder of the Robert F. Kennedy Center for Human Rights; Christopher George (born Boston, Massachusetts 4 July 1963); Matthew Maxwell Taylor (born New York 11 January 1965); Douglas Harriman (born Washington DC 24 March 1967) is a journalist; and Rory Elizabeth Katherine (born Washington DC 12 December 1968), a radical feminist, she is a prize-winning documentary film-maker.

David Beck, the president of the International Brotherhood of Teamsters, who eventually went to prison for larceny and tax evasion. On national television, Kennedy dissected Jimmy Hoffa, Beck's successor as the Teamsters' president. In April 1959, he left the McClellan committee to run the presidential campaign of his brother, John. Bobby wrote a book entitled *The Enemy Within* (1960) about his time on the committee.

When his brother was elected president, Bobby Kennedy became Attorney General on 21 January 1961. He is the only "First Brother" to have held a Cabinet post. JFK joked that he wanted "to give [Bobby] a little experience before he goes out to practise law". It was also a reward for running successful campaigns and also because their father, Ambassador Joseph P. Kennedy, had told him to. President Kennedy had wanted to make his brother assistant secretary of defence but Ambassador Kennedy would have none of it. Bobby was his brother's leading advisor on foreign affairs, national security, domestic policy and political management. From 1961, Kennedy encouraged the CIA to carry out covert missions to destabilize Fidel Castro, although there is no evidence he was aware of the agency's attempts to assassinate the Cuban leader. In 1963 the rising violence of the civil rights movement and allegations of communist infiltration led to Kennedy publicly defending Martin Luther King, but privately allowing FBI chief J. Edgar Hoover to secretly tap King's phones. Kennedy was confident nothing incriminating would be found.

Kennedy remained Attorney General under President Johnson for ten months following his brother's assassination, but resigned on 2 September 1964 to run for the Senate. He had announced his candidature the previous week on Tuesday 25 August. He was elected as senator from New York that November by 719,693 votes. In June 1967 Kennedy addressed a meeting of Jewish labour leaders and, clearing his throat, coughed and said, "I've just drunk a cup of bitter Arab coffee and have not had time to wash my mouth." The remark got

Bobby Kennedy supported Martin Luther King but nonetheless gave the FBI permission to tap his phones.

a laugh among his Semitic audience but caused outrage in the Arab world, seeming to be an insult to Arab hospitality. The remark dogged the rest of his days and was even mentioned in his obituary in Arab newsapers.

It was assumed that Kennedy would at some stage run for the White House, but he seemed reluctant to take on President Johnson. On 16 March 1968, Kennedy announced that he would indeed run, after Senator Eugene McCarthy won 42 per cent to the sitting president's 49 per cent in the New Hampshire primary. Bobby Kennedy made his announcement in the Senate Caucus room, the same place John Kennedy had announced his candidacy for the White House eight years earlier. Ambassador Kennedy and Bobby's younger brother, Ted Kennedy, were both opposed to Bobby running and Jackie Kennedy did not want him to run for fear he, too, would fall to an assassin's bullet. Fifteen days later, Lyndon Johnson, in a televised address, surprised the nation and the world by giving up politics and removing himself as a candidate for a second full term, recognizing that he was the symbol of the dissent that was dividing the country.

What we won when all of our people united just must not now be lost in suspicion, distrust, selfishness, and politics among any of our people. Believing this as I do, I have concluded that I should not permit the presidency to become involved in the partisan divisions that are developing in this political year. With America's sons in the fields far away, with America's future under challenge right here at home, with our hopes and the world's hopes for peace in the balance every day, I do not believe that I should devote an hour or a day of my time to any personal partisan causes or to any duties other than the awesome duties of this office – the presidency of your country. Accordingly, I shall not seek, and I will not accept, the nomination of my party for another term as your president.

On 3 April, President Johnson and Senator Kennedy met for the last time. It seems a deal was done. The president would allow Bobby to be only specifically critical of him, in return for which he would not reveal any of the unsavoury secrets he knew about JFK. Reluctantly, Bobby told Johnson, "You are a brave and dedicated man." Johnson then held a meeting with his vice president Hubert Humphrey and gave him his secret backing. The same day, Johnson also met muckraking journalist Drew Pearson and told him that Bobby was responsible for the Bay of Pigs.

In May, Kennedy won primaries in Indiana and Nebraska but lost to McCarthy in Oregon on 28 May by 44.7 to 38.8 per cent. On 26 May in Oregon, Bobby Kennedy gave a speech that was more pro-Israel than any presidential candidate had ever made. "The US must defend Israel against aggression from whatever source. Our obligations to Israel, unlike our obligations to other countries, are clear and imperative. Israel is the very opposite of Vietnam. Israel's government is democratic, effective, free of corruption, its people united in its support," he said. His candidacy made Kennedy a target not only for his sworn enemies (organized crime, gangsters Hoffa and Giancana etc.) but also for any individuals that wanted to get their name in the history books by killing a Kennedy. Despite this, he would often expose himself to danger on his campaigns. Some even believed that he had a subconscious desire to join John F. Kennedy. What made his campaign even more courageous was that Bobby Kennedy was basically a shy man who was only really happy when he was with members of his family. One aide noticed that when he spoke in public, his hands shook.

Date and Place of Assassination

5 June 1968, Ambassador Hotel 3400, Wilshire Boulevard (between Catalina Street and Mariposa Avenue), Los Angeles, California, USA.

The Event

Bobby Kennedy spent the day of Tuesday 4 June 1968 relaxing and having fun with his family at the Malibu home of film director John Frankenheimer. He went to the beach and then had an early supper with Frankenheimer, director and producer Roman Polanski and his actress wife, Sharon Tate. The campaign had been a hard-fought contest and he was not in the mood for a celebratory party that night. He was persuaded to go to Los Angeles because the television crews would not go to Malibu to interview him should he win. Reluctantly, he agreed to let Frankenheimer drive him to the Ambassador Hotel at 7pm where he kept a suite. The vote count was running late so he went upstairs to the Royal Suite on the fifth floor. At 11.40pm the news broke that Kennedy had unexpectedly won California by a margin of 46.3 per cent to McCarthy's 41.8, and had beaten Vice President Hubert Humphrey in South Dakota by 49.5 to 30 per cent. His party went down to the Embassy Ballroom where he made a brief speech thanking the campaign team, "We are a great country, an unselfish country, and a compassionate country, and I intend to make that my basis for running over the peri-

od of the next few months ... My thanks to you all," ending with a V-sign and the words, "and now it's on to Chicago and let's win there."

There was very little security around (the Secret Service did not provide protection for presidential candidates in 1968) and the Kennedy campaign team had hired a bodyguard from Ace Security, a local company. William Gardner, the hotel's head of hotel security, said that he had received no request to provide personal security for Robert Kennedy, but he had anticipated security problems and hired eight guards in addition to the ten plainclothes hotel security staff. Kennedy began heading for the Colonial Room where he was to give a press conference. He moved through the crowds until his press secretary, Frank Mankiewicz, took charge and headed towards the pantry, a less crowded but ultimately fatal route. Assistant maître d'hôtel Karl Uecker moved in front of Kennedy and Thane Eugene Cesar, 26, a part-time bodyguard from Ace Security, followed. Kennedy shook hands with kitchen staff as he walked. Female Kennedy supporters cried out, "We love you!" As Juan Perez shook the senator's hand, he said, "Señor Kennedy, mucho gusto!" Kennedy moved on to shake hands with some cooks and 17-year-old busboy Juan Romero. Suddenly, a young man moved from the vicinity of the ice machine toward the steam table where Kennedy was shaking hands. Concurrently, the young man brushed past photographer Virginia Guy, his gun chipping one of her teeth. At 12.15am, he pulled an Iver-Johnson Cadet .22 calibre revolver from the waistband of his jeans, shouted, "Kennedy, you sonofabitch," and fired eight rounds.

As Kennedy fell to the floor, he grabbed the security guard Thane Cesar's clip-on tie. The shooter, Sirhan Sirhan, was grabbed and restrained by Karl Uecker, the writer George Plimpton, the Olympic gold medallist decathlete Rafer Johnson and the professional football player Rosey Grier. Grier jammed his thumb behind the trigger of the revolver to prevent further shots from

On the campaign trail: RFK was a popular choice for the White House.

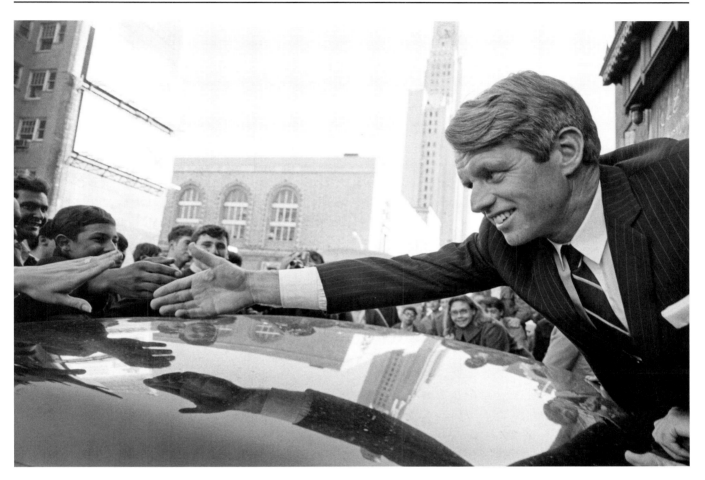

being fired. Kennedy and five other people were hit: William Weisel of ABC News, 30; Paul Schrade, 43, of the United Auto Workers; Democratic Party activist Elizabeth Evans, 43; radio reporter Ira Goldstein, 19; and Kennedy volunteer Irwin Stroll, 17. Juan Romero put his rosary beads into Kennedy's hands and said, "Come on, Mr Kennedy, you can make it."

The crowd parted to let Ethel through to see her husband. The senator lay on the floor, blood pouring from his head, his eyes staring blankly and muttering unintelligibly. Mrs Kennedy cradled her husband's head, unbuttoned his shirt and rubbed his chest. As people took pictures, Ethel said, "Get back. Give him room to breathe," only for a cameraman to curtly reply, "This is history, lady." Stephen Smith, married to the youngest

Kennedy daughter, Jean, and Bobby's campaign manager, used the hotel PA system to ask if there was a doctor in the house. Dr Stanley Abo, a diagnostic radiologist, answered the call and examined the senator. One of Bobby's eyes was closed while the other stared vacantly. His pulse was slow but strong. He spotted his wife and called her name. He lifted his hand and Ethel grasped it. The police arrived to take away Sirhan who claimed, "I did it for my country." As he was being led away, the ambulance arrived and two attendants, Max Berhman and Robert Hulsman, fought their way through the crowd. They wrapped a blanket around him. "Don't lift me," said the senator weakly. "Don't lift me." Ethel pushed at the ambulance men, "Don't touch him. I'm Mrs Kennedy." The medical team ignored her and lifted Kennedy onto a wheeled stretcher. "No, no, no... don't," said Kennedy. They were the last words he uttered in public.

The stretcher was wheeled out with the Kennedy entourage following. By the time they reached the lift, the Kennedys and the ambulance men were at loggerheads. In the lift an argument broke out and Ethel shouted at Max Berhman. When they reached the exit, Berhman tried to stop anyone apart from Mrs Kennedy getting into the ambulance. Ethel would have none of it and three male friends clambered on board. The trip to the Central Receiving Hospital was just a mile and took two minutes but still the arguments continued. When Max Berhman tried to put an oxygen mask on Senator Kennedy, Ethel stopped him. In a temper she threw his logbook out of the ambulance window. Finally, she allowed the medic to place the mask on her husband. The ambulance was met at the hospital by Dr Vasilius Bazilauskas, 53, who said, "When [Bobby] was on the platform I could see that he was like a blob of Jell-O that you took out of the refrigerator. I immediately realised that he was probably gone but of course I couldn't be sure of it. There was an oxygen mask on his face, put there in the ambulance. I put my hand in underneath his shirt, which had been partially opened, to feel his chest for warmth and it was halfway to the coldness of death."

In Emergency Room 2, nurses began to remove the senator's clothes while Dr Bazilauskas, not hearing a heartbeat, began to massage his chest. Dr Bazilauskas had earlier slapped Bobby's face to see how he reacted to pain stimulus and Ethel screamed at him to stop being so rough. Dr Bazilauskas injected adrenaline into the senator's arm and his heart began to beat on its own. Father James Mundell, a family friend, was allowed into the room and gave Bobby absolution. Father Thomas Peacha, 36, of St Basil's, performed the last rites. A decision was made to transfer Bobby to the Good Samaritan Hospital, at 1212 Shatto Street, Los Angeles, because it had a better reputation for brain surgery. With

tubes in his body, Bobby was sneaked out of the Central Receiving Hospital at 1am by a side door to avoid the crowd of more than a thousand who had gathered outside. Ethel asked Dr Bazilauskas if her husband would be okay. He replied that there was hope but admitted later, "I had seen the senator's legs go into convulsions which meant that the damage to the switchboard, or nerve centre, was just too much. He could not survive. But, of course, I didn't want to tell her that."

At 2.45am doctors began operating on the senator. They discovered that one of the bullets had penetrated the brain but did not have the power to exit the skull. (The fatal bullet entered the right rear mastoid area of the head and splintered.) It hit the other side of the skull, ricocheted back and caused yet more cerebral damage. Surgery lasted 3 hours and 40 minutes and Ethel spent that time pacing the room and praying. At 7.20am, Ted Kennedy arrived at the hospital. Bobby's press secretary Frank Mankiewicz told the press that the next "12 to 36 hours [were] crucial", but in fact he knew that the situation was hopeless and it was only a matter of time before the senator died.

Senator Robert Francis Kennedy died, aged 42, at 1.44am on 6 June, a few minutes after being taken off a life support machine. The autopsy (Medical Examiner's Case No 68-5731) by Dr Thomas Noguchi showed that Kennedy had been shot three times – once behind his right ear, secondly near his right armpit and thirdly about 1½ inches (4 centimetres) below the second wound. The freelance journalist and assassination researcher Mel Ayton reports on the wounds:

1) the fatal wound to the head. The bullet entered the brain and fragmented into two large and many tiny pieces. Fragments of the mastoid bone were scattered in the brain. Two wound tracks were visible in the X-rays. According to coroner Thomas Noguchi, who performed the autopsy, powder burns on the right ear area indicated Kennedy had been shot from a distance of 1 to 1½ inches; 2) a wound to the shoulder. The bullet entered from the back of Kennedy's armpit, through soft tissue, and travelled upward at an angle of 59 degrees to the vertical moving back to front and 3) a wound to the neck. The bullet entered from the back of Kennedy's armpit at an angle of 67–70 degrees to the vertical in a path nearly parallel to the path of the bullet that caused wound two. The bullet did not exit the skin and lodged near the sixth vertebrae, where the neck meets the back, an inch from the spine. According to Noguchi, both wounds in the area of Kennedy's armpit and right side were the results of shots fired at very close range. All three bullets travelled back to front, right to left and upward. A fourth bullet passed through Kennedy's jacket without causing injury; it travelled the same path as the bullets that caused wounds two and three. Later, Noguchi said it was impossible to determine which bullet hit Kennedy first. There were five holes in Kennedy's coat: an exit hole at the right front of the shoulder – no nitrate; an exit hole ¾ of an inch to the rear of the right shoulder seam – nitrate particles present; an entrance hole 2 inches below the shoulder seam in the right sleeve – nitrate deposits; and two holes in the rear right sleeve 7 inches below the shoulder seam – nitrate deposits. Noguchi later stated that despite his efforts he could not accurately trace the flight pattern of so many bullets.

All the bullets entered the body on an upward trajectory moving right to left. Despite 76 witnesses and the aftermath being shown on television, much mystery appeared to surround the assassination of Bobby Kennedy. Based on Noguchi's examination, he later said, "Until more is precisely known ... the existence of a second gunman remains a possibility. Thus, I have never said

DR THOMAS NOGUCHI

Thomas T. Noguchi was born on 4 January 1927 in Japan. He emigrated to the USA in 1952 to complete his residency in pathology at Orange County General Hospital. He was Chief Medical Examiner-Coroner for the County of Los Angeles from 1967 to 1982. Known as the "coroner to the stars", he performed autopsies on Marilyn Monroe, Janis Joplin, Albert Dekker, William Holden, John Belushi, Natalie Wood and Sharon Tate. The autopsy on Kennedy was the first and only time in Noguchi's career that he asked for the decedent's face to be covered during the operation. He was sacked in 1982 after being accused of being publicity hungry. Noguchi is said to be the prototype for television's *Quincy, M.E.*

that Sirhan Sirhan killed Robert Kennedy." Witnesses said that Sirhan had been in front of Kennedy and was not closer than a few feet. These inconsistencies have caused many to posit a suspicion that there had been a second gunman behind Kennedy. The conspiracy theorists point to the number of shots fired. Sirhan's .22 calibre revolver held eight bullets and all were fired – three hit the senator, and the others hit bystanders, the ceiling and one was lost. Crime scene photographs and Los Angeles Police Department's (LAPD) investigators' memories appear to show two more bullets embedded in the wooden frame of the pantry's swinging doors. So, if there were ten bullets fired that night then there must have been a second gunman present. Further, a 1975 judicially appointed panel found bullet markings that were different from the markings on Sirhan's gun.

However, thanks to the sleuthing of author Dan Moldea, many of the questions from that night can be answered. The reason why the 1975 inquiry found different markings was simply because Sirhan's gun had been damaged by "heavy leading" (barrel fouling) that compromised the further tests. The heavy leading, Moldea discovered, was caused by numerous test firings of Sirhan's gun by LAPD members who wanted souvenirs. "Thus, [LAPD ballistics expert DeWayne] Wolfer and only Wolfer could have positively matched the three victim bullets," wrote Moldea, "before the leading of and permanent damage to the barrel of Sirhan's gun. Wolfer legitimately made these matches and testified honestly. His analysis could not be confirmed by the firearms panel or anyone else, because the barrel became damaged immediately after he conducted the tests."

One witness in 1968, Kennedy campaign supporter Sandra Serrano, told Sergeant Paul Scharaga of the Los Angeles Police Department about the pretty girl in a "polka dot dress" who was seen in the pantry and later leaving the Ambassador shouting, "We shot him! We shot him!" Pantry eyewitness Vincent DiPierro also supported the story. DiPierro, the son of the Ambassador's maître d'hôtel, said that he had seen a "pretty girl" standing next to Sirhan seconds before the shooting. She was "wearing a polka dot dress". DiPierro, however, later identified the girl as Valerie Schulte. Schulte had been wearing a bright green dress with yellow polka-dots, was pretty and blonde and, as DiPierro stated, had a "pug-nose". Serrano later withdrew her story and, on 20 June 1968, she underwent a lie detector test administered by a Sergeant Hernandez. Asked if she sat down on the staircase at the time of the shooting she replied, "Yeah, I think I did … people messed me up … stupid people … just in all the commotion and everything … I was supposed to know more than I knew … I told [D. A. staffer John Ambrose] I heard the people say 'We shot him' or 'They shot him' or something. And I remember telling him that I had seen these people on the … on the stairway." According to the LAPD Summary Report, "Polygraph examination disclosed that Serrano has never seen Sirhan in person; further, that Miss Serrano fabricated, for some unknown reason, the

story about the girl in the polka dot dress. Responses to relevant questions indicate that no one made statements to Miss Serrano telling her that they had shot Kennedy or that she heard any gunshots during the late evening of 4 June or early morning of 5 June 1968. Miss Serrano was informed of the results of the polygraph examination." She later admitted that her statement was based more on guesswork "… two reasons, so I didn't look like a fool, which I look like now. Another reason, because everybody figures … you know … I was sitting [in the police station] hearing descriptions and descriptions of these people. Oh God, no, maybe that's what I'm supposed to see … more than I did. It messed me up, that's all, and I figured, well, they must know what they're doing – I mean, they are police, after all. They have to know what they're doing." A fire marshal further swore Serrano was not on the outside stairs at the Ambassador at the time she stated. It should also be remembered that people had been drinking that night and alcohol is notorious for creating false memories. The right-wing supporters of Senator Max Rafferty and Senator Alan Cranston were also at the hotel that night and it is believed that the shouts of "We shot Kennedy" probably originated there.

The conspiracy theorists have identified Kennedy's bodyguard Thane Cesar as the second gunman and firer of the fatal bullets. He worked for the Lockheed Corporation. Cesar admitted on tape that he had removed his gun from his holster during the shooting in the pantry but insisted he never fired it. Cesar also admitted to investigator Theodore Charach that he had owned a .22 calibre revolver similar to Sirhan's, but said he had sold it in February 1968, a claim eventually proven to have been false, as it was later discovered that Cesar had instead sold the gun three months after the assassination (if Cesar had been the second gunman, he would have been extremely foolish to hold on to a murder weapon). The buyer of that revolver later reported it stolen.

Dan Moldea discovered Cesar's whereabouts and subjected him to a lie detector test, which he passed. Further, if Cesar had been the killer he would have had to have been a solitary opportunist because he did not know he was due to work that day, being called in at the last minute. The other possibility is that Sirhan had several accomplices, but this does seem nonsensicial. Moldea also explains the apparent discrepancy regarding Sirhan's proximity to Kennedy. When he investigated the dynamics of the shooting Moldea concluded that Kennedy had been turning to his left when Sirhan fired the fatal shot. Furthermore, Moldea pointed out that the reliable witnesses to the shooting had all said the distance from Kennedy to Sirhan's gun was between 1½–3 feet (50–90 centimetres). Therefore, it was not far-fetched to say that the muzzle of Sirhan's gun had or nearly touched Kennedy's head in the chaos that ensued. As Moldea explained, "All twelve of the eyewitnesses' statements about muzzle distance is based on – and only on – their view of Sirhan's first shot." The shot, which Moldea has argued, did not hit Kennedy in the head. "After the first shot, their eyes were diverted as panic swept through the densely populated kitchen pantry. The people in the area began to run, duck for cover and crash into each other."

One of the most reliable witnesses, Lisa Urso, who could see both Kennedy and Sirhan, saw Kennedy's hand move to his head behind his right ear. As the distance from Kennedy to the gun after the first pop was 3 feet (90 centimetres), it is likely he had been simply reacting defensively to the first shot fired. Urso described Kennedy's movements as "… [jerking] a little bit, like backwards and then forwards." In Moldea's opinion the backwards and forwards jerking, "... came as Kennedy had recoiled after the first shot; he was then accidentally bumped forward, toward the steam table and into Sirhan's gun where he was hit at point-blank range." Boris Yaro, a photographer for *The Los Angeles Times*, said, "Kennedy backed up against the kitchen freezers as the gunman fired at him [at] point-blank range." This claim is also supported by key witness Frank Burns, who was identified as one of the five in the group (the others were Karl Uecker, Juan Romero, Jesus Perez, Martin Patrusky) that was closest to the senator. Burns said that the gun was never less than 12 or 18 inches (30–45 centimetres) from Kennedy. He described the shooting in such a way as to make it entirely plausible that Sirhan's gun moved to an area inches away from Kennedy. Burns had suffered an abrasion on his face that he thought was caused by a bullet passing near his cheek. It was likely a powder burn from Sirhan's pistol. Burns said:

I had just caught up with him [in the pantry], and he was a step or so past him. And I'd turned around facing the same way as he turned toward the busboys, I was just off his right shoulder, a matter of inches behind him … The noise was like a string of firecrackers going off, it wasn't in an even cadence. In the process, a bullet must have passed very close to my left cheek because I can remember the heat and a sort of burn. I remember an arm coming towards us, through the people, with a gun in it. I was putting together the burn across my cheek, the noise and the gun and I was thinking, 'My God, it's an assassination attempt.' I turned my head and saw the gun and quickly looked back to the senator and realised he'd been shot because he'd thrown his hands up toward his head as if he was about to grab it at the line of his ears. He hadn't quite done it. His arms were near his head and he was twisting to his left and falling back. And then I looked back at the gunman, and at that moment he was almost directly in front of me. He was still holding the gun and coming closer to the senator, pursuing the body so that the arc of the gun was coming down to the floor as the body was going down.

The Assassin

Sirhan Bishara Sirhan was born on 19 March 1944 in Jerusalem, Palestine, the fifth son and sixth of the seven children of Mary Muzher and Bishara Sirhan, a master mechanic. His family became refugees on the formation of Israel in 1948. In 1956 the family moved to California but Sirhan maintained an interest in his homeland. In 1962 the family bought a house at 696 East Howard Street in Pasadena. Despite living in America, he and his brothers could not, or would not, assimilate into American society. They abhorred US culture, disliked the mores of the American people and, most importantly, hated the support Americans gave to the state of Israel. The family felt they were part of a minority group, alienated and misunderstood within the larger community. They kept themselves apart and while they could all speak English, spoke only Arabic at home. They also ate and drank the same food and drinks that they had enjoyed in Jerusalem. They subscribed to a weekly Arabic newspaper *Al Bayan*.

Sirhan was to later claim that Arabs were treated like second-class citizens in the United States. "Just because we're Arabs in this country," he said, "we have no power, no prestige, no influence, no money – nothing really. We can be treated like dogs, like ants. Had it not been for me … Munir [Sirhan's youngest brother] would be out there in one of those [Palestinian refugee] camps. He would have been deported [for having a criminal conviction] … The whole world knows Sirhan now. If they had deported his younger brother from America that would show an injustice on the part of America … But even without me, what's all the difference? Munir [is] just a good-for-nothing Aye-rab."

On leaving high school Sirhan was sacked from a number of jobs, which further fuelled his sense of alienation. Sirhan was a student at Pasadena City College from September 1963 until May 1965. During this period two Arab groups were active on campus – the International Club and the Organization of Arab Students in the United States and Canada (OAS) – but they were not recognized by the college. According to the OAS's president, Kanan Abdul Latif Hamzeh, Sirhan had intense feelings against the Israelis. According to writer James H. Sheldon, in a contemporary article entitled *Anti-Israeli Forces on Campus*, the OAS was dangerously active in spreading extremist and violent ideas during this period. "Based on my research into the groups and individuals he conversed with, I have no doubt Sirhan saw himself as an 'avenger' for perceived wrongs against the Palestinian people," he wrote. In June 1966, Sirhan joined the Ancient Mystic Order Rosae Crucis, commonly known as the Rosicrucians, paying the $20 initiation fee. On 7 March 1968, Sirhan left his job at a Pasadena health food shop.

Sirhan had been a supporter of John F. Kennedy and was originally in favour of Bobby Kennedy. However, in April 1968, he told a dustman, Alvin Clark, of his hatred of Kennedy (Mr Clark testified to this at Sirhan's trial). Sirhan's mind was changed permanently on 20 May 1968 when he saw a film *The Story of Robert Kennedy* made by the Jewish filmmaker John Frankenheimer. It was the story of Kennedy's visit to war-torn Palestine when he was at Harvard and how he had written up his experiences for a Boston newsaper. The narrator said, "Bob Kennedy decided his future lay in the affairs of men and nations." In the background flew an Israeli flag leaving Sirhan in no doubt where Kennedy's sympathies lay. He was further upset when he learned of Kennedy's support for Israel during the 1967 Six Day War. It's possible that Sirhan's feelings towards Bobby Kennedy had changed even earlier, in January 1968, when he read of Senator Kennedy's support for sending more armaments to Israel. Sirhan was an avid reader of political periodicals and could not have failed to notice that Kennedy met the Israeli Premier, Levi Eshkol, in January 1968 and expressed his support for Israel. In January and February of 1968, Bobby made at least three statements recommending arms aid to Israel.

Sirhan dropped out of Pasadena College and was an unemployed horse trainer. On 26 May he read an article in which Kennedy advocated withdrawal from Vietnam but the total arming of Israel. On 1 June, he spent two hours practising pistol shooting at the horse ranch where he had worked. On 4 June from 11am until 5pm, he again practised his shooting. He fired more than 400 rounds. On leaving the range, he drove to Bob's Big Boy restaurant where he bought a hamburger and a coffee. He gatecrashed a party at the Ambassador for Max Rafferty, another senatorial candidate. He drank two Tom Collinses before he was ejected. Outside, he met two Kennedy supporters and they discussed whether Kennedy could win. Sirhan said, "Don't worry about him if he doesn't win, that son of a bitch. He's a millionaire and he doesn't need to win. He just wants to go to the White House, but even if he wins he's not going to do anything for you or for any of the poor people." Leaving the two supporters, Sirhan wandered around the hotel. By 11pm he had drank two more Tom Collinses. He walked to his car and collected his gun. He left his wallet in the vehicle before returning to the hotel with murder on his mind.

The Aftermath

Sirhan Sirhan was arraigned at 7.40am on 5 June with six counts of assault with intent to murder. Some authorities believe that the date of the shooting is significant. It was the first anniversary of the first day of the Six Day War between Israel and its Arab neighbours, which began on 5 June 1967. One writer suggested that the assassination may have been the first Arab terrorist act to happen on American soil (the 11 September 2001 attacks being the most recent). A diary was reputedly found at Sirhan's home in which he had written: "My determination to eliminate RFK is becoming more and more [sic] of an unshakable obsession. RFK must die. RFK must be killed. Robert F. Kennedy must be assassinated … Robert F. Kennedy must be assassinated before 5 June 1968." It is now believed that the diary was a forgery.

On 7 June, Sirhan was charged with first-degree murder. At his trial, which began before Judge Herbert V. Walker in Los Angeles on 13 January 1969, one of his lawyers said, "[Sirhan] was disturbed that both his mother and his brothers did not see Senator Kennedy as the same destructive and malevolent and dangerous person as Sirhan perceived him to be; and I gather that he and his family … had some arguments about this." Sirhan believed he was an important revolutionary; he was in the vanguard of the Third World as he expressed it. He thought RFK would be "like his brother", the president, and help the Arabs but, "Hell, he fucked up. That's all he did … He asked for it. He should have been smarter than that. You know, the Arabs had emotions. He knew how they felt about it. But, hell, he didn't have to come out right at the fucking time when the Arab-Israeli war erupted. Oh! I couldn't take it! I couldn't take it!" Sirhan went on to claim that he acted unconsciously, and that he has no memory of the shooting.

One theory is that he was brainwashed into killing Kennedy (similar to the plot of the 1962 film *The Manchurian Candidate*). However, a majority of hypnosis and mind-control experts dismiss the notion that subjects can be hypnotized to commit murder. They say that such programming of an unwitting and unwilling subject is not possible. Furthermore, there would be no guarantee of success for a robotic assassin; it is an erratic tool. A hypnotist can plant a suggestion in the subject's mind and ask him to forget that suggestion but there is no foolproof way of preventing another hypnotist coming along and recovering that memory. Sirhan told defence investigator Michael McCowan that he remembered shooting Kennedy. In the pre-trial period, McCowan had spoken to Sirhan about the shooting. McCowan had been startled when Sirhan related to him how his eyes had met Kennedy's in the moment just before he shot him. McCowan asked Sirhan, "Then why, Sirhan, didn't you shoot him between the eyes?" Without hesitating, Sirhan replied, "Because that son-of-a-bitch turned his head at the last second." When asked by a police sergeant if he was ashamed of what he did, Sirhan said, "Hell, no!" In fact, he was proud of his action and the next morning he asked jail guards for a newspaper so he could see what had been written about him. When no stories of the assassination appeared because of press deadlines, he became upset.

So why did Sirhan choose Senator Kennedy? Initially, Sirhan would likely have been satisfied with any opportunity to kill a prominent US politician. At one point, he even had UN Ambassador Goldberg in his sights. Sirhan said that he first considered killing Vice President Humphrey. However, the rise of the Kennedy Camelot legend was in full flow between 1963 and 1968. As the distinguished researcher, Mel Ayton, says:

Sirhan, too, desired fame. Killing any of the other candidates would certainly have given him status throughout the Arab world. But his true target had an even greater symbolism attached to it. Sirhan would become the 'Second Kennedy Assassin'. He knew that killing RFK would give him greater world exposure that the other candidates could not provide. It was no accident that Sirhan set his sights on the candidate who was the brother of the martyred president. It was no accident that Sirhan chose the candidate who was most likely to become the next president. There is no evidence that Sirhan met any terrorist group representatives, but the Arab community in the Los Angeles area gave its wholehearted support to a violent solution to the Palestinian problem.

On 10 February 1969, a motion by Sirhan's lawyers to enter a plea of guilty to first-degree murder in exchange for life imprisonment (rather than the death penalty) was made in chambers and denied. The court judge Herbert V. Walker ordered that the record pertaining to the motion be sealed. A month later, on 3 March 1969 in a Los Angeles courtroom, Sirhan claimed that he had killed Kennedy "with 20 years of malice aforethought", contradicting his statements that he had no memory of the crime. The judge did not accept this confession and it was later withdrawn. Sirhan was convicted on 17 April 1969 and was sentenced to death six days later. He moved into death row in San Quentin on 23 May 1969. The sentence was commuted to life in prison on 17 June 1972. Senator Ted Kennedy made several pleas on Sirhan's behalf for leniency.

Senator Kennedy's body was returned to New York City on 6 June, where he lay in state at St Patrick's Cathedral at Fifth Avenue and East 51st Street, before the funeral Mass the next day. Senator Ted Kennedy did the eulogy, "My brother need not be idealized or enlarged in death beyond what he was in life, to be remembered simply as a good and decent man, who saw wrong and tried to right it, saw suffering and tried to heal it, saw war and tried to stop it." Ted Kennedy finished by paraphrasing Bobby quoting George Bernard Shaw, "Some men see things as they are and say 'Why?' I dream things that never were and say, 'Why not?'"

After the Mass, a special train (number 4901) took the body 226 miles (364 kilometres) to Washington DC. Thousands of mourners lined the tracks and stations to pay their respects. Tragically, one couple who had stood on the tracks to watch the train go by were killed when they were struck by a train coming the other way. Senator Kennedy was buried near his brother, the president, in Arlington National Cemetery on 8 June 1968. He had always said that he would like to be buried in Massachusetts, but his family believed that the brothers, who had been so close in life, should be buried next to each other. Robert Kennedy's burial at Arlington National Cemetery is the only one to ever take place at night.

On 7 June 1968, President Johnson signed legislation that the Secret Service would protect presidential candidates. On 9 June 1968, he declared an official day of national mourning following Kennedy's death.

Che Guevara (1928–1967)

The Victim

There are probably millions of people worldwide who know the face of Che Guevara, thanks to an iconic picture on a T-shirt, but most of them will have no idea who he was. Ernesto Guevara de la Serna was born on 14 June 1928 in Rosario, Argentina. He was the eldest of five children of Ernesto Guevara Lynch and Celia de la Serna y Edelmira Llosa. Both parents were card-carrying members of the Argentine communist party.

As a child he began to suffer from asthma. The first attack occurred on 2 May 1930, six weeks shy of his second birthday and the affliction plagued him throughout his life. Despite the illness, he was a keen rugby player and was nicknamed Fuser – a contraction of El Furibundo, meaning "The Raging" and his mother's surname, Serna – for his aggressive style of play. Another less pleasant nickname was Chancho – pig – because he stank through lack of familiarity with soap and water. Oddly, Guevara was proud of his baseness. As a child his hobbies were chess, poetry and photography.

In 1932, the family moved to Alta Gracia, Cordoba. In 1948, Guevara enrolled in the University of Buenos Aires to study medicine. In 1951, he spent a gap year travelling with an older friend Alberto Granado, 29, a biochemist. They rode a 1939 Norton 500cc motorcycle they named La Poderosa II, "The Second Mighty One". Guevara kept a record of the journey (see box on right). On his travels he saw much poverty and hardship and

PARENTS AND SIBLINGS

Father – Ernest Guevara Lynch: born 1900, died 1987.

Mother – Celia de la Serna y Edelmira Llosa: born 1906, died in Buenos Aires 1965.

Siblings – Celia: born 31 December 1929; Roberto: born 1932; Ana Maria: born 1934; Juan Martin: born at Cordoba May 1943.

THE MOTORCYCLE DIARIES

Guevera's record of his travels was published as *The Motorcycle Diaries*. The journal was translated into English in 1996 and formed the basis for a film, directed by Walter Salles and released on 27 August 2004. Gael García Bernal played Guevara and Rodrigo De la Serna portrayed Alberto Granado.

came to the conclusion that only an armed revolution could end the suffering. He also believed that Latin America was one entity not a group of discrete nations.

Back in Argentina, he returned to his studies and received his medical diploma on 12 June 1953. Twenty-five days later, on 7 July 1953, he set off on a journey that would take him through Bolivia, Peru, Ecuador, Panama, Costa Rica, Nicaragua, Honduras and El Salvador. In December he landed in Guatemala where he decided to become a "real" revolutionary. There he met (and later married) the Peruvian economist Hilda Gadea Acosta. She was a member of the socialist American Popular Revolutionary Alliance, led by Víctor Raúl Haya de la Torre. Through her he met some high-ranking government officials and he also re-established contact with a group of Cuban exiles with links to Fidel Castro, whom he had initially met in Costa Rica. It was in this period that he acquired his famous nickname, Che, due to his frequent use of the Argentine word *che*, which roughly translates as "mate" or "hey".

Despite his qualifications, he found medical work difficult to come by in Guatemala, so he briefly left for El Salvador to pick up a new visa, but returned only a few days before the CIA-sponsored coup attempt led by Carlos Castillo Armas began. Guevara fled to Mexico where his hatred of America continued to fester. On 21 September 1954, Guevara arrived in Mexico City to meet again with the Cuban exiles, including Ñico López, whom he had known in Guatemala. In June 1955, López introduced him to Raúl Castro, the brother of Fidel (the

Despite being a revolutionary, Che Guevara would often give
speeches to world organizations.

man who on 31 July 2006 temporarily took over the running of the communist state when Fidel fell ill). On the
evening of 8 July (some historians place the date as
later in the month, August or even September) Raúl supposedly introduced Guevara to his older brother. The
men spent all night locked in discussions and Guevara

became convinced that Fidel Castro was the revolutionary leader for whom he had long been searching.

Guevera joined the 26th of July Movement (named
for a failed attack on the Moncada barracks in Santiago
on 26 July 1953), whose aim was to overthrow the
regime of Fulgencio Batista (see box on page 161). It

was intended that Guevara work as the organization's doctor, but when he took part in the military training, it was soon realised that he was probably their best recruit. That same summer, Guevara resumed his relationship with Hilda Gadea and when she fell pregnant, they married on 18 August 1955. Their daughter, Hilda Beatríz, was born on 15 February 1956.

Nine months later, on 25 November 1956, the expedition to overthrow Batista set off for Cuba from Tuxpan, Veracruz, Mexico aboard the cabin cruiser *Granma*. Guevara was one of only four non-Cubans on the vessel. The voyage was a nightmare – Guevara suffered a crippling asthma attack and discovered that the seasickness pills for the crew had been left behind. The landing on 2 December was not successful and almost half of the revolutionaries were killed then, or executed upon capture. Only 15 rebels, including Guevara, survived and they fled into the mountains of the Sierra Maestra to wage guerrilla warfare against the Batista regime.

Guevera emerged as a leader of the rebels and ruthlessly ordered the executions of any of them he believed were informers, deserters or spies. On 21 July 1957, Guevara was promoted to *comandante*. In December 1957, he was wounded in the foot during fighting at Altos de Conrado and, in March 1958, he began to train new volunteers at a military school set up in Minas del Frío in the Sierra Maestra. He also had a five-month affair with Zoila Rodríguez Garcia, the 18-year-old daughter of a local man.

In July 1958, he demonstrated his military abilities at the Battle of Las Mercedes when he saved Castro from imminent disaster. On 28 December 1958, Guevara's fighters attacked Santa Clara and Batista discovered that some of his generals had been negotiating a secret peace treaty with the rebels. The Cuban leader fled to the Dominican Republic at 2am on 1 January 1959. The next day, Guevara was appointed commander of the La Cabaña Fortress prison. The following month, on 7 February, Guevara was named "a Cuban citizen by birth" because of what the rebels saw as his sterling work in bringing about Batista's downfall. He divorced his wife on 22 May 1959 and, on 2 June 1959, he married Aleida March, a Cuban-born member of the 26th of July Movement, with whom he had been living since late 1958.

On 12 June, he left his position at the prison. During his five months in charge, up to 550 people had been executed on Guevara's direct orders. On 7 October, he became an official at the National Institute of Agrarian Reform. From 26 November 1959 until 23 February 1961, he was the president of the National Bank of Cuba, signing all the banknotes "Che" rather than Ernesto Guevara. During his time in office, he did not draw a ministerial salary preferring his army wages as a "revolutionary example". What had succeeded in Cuba, however, did not translate to other Latin American countries. Revolutions organized by Guevara in Panama and the Dominican Republic failed.

At 3.10pm on 4 March 1960, the French munitions freighter *La Coubre* exploded in Havana harbour as its cargo was being unloaded. As rescuers went to help the injured, a second explosion occurred leaving more than 100 people dead and double that number injured. It was at the improvised memorial service on 5 March for the victims of this explosion, that Alberto Korda took the iconic photograph of Guevara (see box on page 163).

CHE'S CHILDREN

Mother – Hilda Gadea (one child)
Hilda Beatríz – born 15 February 1956, died 1995

Mother – Aleida March (four children)
Aleida – born 24 November 1960
Camilo – born 1962
Celia – born 1963
Ernesto – born 24 February 1965

Mother – Lilia Rosa Perez (one child)
Omar – born 19 March 1964

Omar was the only child out of wedlock that Guevara acknowledged.

When Cuban exiles attempted to recapture their homeland during the Bay of Pigs fiasco on 22 April 1961, Guevara was not involved in the fighting. Castro had sent him to Pinar del Río where a decoy force had landed. During that time, he was shot in the face but claimed that he had accidentally discharged his own gun. He was involved in the Cuban Missile Crisis, however, and later told the *Daily Worker* that, if the missiles had been under Cuban control, they would have fired them against major American cities.

On 9 December 1964, he arrived in New York as the leader of the Cuban delegation to address the United Nations. He also appeared on CBS's *Face the Nation* and met Senator Eugene McCarthy, several associates of Malcolm X and Canadian radical Michelle Duclos. On 17 December, he flew to Paris and then embarked on a three-month international tour to the People's Republic of China, the United Arab Republic (Egypt), Algeria, Ghana, Guinea, Mali, Dahomey, Congo-Brazzaville and Tanzania, and stopped off in Ireland and Prague. He also visited Pyongyang and told the press that North Korea was the ideal to which Cuba should aspire. In Algiers on 24 February 1965, he made his last public appearance on the international stage when he delivered a speech to the Second Economic Seminar on Afro-Asian Solidarity. He said, "There are no frontiers in this struggle to the death. We cannot remain indifferent in the face of what occurs in any part of the world. A victory for any country against imperialism is our victory, just as any country's defeat is our defeat. The socialist countries have the moral duty of liquidating their tacit complicity with the exploiting countries of the West."

On 14 March, he returned to Cuba where he was met by Fidel and Raúl Castro, Osvaldo Dorticós and Carlos Rafael Rodríguez at Havana airport. At the end of the month, Guevara dropped out of sight. The reasons for his disappearance remain a mystery but various theories include the failure of the industrial scheme he had propounded, ideological differences between Guevara and Castro and Castro being told to remove Guevara from power by the Soviet Union, angry at Guevara's pro-China line. As speculation grew as to Guevara's health and whereabouts, Castro made an announcement on 16 June 1965 in which he said that all would be revealed about Guevara when he (Guevara) wanted it known. On 3 October 1965, Castro revealed the existence of a handwritten, undated letter from Guevera in which Che had said that while he fully supported Castro and his aims, he (Guevara) felt the need to go and fight "on new battlefields". In the letter Guevara announced his resignation from all his positions in the government, in the party and in the army, and renounced his Cuban citizenship. He wrote, "I have fulfilled the part of my duty that tied me to the Cuban revolution... and I say goodbye to you, to the comrades, to your people, who are now mine."

When Guevara landed at Havana airport the previous March, he went into conference with the Cuban leadership and it was decided that he should lead Cuba's first military action in sub-Saharan Africa. On 24 April 1965, Guevara, his second-in-command Victor

Dreke, and 12 Cubans arrived in the Congo in support of the pro-Patrice Lumumba Marxist Simba movement. Around 100 additional Cubans later joined Guevera. The Cubans worked with guerrilla leader Laurent-Désiré Kabila but the Lumumba revolt was suppressed in November by the Congolese army. Guevara did not know that South African mercenaries and Cuban exiles joined forces with the Congolese to thwart his plans. Guevara left the Congo with the six remaining members of his original force.

The plan had been for Castro to only reveal the contents of the letter Guevara had written him after the latter's death. When Castro pre-empted the idea, Guevara felt unable to return to Cuba and so spent six months living secretly in Dar-es-Salaam and Prague. Guevara's next port of revolution was Bolivia, where he arrived on 4 November 1966 using a fake name and passport. Three days later, 7 November, Guevara arrived at the rebel camp and made the first entry into his Bolivian diary. After an initial skirmish on 23 March 1967, President René Barrientos said that he wanted Guevara's head displayed on a spike in downtown La Paz. Despite having a band of only 50 men, Guevara did score some early successes. On 31 August 1967, the army hit back and destroyed two guerrilla groups. The Bolivian revolt failed as much because of Guevara's enormous ego as the incompetence of the men around him. In Cuba, Castro had managed to keep a tight rein on some of Guevara's wilder schemes – away from Cuba, there was no holding him back.

Date and Place of Assassination

9 October 1967, La Higuera, Bolivia.

The Event

Guevara was captured in a CIA-aided operation at 3.30pm on 8 October 1967 while leading a detachment with Simeón Cuba Sarabia in the Quebrada del Yuro ravine. The Bolivian Special Forces surrounded his hideout and

ALBERTO KORDA'S ICONIC IMAGE

The picture was not published until six years later. Korda's newspaper, *Revolución*, preferred pictures of Castro and French writers Jean Paul Sartre and Simone de Beauvoir. In 1966, Korda gave a copy to the Italian publisher and terrorist Giangiacomo Feltrinelli (born 19 June 1926, died near Milan 14 March 1972). When Guevara died, the Italian quickly began distributing the picture. Korda, a life-long communist, never received any royalties.

Guevara offered to surrender after being shot in the legs. According to military personnel present at the capture, during the skirmish, as soldiers approached Guevara, he allegedly shouted, "Do not shoot! I am Che Guevara and worth more to you alive than dead." Guevara was taken to a dilapidated, one-room schoolhouse in the nearby village of La Higuera where he was held overnight.

Early the next afternoon he was executed, bound by his hands to a board. The executioner was Mario Terán, a sergeant in the Bolivian army who had drawn the short straw and had to shoot Guevara. Several versions exist about what happened next. One has it that the executioner was too nervous and left the hut before being forced back inside by Colonel Selich and Colonel Zenteno. Another version is that he was so nervous he refused to look Guevara in the face and shot him in the side of the throat, which was the fatal wound. The most widely accepted account is that Guevara received multiple shots to the legs, so as to avoid maiming his face for identification purposes and simulate combat wounds in an attempt to hide the details of his assassination. Guevara is supposed to have said, "I know you are here to kill me. Shoot, coward, you are only going to kill a man." Biting his arm to avoid crying out, Guevara was eventually spared his pain and shot in the chest at 1.10pm, filling his lungs with blood. His body was tied to the landing skids of a helicopter and taken to neighbouring Vallegrande where it was laid out on a laundry tub in the local hospital and displayed to the press. Two doctors, Moisés Abraham Baptista and José Martínez Cazo, at the Hospital Knights of Malta, Vallegrande, signed Guevara's death certificate. Bolivian army officers transferred Guevara's corpse to an undisclosed location after a military doctor had surgically amputated his hands.

Stories as to what then happened are confused. General Ovando claimed that Guevara's corpse was buried in the Vallegrande on 11 October. Later, President Barrientos said that Guevara had been cremated and his ashes buried in Vallegrande.

The agent charged with tracking down Guevara was Félix Rodríguez. After Guevara's death, Rodríguez took the dead man's Rolex and other personal items. During press interviews he would display his trophies. A few of these are now on display at the CIA headquarters in Langley, Virginia.

The Assassins

The man who fired the fatal shot was Mario Terán, a sergeant in the Bolivian army. Terán is still alive and lives in the Santa Cruz Mountains. He has given several interviews since 1967.

The Aftermath

On 15 October 1967, Fidel Castro announced three days of public mourning for Guevara's death.

In July 1997, the skeletal remains of Guevara's handless body were exhumed from beneath an airstrip near Vallegrande, positively identified by DNA matching and returned to Cuba. On 17 October 1997, the remains of Ernesto "Che" Guevara, along with those of six of his men – including Octavio de la Concepcion y de la Pedraja, Edilberto Lucio Galvan Hidalgo, Jaime Arana Campero and Francisco Huanca Flores – killed in Bolivia, were buried with full military honours in a specially built mausoleum in the city of Santa Clara. A crowd estimated at 100,000 attended the ceremony.

As the 1960s wore on, Guevara became to be revered as the ideal revolutionary, and Jean-Paul Sartre described him as "the most complete human being of our age".

Perhaps the last words should go to the journalist Christopher Hitchens. He said, "Che's iconic status was assured because he failed. His story was one of defeat and isolation, and that's why it is so seductive. Had he lived, the myth of Che would have long since died."

Martin Luther King (1929–1968)

The Victim

Martin Luther King, Jr was born in Atlanta, Georgia, on 15 January 1929, as Michael Louis King (his name was changed in 1934), the elder son of three children of Martin Luther King and Alberta Christina Williams. Known as "ML", King was a sensitive boy and twice attempted suicide by leaping from a first floor window – once when he thought his grandmother had died, and the second time when she actually did.

Growing up in a racially segregated area, he recalled his "determin[ation] to hate every white person". After a second-class "coloured" education, he abandoned plans to become a lawyer or doctor, and in 1947 was ordained a minister. He became assistant pastor of the Ebenezer Baptist Church in Atlanta. His father was the pastor. King, who stood 5 feet 7 inches (1 metre 68 centimetres), claimed that women and food were his weaknesses. In 1948, he graduated from Morehouse College with a degree in sociology and three years later he obtained a BA in divinity from Crozer Theological Seminary in Chester, Pennsylvania. At Crozer, he became a follower of the teaching of M. K. Gandhi. In September 1951, he entered Boston University to study for a PhD in systematic theology. He received his doctorate in 1955.

On 18 June 1953, he married a promising young concert singer named Coretta Scott and they had two sons and two daughters (see box on page 169). Later that year, the couple moved to Montgomery, Alabama, where he became pastor of the Dexter Avenue Baptist Church. A year later, on 1 December 1955, Rosa Parks, a seamstress and official of the National Association for the Advancement of Colored People, refused to give up her seat on a Montgomery bus to a white person and was consequently arrested. Martin Luther King organized a boycott of the bus service that lasted 382 days and that brought the world's attention to the racial segregation that was still prevalent in the American south. On 13 November 1956, the United States Supreme Court overturned the Alabama laws that enforced segregation on buses.

In January 1957, the Kings' family home was fire-bombed by white supremacists. In August 1957, Martin Luther King and 115 other black leaders founded the Southern Christian Leadership Conference and Coretta Scott King used her artistic talents to create Freedom Concerts, at which poetry, narrative and music were used to tell the story of the civil rights movement. In 1957, King travelled 780,000 miles (1,255,285 kilometres) delivering 208 speeches, and this was before he went into civil rights full time. In 1958, he published *Strides Toward Freedom: The Montgomery Story*. In September of that year, he narrowly escaped death in New York when a mad black woman stabbed him in the chest with a letter opener. The surgeon who operated said that if King had even sneezed he would have drowned in his own blood through a ruptured aorta.

PARENTS AND SIBLINGS

His father was born as Martin King at Stockbridge, Georgia, on 19 December 1897. He added Luther to his name after a trip to Europe and the Holy Land in 1934. He died in Atlanta, Georgia, on 11 November 1984.

Born at Atlanta, Georgia, on 13 September 1904, his mother married Michael King on 25 November 1926. She was shot and killed on 30 June 1974 by Marcus Wayne Chenault, as she sat at the organ of the Ebenezer Baptist Church where she had played the organ since 1932 and where her father had been pastor before her husband took over.

His sister, Willie Christine King, was born on 11 September 1927 and his brother, Albert Daniel Williams King (nicknamed "AD"), was born on 30 July 1930. AD died in a swimming pool accident on 21 July 1969.

In 1959, he made a pilgrimage to India and rededicated his Gandhian principles. It should be noted that although King tried to help the poor, it did not stop him staying in fancy hotels, dressing well or accepting the largess of wealthier members of the Southern Christian Leadership Conference. In 1960, he resigned his pastorship and devoted his energies full time to the civil rights movement. In October, he was arrested during a sit-in at a segregated snack bar in Atlanta. He was released when John F. and Bobby Kennedy interceded on his behalf. In 1961 and 1962, he pressurized President Kennedy to support a tough civil rights bill and insisted that he issue a second Emancipation Proclamation to wipe out segregation. When the president refused, King and his men arranged a series of mass protests in the American south. In Albany, Georgia, in 1962, the police refused to rise to the bait and treated the demonstrators with decorum. "We killed them with kindness", said one city official.

The following year, Birmingham, Alabama, was a different matter and police chief Eugene Connor made the mistake of turning fire hoses and dogs on the protesters in view of the television cameras. Jailed during the demonstration, King wrote his celebrated "Letter from Birmingham Jail", regarded as perhaps the most eloquent expression of the goals and philosophy of the non-violent movement. On 28 August 1963, at the Lincoln Monument in Washington DC, King made his most famous speech. Around 250,000 people – 60,000 of them white – were at the then-largest civil rights demonstration ever held. King said:

The marvellous new militancy which has engulfed the Negro community, must not lead us to a distrust of all white people. For many of our white brothers as evident by their presence here today have come to realise that their freedom is bound to our freedom. I have a dream that one day this nation will rise up and live out the true meaning of

28 August 1963: Martin Luther King told the world of his dream.

its creed: "We hold these truths to be self-evident, that all men are created equal." I have a dream that my four little children will one day live in a nation where they will not be judged by the colour of their skin but by the content of their character. I have a dream that one day on the red hills of Georgia the sons of former slaves and the sons of former slave owners will be able to sit down together at a table of brotherhood. This is our hope. This is the faith with which I return to the South. With this faith we will be able to hew out of the mountain of despair a stone of hope. With this faith we will be able to transform the jangling discords of our nation into a beautiful symphony of brotherhood. With this faith we will be able to work together, to pray together, to struggle together, to go to jail together, to stand up for freedom together, knowing that we will be free one day. Let freedom ring. And when this happens, and when we allow freedom ring – when we let it ring from every village and every hamlet, from every state and every city, we will be able to speed up that day when all of God's children – black men and white men, Jews and gentiles, Protestants and Catholics – will be able to join hands and sing in the words of the old Negro spiritual: "Free at last! Free at last! Thank God Almighty, we are free at last!"

In January 1964, *Time* nominated King as their "Man of the Year" for 1963. In that same year he was granted an audience by the Pope, preached at St Paul's Cathedral and predicted that there would be a black president of the United States within 25 years. On 10 December 1964, King was awarded the Nobel Peace Prize by Gunnar Jahn, the president of the Nobel Committee. At 35, King was the youngest, third black, and fourteenth American laureate. As he accepted the prize, he said, "I do not consider this merely an honour to me personally, but a tribute to the discipline, wise

restraint and majestic courage of the millions of gallant Negro and white persons of goodwill who have followed a non-violent course in seeking to establish a reign of justice and a rule of love across this nation of ours." The prize was worth $54,123. King donated it to the Southern Christian Leadership Conference who used $12,000 of it to put Mrs King on the payroll and took out a $15,000 life insurance policy on Dr King. (His friend, the singer Harry Belafonte, took out a similar policy on Dr King's life but worth $50,000.)

On 7 March 1965, almost 600 civil rights marchers, led by John Lewis and the Reverend Hosea Williams, headed east out of Selma for Montgomery, in support of federal voting rights for blacks. Governor George Wallace denounced the march as a threat to public safety and declared he would take all measures necessary to prevent it. The protesters only reached the Edmund Pettus Bridge, six blocks away, before state troopers and the Dallas County Sheriff's Department, some mounted on horseback, forced them back.

On 9 March, King organized a second march but Federal District Court Judge Frank Minis Johnson issued a restraining order, preventing the march from taking place until he could hold additional hearings later in the week. King and the marchers walked to the Edmund Pettus Bridge where they held a short prayer session before turning back, thereby not breaking the court order preventing them from marching all the way to Montgomery. A third and comprehensive march went ahead on 25 March. It was during this march that Willie Ricks coined the phrase "Black Power". After Selma, Congress passed the 1965 Voting Rights Act to outlaw impediments to black voting.

Leadership of the civil rights movement was a heavy burden to bear and King suffered personally and emotionally. He suffered from stomach aches and insomnia. He slept with other women and felt guilty about his infidelities. The FBI, under J. Edgar Hoover, discovered King's indiscretions in 1963 when they bugged his telephone and those of the Southern Christian Leadership Conference. The evidence gathered by the bureau was sent to Senator Strom Thurmond, white supremacists, reporters, trade union leaders and the president. In 1964, a special agent sent a tape recording of King having sex to the Southern Christian Leadership Conference with a note suggesting that King kill himself. When King opposed the Vietnam War in a speech on 4 April 1967, the Johnson White House co-operated with the FBI to discredit him. In 1966, the civil rights movement split with young militants advocating the use of "black power" and rejecting King's teachings. In February 1968, King launched the Poor People's Campaign to highlight the plight of the poor. He travelled to Memphis in late March 1968 to help black dustmen who were striking for the right to form a trade union.

Date and Place of Assassination

4 April 1968, Lorraine Motel, 450 Mulberry Street, Memphis, Tennessee, USA.

The Event

On Wednesday 3 April 1968 at the Bishop Charles J. Mason Temple, King gave his last public speech. He said:

It really doesn't matter what happens now … some began to … talk about the threats that were out – what would happen to me from some of our sick white brothers … Like anybody, I would like to live a long life. Longevity has its place, but I'm not concerned about that now. I just want to do God's will. And He's allowed me to go up to the mountain! And I've looked over, and I've seen the Promised Land. I may not get there with you. But I want you to know tonight, that we, as a people, will get to the Promised Land. And so I'm happy tonight. I'm not worried about anything. I'm not fearing any man. My eyes have seen the Glory of the coming of the Lord!

WIFE AND CHILDREN

Coretta Scott King was born at Heiberger, Alabama, on 27 April 1927. She died at Rosarito Beach, Mexico, on 31 January 2006.

Children – Martin Luther King III (born in Montgomery, Alabama, 23 October 1957); Dexter Scott King (born 30 January 1961); Yolanda Denise King (born in Montgomery, Alabama, 17 November 1955, died in Santa Monica, California 15 May 2007); Bernice Albertine King (born in Atlanta, Georgia 28 March 1963).

James Earl Ray spent the night of 3 April in the New Rebel Motel. At 1pm he checked out and at 3pm booked into room 5B on the second floor of a doss house, located at 422 1/2 South Main Street, which provided an unobstructed view of the Lorraine Motel. (Landlady Bessie Brewer later positively identified him – he used the alias John Willard.) The press had revealed exactly where King was staying, even down to his room number. Ray locked himself in the doss house's one bathroom and, armed with his rifle, waited. At 6.01pm King stood on the balcony outside room 306 of the Lorraine Motel, waiting for an aide to fetch him a coat. He was shot in the throat and rushed to St Joseph's Hospital where he was pronounced dead at 7.05pm. Ray fled the doss house carrying the murder weapon and headed for his Mustang, but when he spotted a police car, he dumped the rifle in the doorway of the Canipe Amusement Company.

The Assassin

James Earl Ray was born on 10 March 1928 in Alton, Illinois, 20 miles (32 kilometres) north of St Louis, one of nine children of George and Lucille Ray. His father's family had a long history of violence and run-ins with the law; his great-grandfather was hanged, his grandfather was an alcoholic bootlegger and his own father was convicted on a charge of breaking and entering.

By the mid-1940s, Ray had developed right-wing views and was pro-German with a particular penchant for Adolf Hitler's view of a world without blacks or Jews. In February 1946, he joined the army and asked to be stationed in Germany. In December, he was transferred to the 382nd Military Police Battalion in Bremen. His service record was less than distinguished. He became involved in black marketeering, frequented local brothels, caught syphilis once and gonorrhoea twice, and started drinking and using amphetamines. In 1947, he joined the 18th Infantry Regiment, First Infantry Division. In November 1948, he was court-martialled after going AWOL. He had fallen ill, missed a shift and rather than lying low and waiting for the problem to blow over, had hitchhiked to Nuremberg. There, he was caught along with other GIs by military police. He was demoted to private, fined $45 and sentenced to three months' hard labour. On 23 December, having served around half of his sentence, he was discharged "for ineptness and lack of adaptability for military service".

Back in the States, he moved from one menial job to another and in October 1949 was arrested for burglary in Los Angeles. He received a short jail sentence and was back on the streets in December. He served three weeks in a Marion, Iowa, jail for vagrancy before returning to Quincy, Illinois. He landed a job at a local plastics factory but handed in his notice after ten months and received another prison sentence (this time for 90 days) for vagrancy. Ray moved to Chicago. On 6 May 1952, Ray was arrested for robbing a taxi driver at gunpoint. Pleading guilty, he served most of his term in the Pontiac prison. On 12 March 1954, he was released. His probation report noted that his "prognosis seems to be problematic to doubtful". Back in Alton, Ray tried to go straight but in August he robbed a local dry cleaner of $28. In March 1955, Ray travelled across America with a friend, Walter Rife, using 66 blank money orders that they had stolen from a post office in Kellerville, Illinois. Arrested, he was sentenced to 45 months in Leavenworth Penitentiary. During his sentence he refused to go to the prison farm because black men worked there, preferring his all-white cellblock. In April 1958, he was released after serving 33 months and went back to crime, specializing in burglary.

In July, he and an ex-con by the name of Joseph Elmer Austin held up a Kroger's supermarket for $1,200. Austin was caught and went back to prison but Ray stayed at large. Eight weeks later, Ray and James Own robbed another Kroger's supermarket and got $120 for their troubles. They did not know it, but in the company safe lay $18,000. They were caught and on the opening day of the trial, 15 December 1959, Ray tried and failed to escape. When the case began, Ray conducted his own defence. He really was the lawyer with a fool for a client. The jury returned a guilty verdict in less than 20 minutes. On 17 March 1960, Ray arrived to begin a 20-year sentence at the Missouri State Penitentiary, as inmate number 00416J. In prison, he became a drug dealer selling amphetamines. He also told fellow inmates of his hatred for black people.

In 1961, and again in 1966, Ray tried to escape, finally succeeding on Sunday 23 April 1967. He kept one step ahead of the law, spending time with his brothers, John Larry and Jerry, before he left for Canada on 16 July. He rented a room at $75-a-month in Windsor, Ontario, and called himself Eric S. Galt. It was in Canada that Ray claimed he first met a mysterious man called Raoul (see page 172). From August to 6 October 1967, Ray lived in Birmingham, Alabama. He then moved to Mexico, where he stayed in Puerto Vallerta until 19 November 1967, when he moved to Los Angeles. On 15 December 1967, he drove to New Orleans to meet his brother Jerry (Jerry Ray has denied this was the case) and stayed at the Provincial Motel on Chartres Street in the French Quarter for two nights, 17 and 18 December. Back in Los Angeles by 21 December, and still using the name Eric Galt, he lived in apartment number six at 1535 North Serrano Avenue. He enrolled on a barman's course on 19 January 1968, underwent a rhinoplasty on 5 March at a cost of $200 (he did not return for the post-operative check-ups), joined a correspondence school for locksmiths and placed a lonely hearts' advertisement. The advertisement read: "SINGLE MALE. Cauc. 36 yrs. 5'11" [sic]. 170lbs. Digs Fr. cult. Desires discreet meeting with passionate married female for mutual enjoyment and/or female for swing sessions."

On 18 March, Ray left the City of the Angels and on 22 March turned up in Selma, Alabama, calling himself Eric S. Galt. By coincidence, or perhaps not, Martin Luther King arrived in the city the same day. Both men stayed for just a day before Ray drove to Atlanta, King's hometown. On 29 March, Ray bought a powerful .243 calibre Remington Gamemaster rifle with a 7-power Redfield variable telescopic sight and a box of 20 Norma hollow-point bullets for cash. For the first and only time he used the alias Harvey Lohmeyer. Later that day Ray exchanged the rifle for the more powerful 30.06 calibre Remington Gamemaster and bought new bullets. Ray left Atlanta for Memphis on 3 April and at 7pm checked into the New Rebel Motel under the name Eric Galt.

The Aftermath

James Earl Ray drove to Atlanta and boarded a bus to Canada. The rifle that he had carelessly abandoned in the shop doorway put the FBI on his trail. He stayed in Canada for a month at a ski resort called Grey Rocks. While there, he had a brief affair with Claire Keating, a civil servant. She later said, "I can't remember how the subject came up but he said something like, 'You got to live near niggers to know 'em.' He meant that he had no patience with the racial views of people like me who don't 'know niggers' and that all people who 'know niggers' hate them."

Ray decided that his future lay in Rhodesia or South Africa where, he believed, his racial views would make him seem a hero. However, he did not have enough money for the flight and instead, on 6 May, flew to

London. He then flew to Lisbon and spent 11 days there but returned to London because he could speak the language and thought it would be easier to commit crimes there. In the capital he began to run low on money and robbed a jeweller's.

The FBI discovered that Ray was travelling on a false passport made out in the name Ramon George Sneyd (the real Ramon Sneyd was a Toronto policeman) and alerted New Scotland Yard. A warning was issued to all ports and airports. On 8 June, 65 days after King's assassination, Ray was arrested at Heathrow airport, trying to fly to Brussels where he hoped to join mercenary groups. He was extradited to Tennessee on 19 July where he was charged with Dr King's murder.

In custody Dr McCarthy DeMere examined James Earl Ray in the Shelby County Jail and asked the $64,000 question, "Did you really do it?" Ray replied, "Well, let's put it this way, I wasn't in it by myself." On 10 November 1968, a mere two days before his trial was due to start, Ray sacked his first defence lawyer, Arthur Haynes, who had already entered a plea of not guilty to the charge of murdering King. His brother, Jerry, persuaded Ray that the celebrated Houston lawyer Percy Foreman (whose other most notorious client was Charles Harrelson, the father of *Cheers* actor Woody), would be able to provide a better defence case.

The district attorney offered Ray a deal: plead guilty and the state would not ask for the death sentence. Foreman explained to his client that Tennessee juries were tough on first-degree murder defendants. Ray would, in all probability, be sentenced to 99 years in prison, said Foreman. On 6 March 1969, four days before his 41st birthday, Ray confessed to the assassination in a 55 paragraph-long document. The prosecution presented their evidence and the judge, W. Preston Battle, passed the sentence. Then, three days later, he refuted his confession claiming that he had been pressurized into the guilty plea by his lawyer. The court refused to act after Mr Justice Battle died on 31 March so Ray began telling anyone who would listen of his innocence. He gave dozens of interviews and wrote two books.

In all of his tales, he claimed that the real killer was a mystery man called Raoul. Ray admitted buying the murder weapon and renting the room at the doss house, but only so that the mysterious Raoul could carry out the assassination. He, Ray, had left the doss house before the shooting. Raoul has been thoroughly investigated by several Memphis district attorneys, Tennessee attorneys general, divisions of the US Justice Department, and the House Select Committee on Assassinations (1976–1979). All have come to the conclusion that Raoul was nothing more than a figment of Ray's imagination. The House Select Committee on Assassinations believed, without definite proof, that Raoul was, in fact, Jerry Ray. Testifying before the House Select Committee on Assassinations, Percy Foreman said, "[I] cross-examined James Earl Ray for hours and the only name that he ever mentioned other than his own at any phase of his preparation for the killing … was his brother Jerry … Jerry was with him when he bought the rifle in Birmingham, the one he did not use because it was low calibre. He took it back … and Jerry was not with him … but he was with him the day before at the same place where he bought another rifle [to kill King]."

However, certain members of the King family do believe Ray's tale. In 1997, Dexter King met Ray and supported his attempts to get a new trial. On 10 June 1977, shortly after Ray had testified to the House Select Committee on Assassinations that he did not shoot King, he and six other convicts escaped from Brushy Mountain State Penitentiary in Petros, Tennessee. (On 11 June 1977, Ray made his second appearance, this time as the 351st entry, on the FBI Most Wanted Fugitives' list.) They were recaptured three days later and sent back to prison. In 1978, Ray married court artist Anna Sandhu. A friend of Martin Luther King performed the ceremony.

In 1979, the US House of Representatives reported on a Congressional investigation into King's assassination. Their findings were that Ray had been the assassin but there was a likelihood he had been part of a conspiracy that had been planned by a group of right-wing Southerners. The Justice Department investigated further but could find no evidence for charges. The two suspects were named by the House Select Committee on Assassinations as the St Louis businessmen John Sutherland and John Kauffmann, who had both died of natural causes in the early 1970s. The two men were racists who had put a price on Dr King's head, said the House Select Committee on Assassinations. Apparently, Kauffmann had links with the Missouri State Penitentiary where Ray had been imprisoned before his 1967 escape. Kauffmann was a friend of the prison doctor, Hugh Maxey, who had treated Ray at the prison. It was further alleged that Kauffmann, who would later be tried for drug dealing, supplied illegal drugs to the prison through a third party. The House Select Committee on Assassinations was unable to establish conclusively the truth about the alleged St Louis-based conspiracy. In 1998, the chief counsel for the House Select Committee on Assassinations, G. Robert Blakey, said:

What we came up with was the possibility of a race-based conspiracy in St Louis where a $50,000 bounty had been offered on Dr King's life involving two men, Sutherland and Kauffmann. It was only a possibility; we couldn't prove it and both of them were dead before our investigation started. But we were able to trace Kauffmann to the Grapevine Tavern in St Louis, where he used to hold meetings of the American Party. James Earl Ray's brother, John, owned the tavern. Was it possible that the $50,000 bounty was discussed in the tavern and heard by John Ray, and that John Ray then conveyed it to James Earl? Yes. Were we ever able to say definitively that John Ray was the conduit from the Kauffmann group to James Earl? No.

However, despite the lack of credible material evidence, it would seem likely that James Earl Ray was aware that certain groups in the south were offering money to anyone who could kill Martin Luther King. It is further possible that one or both of Ray's brothers helped him in the assassination, and that the three of them had spoken of the murder of King. John Ray ran the Grapevine Tavern in St Louis and was in touch with members of the "George Wallace for President" campaign because they used his bar, situated as it was, conveniently, on the same block as their headquarters. John Sutherland was an unpleasant man who often dressed in a Confederate outfit and was a member of the White Citizens Council of St Louis. It is possible that Sutherland and his friends, while in the Grapevine, discussed wanting King dead and mentioned a reward.

However, if there was a reward, it was never collected. When James Earl Ray was in custody in Memphis, his brother, Jerry, approached Kent Courtney, the leader of a right-wing political organization in New Orleans, and attempted to solicit funds for his brother. If Ray had been paid to kill Martin Luther King he would have had no need for his brother to get out the begging bowl. Ray's fingerprints were on the rifle found in the shop doorway but the bullet that killed King could not be matched to the weapon. However, further tests carried out in 1997 proved that the rifle cannot be definitively ruled out as the murder weapon. (There is a common misconception that a bullet can always be matched to the weapon that it was fired from. Some weapons do not leave distinctive marks on projectiles.)

In 1995, Ray's lawyer, William F. Pepper, based in London, again protested his client's innocence but further claimed that the American government had been behind the killing. According to Pepper, the government got in touch with the Mob in Memphis, who then hired Loyd Jowers who owned and ran Jim's Grill, which was situated under the doss house that Ray had booked into. Jowers was also entrusted with getting rid of the rifle. Pepper claimed that a marksman from the American army was also in place in case the Mafia plan went awry. Added to this unlikely scenario, Pepper further alleged that the FBI, CIA, the media, Army Intelligence, and state and city officials helped cover up the assassination. The excellent and hard-hitting freelance journalist and author Mel Ayton comprehensively knocked down that ridiculous theory. He wrote:

Because Ray had proclaimed the existence of a conspiracy during his trial, it is far-fetched that conspirators would have allowed him to remain alive during the three decades he spent in prison prior to his death. There were simply too many risks attached to this scenario. If conspirators, especially government-led killers, could successfully murder America's foremost civil rights leader and then cover up the circumstances surrounding the act, they would assuredly have had little problem in eliminating Ray. If co-conspirators had indeed aided Ray, they would have spirited him away and placed him in hiding as soon as the murder had been carried out. They would not have allowed him to be exposed so many times during his two months on the run. Conspirators would not have put themselves in jeopardy by allowing Ray the opportunity to identify fellow conspirators. And, if Ray had been an unwilling patsy, conspirators could not have been certain that Ray would flee the scene of the crime. Under these circumstances, had Ray stayed put, the whole conspiracy may have collapsed. Why would the government employ so many people in the conspiracy when the risk of leakage would have been so much greater? Had President Johnson wanted to eliminate King all that was required was for him to request the CIA Director or private parties to arrange a contract and that would have been the end of it. This was no sophisticated murder, as conspiracy advocates maintain.

King was an easy target for any killer bent on eliminating him. King did not have an armed guard; he frequently left his home on foot; and his travel arrangements were well publicized. The government could also have destroyed King by simply arranging for all the scandal-filled surveillance tapes to be released to a friendly journalist to publicize them. This would not have been at all unusual. In the 1960s, the CIA enlisted the assistance of journalists and student groups to promote the government's policies.

In June 2000, a Department of Justice inquiry appointed by Janet Reno, the attorney general, rejected out of hand all Pepper's allegations. Despite the fact that they spied on King and thought him a degenerate, the FBI kept an open mind on the killing. At one time more than 3,000 agents were assigned to the case. They discovered dozens of witnesses including Ray's uncle, William E. Maher, who could testify that Ray hated black people and Martin Luther King in particular. Deputy Sheriff William DuFour, who guarded Ray after his capture, said that he would regularly refer to "Martin Lucifer King". Walter Rife, an ex-con friend of Ray's, stated, "Yeah, Jimmy was a little outraged about Negroes. He didn't care for them at all. There was nothing particular he had against them, nothing they had done to him. He said once they ought to be put out of the country. Once he said, 'Well, we ought to kill them, kill them all ...' He was unreasonable in his hatred for niggers. He hated to see them breathe. If you pressed it, he'd get violent in a conversation about it. He hated them! I never did know why." On the evening following Ray's guilty plea his brothers said, "All his life Jimmy has been wild on two subjects. He's been wild against niggers, and he's wild on politics. He's wild against any politician who's for niggers, and he's wild for any politician who's against niggers. Nobody can reason with Jimmy on the two subjects of niggers and politics."

FBI chief J. Edgar Hoover wrote in a memo, "I said [to Attorney General Ramsay Clark] ... there will be efforts to kill [James Earl Ray] if there is a conspiracy and if there is no conspiracy, the supporters of Dr King will do everything in their power to kill him ... I said I think he acted entirely alone but we are not closing our minds that others might be associated with him and we have to run down every lead."

James Earl Ray died of kidney failure in prison on 23 April 1998 still protesting his innocence.

On 9 April 1968, the day of King's funeral, President Johnson announced a day of national mourning for the slain leader. Three hundred thousand people attended the funeral and Vice President Hubert Humphrey represented the White House. King himself delivered the eulogy – from a recording of the last sermon he had given at Ebenezer Baptist Church.

The assassination led to riots in more than 60 cities.

The dustmen's strike, King's reason for being in Memphis, was settled very quickly after the assassination.

IN MEMORY OF MARTIN LUTHER KING

• Coretta Scott King continued to play a leading role in the civil rights movement. In 1981 the Martin Luther King Center for Nonviolent Social Change opened in Atlanta, Georgia and Coretta was its president until 1995 when she handed the reins over to her son, Dexter.

• The Lorraine Motel is now the site of the National Civil Rights Museum.

• In 1977 Martin Luther King was posthumously awarded the Presidential Medal of Freedom by Jimmy Carter.

• In 1986 Congress voted to make 15 January, Martin Luther King's birthday, a national holiday.

• Martin Luther King was posthumously awarded the Congressional Gold Medal in 2004.

Benazir Bhutto (1953–2007)

The Victim

Benazir Bhutto was born at Karachi on 21 June 1953, the first of four children; Murtaza (born 18 September 1954), Sanam (born 1957) and Shahnawaz (born 1958) being the others. She was the granddaughter of Sir Shahnawaz Bhutto (1888–1957), the founder of the Bhutto dynasty, which dominated the province of Sind for more than a century. Her father Zulfikar Ali Bhutto (born Larkana 5 January 1928) was married to a first cousin when he was only 13. His second wife, Benazir's mother, whom he married on 8 September 1951, is Nusrat Sabunchi (born Kurdistan 21 September 1929), the daughter of an Iranian Shia trading family. Benazir was named for her aunt who died in adolescence and the name means "unique" or "without equal". By her own admission she was a shy child and her upbringing was privileged. When her father returned from Pakistan's mission to the United Nations he would be laden with gifts of chocolates and fancy clothes from Fifth Avenue shops. At the age of 16, Benazir Bhutto was sent to school in America – a hardship, she claimed, because it was the first time she had to walk to school. "I hated it. It was tough," she recalled, "but it forced me to grow up." Her education abroad lasted until 1977 and included a stint at Lady Margaret Hall, Oxford where she gained a second in Philosophy, Politics and Economics and became president of the union.

Benazir, who stood 5 feet 8 inches (1 metre 7 centimetres) worshipped her father and to her dying days would not hear a word against him. However, his administration was not always widely praised, especially overseas. He arranged for political opponents to be beaten up (murdered said his enemies), rigged elections, was partly responsible for the Bangladeshi civil war and pledged a "1,000-year war" against India. Two days after Benazir's return to Pakistan in July 1977, Zulfikar Ali Bhutto was deposed as prime minister by the army and put in prison. The new leader, General Zia ul-Haq, charged him with conspiring to murder a political opponent. Ironically, Bhutto had promoted Zia to

be his chief of staff because he thought him malleable. Bhutto was tried, sentenced to death in March 1978 and hanged in the early hours of 4 April 1979 at Rawalpindi Central Jail. His daughter spent six of the next nine years in jail or under house arrest. Not long after their father's death Shahnawaz and Murtaza Bhutto founded a terrorist organisation, al-Zulfikar, based in Afghanistan. In 1981 the group hijacked a Pakistan airliner and forced General Zia to release some Bhutto supporters. The incident harmed the Bhutto name in Pakistan and the two brothers quietly left the organization.

On 18 July 1985, Shahnawaz died, aged 27, under mysterious circumstances in his apartment in Nice, France. He was poisoned and died slowly and painfully. His Afghan wife, Rehana, was arrested and later released by the French police. He was buried next to his father in Larkana, the Bhutto family seat, seen off by a large crowd said to number 25,000.

In April 1986, Benazir Bhutto returned to Pakistan. In December 1987, she was married to Asif Zardari in a traditional arranged wedding. They had met on 22 July 1987 and she agreed to marry him seven days later on 29 July. She defended the match in her autobiography while attacking arranged marriages. Throughout her life, Benazir Bhutto tried to hide her contempt for Muslim fundamentalists who were, she believed, most worried about "which nostril you must wash first".

In 1988 General Zia was killed in an aeroplane crash and during the election campaign that followed Benazir Bhutto gave birth to her son Bilawal on 21 September (two more children, Bakhtwar and Aseefa, would be born to the couple). The new mother was elected prime minister of Pakistan on 17 November 1988, winning 92 seats. Under her rule she freed political prisoners, liberalised the media and unshackled trade unions and students. However, there were many within the country implacably opposed to her – indeed in her own Sind province her Pakistan Peoples Party (founded by her father in 1967) only held power by a thread. On 6 August 1990, President

Benazir Bhutto was unharmed by the first suicide bomb attack following her return to Pakistan on 18 October 2007 to contest the general election, but a second attempt, as she left this rally in Rawalpindi, was fatally successful.

Ghulam Ishaq Khan sacked Bhutto as premier claiming that she was corrupt (she faced 19 corruption charges in total, including accusations that she used Swiss banks to launder money). Her husband was nicknamed "Mr 10 Per cent" after allegations that he had illegally profited from government deals. On 19 October 1993, Bhutto became prime minister for a second time but on 5 November 1996 was sacked again for corruption by President Farooq Leghari. In 1998 she went into exile in Dubai.

On 20 September, six weeks before her sacking, Murtaza Bhutto was shot and killed, along with six supporters, outside his home, 70 Clifton Road, Karachi. His death, like his brother's, is mysterious but it is believed that the police assassinated him.

Date and Place of Assassination
27 December 2007, Rawalpindi, Pakistan.

The Event
On 18 October 2007 Benazir Bhutto flew into Quaid-e-Azam international airport in Karachi to contest the forthcoming general election. President Pervez Musharraf had granted her an amnesty and all corruption charges were withdrawn. On the day of her arrival, while en route to a rally in Karachi, she was subjected to an assassination attempt that left 179 of her supporters dead and 600 injured, although Bhutto herself escaped unscathed, apart from a perforated eardrum. Among the dead were 50 of her own security guards who had formed a human chain around her vehicle in an unsuccessful bid to prevent a suicide bomber. Realising that her life was in danger Bhutto asked President Musharraf for help with her security. Before her return Musharraf had told her of his concern for her safety but, as she recalled in her posthumously published autobiography, "His supporters did very little to provide the necessary protection we needed: jammers that worked [to stop bombs being detonated via mobile], street lights that worked, roads that had been cleared of empty cars that could carry improvised explosive devices – protection to which I was entitled as a former prime minister". Bhutto was told that at least four potential suicide bomb squads including one sent by Hamza bin Laden, a son of Osama, intended to attempt to murder her. She wrote to Musharraf and "told him that if I was assassinated by the militants it would be due to sympathisers in his regime... [who] wanted to eliminate me and remove the threat I posed to their grip on power". Two months later, campaigning in Rawalpindi, another assassination attempt was successful. She attended a rally of the Pakistan Peoples Party at Liaquat National Bagh and was leaving when she stood in her bulletproof white Toyota Land Cruiser to wave to crowds. Even now reports are mixed but it is thought that she was shot in the neck and in the chest before a suicide bomb was detonated. Despite her spokesman announcing that she was safe, Benazir Bhutto was pronounced dead at 6.16pm at Rawalpindi General Hospital. Around two dozen people died in the attack. The next day the government announced that Bhutto had died of a fractured skull caused when she was thrown against the inside of the sunroof of her vehicle by the force of the bomb. No autopsy was performed before Bhutto's burial on 28 December 2007 next to her father in the family tomb.

The Assassin
Unknown at the time of writing.

The Aftermath
There were riots in Pakistan following her death, with her supporters accusing President Musharraf of being behind the murder. Around 50 people lost their lives in the riots and 176 banks, 34 petrol stations, 72 train cars, 18 railway stations and hundreds of cars and shops were destroyed.

On 30 December 2007, her son Bilawal Zardawi, a student at Oxford, became co-chairman (with his father) of the Pakistan Peoples Party. It is thought that his protection until his graduation will cost the British taxpayer £1 million a year.

Appendix

PANOPLY OF ASSASSINATIONS AND ASSASSINATION ATTEMPTS

King Ananda Mahidol (1925–1946)

At 6am on 9 June 1946, King Ananda was woken by his mother in his bedroom in the Grand Palace in Thailand. An hour and a half later, But Pathamasarin, his page, came on duty and began to prepare his master's breakfast. At 8.30am, But brought the monarch a glass of orange juice, but Ananda refused the drink and returned to bed. At 9.20am the young king was shot in the forehead. The king was found lying face up in bed by his mother and his other page, Chit Singhaseni. The king had been due to return to Switzerland to finish his law degree at the University of Lausanne on 13 June. UK Home Office pathologist Keith Simpson flew to Thailand to perform an autopsy on the dead monarch.

After protracted and involved legal proceedings King Ananda's secretary, Senator Chaleo Patoomros and his two pages, Chit Singhaseni and But Pathamasarin, were convicted of conspiracy to kill the king in May 1951. The three men were executed. It is generally accepted today that the charges against these men were groundless and the king's death remains unexplained.

Charles de Gaulle (1890–1970)

The French president was subjected to 31 assassination attempts. The most serious, the 22nd, occurred on 22 August 1962. De Gaulle, his wife, son-in-law and driver were motoring in a custom-built Citroën DS through the Paris suburb of Petit-Clamart when their vehicle was sprayed with machine-gun fire. The occupants escaped injury despite the fact that 14 bullet-holes were found in the car; two hit but did not puncture the bullet-proof tyres. Another 20 bullets struck the nearby Café Trianon and 187 were discovered on the pavement. The would-be assassins were led by Colonel Jean Bastien-Thiry (born at Lunéville on 19 October 1927), but he did not actually take part in the shooting. He had been decorated by the president and his father was a friend of de Gaulle's.

Bastien-Thiry, a father of three daughters and one of France's leading experts on guided missiles, was arrested on 15 September and went on trial on 28 January 1963. A practising Catholic who had spent time in a mental hospital, he compared himself to von Stauffenberg (see page 66) and claimed that de Gaulle deserved to die because he was responsible for genocide in Algeria. He was convicted on 4 March 1963 and sentenced to death. De Gaulle pardoned the shooters but refused to extend clemency to Bastien-Thiry, despite an appeal from his old friend, Bastien-Thiry's father, to spare his son's life. Jean Bastien-Thiry was executed by firing squad at Ivry-sur-Seine on 11 March 1963, while clutching a rosary. De Gaulle commented, "The French need martyrs. They must choose them carefully. I gave them Bastien-Thiry. They can make a martyr of him, if they want to, when I'm gone. He deserves it."

Gerald Ford (1913–2006)

Gerald Ford, a member of the Warren Commission (see page 122), is the only American president and vice-president who was not elected to either office. Richard Nixon appointed Ford vice-president on 10 October 1973 after Spiro Agnew resigned when he pleaded guilty to tax evasion while governor of Maryland. Then on 9 August 1974, Ford became president when Nixon resigned to avoid almost certain impeachment over the Watergate affair. Ford subsequently pardoned Nixon for any crimes he "committed or may have committed or may have taken part in," an action that many believe led to him losing the November 1976 election to Jimmy Carter.

Lynette "Squeaky" Fromme (born Santa Monica, California, 22 October 1948) was a member of the Manson Family. On the morning of 5 September 1975, dressed in a nun's habit but with the addition of a .45 Colt automatic, she travelled to Capitol Park in Sacramento and pulled the gun at Ford outside the Senator Hotel. Although there were four bullets in the gun, there were none in the firing chamber. She was taken into custody and after a lengthy trial was sentenced to life imprisonment under a 1965 law (prompted by the assassination of President Kennedy) that specified a maximum sentence of life in prison for attempted presidential assassinations. She is incarcerated at the Federal Medical Center, Carswell, Texas, where she remains a devoted follower of Charles Manson.

Seventeen days later, on 22 September, the five-time married Sara Jane Moore (born Charleston, West Virginia, 15 February 1930) attempted to assassinate Ford outside the St Francis Hotel in San Francisco. She pulled a .38 revolver and fired one shot from 40 feet (12 metres) away, but an alert bystander, Oliver Sipple, nudged her arm and the bullet missed Ford by 5 feet (1.5 metres). Sipple (born in Detroit, Michigan, 20 November 1941) then wrestled her to the ground. Like Fromme, Moore was sentenced to life imprisonment. In 1979 she escaped from the Federal Correctional Institution at Alderson, West Virginia, but was quickly recaptured.

Sipple was a decorated war hero but he was also a closeted homosexual. He asked the press to respect his privacy because his mother was unaware of his sexuality. However, he was outed, much against his will, by gay activist Harvey Milk who said Sipple, "will help break the stereotype of homosexuals". Being forced out of the closet sent Sipple into a downward spiral. He put on weight, reaching more than 294 pounds (133 kilograms), and he became paranoid and suicidal. He was found dead in bed at his home near the Tenderloin District of San Francisco on 2 February 1989.

Mahatma Gandhi (1869–1948)

The Indian spiritual leader faced several attempts on his life before he was assassinated at 5.10pm on Friday 30 January 1948. The first attempt came on 25 June 1934 as he was travelling to give a speech at the Corporation Auditorium in Pune. A bomb was thrown at the first car in his motorcade, which injured ten people when it exploded. Gandhi, in the second car, was unhurt. Another attempt occurred in May 1944 as Gandhi was recuperating from malaria. A group of 20 young men, led by Nathuram Godse (born 19 May 1910), protested against Gandhi. In the evening Godse rushed at Gandhi with a knife but was stopped by two aides, Mani Shankar Purohit and D. Billare Guruji. In September 1944 Nathuram Godse was found carrying a knife with which he intended to kill Gandhi. Godse was a radical Hindu who felt that Gandhi was mollifying minority groups and not serving the interests of the Hindu population. He also blamed Gandhi for the thousands of deaths as a result of Partition.

On 29 June 1946, a train carrying Gandhi was deliberately derailed near Pune. Again, he escaped unharmed. On 20 January 1948, a fifth attempt was made to kill him. A group of seven would-be assassins – Madanlal Kishanlal Pahwa, Shankar Kishtaiyya, Digambar Bagde, Vishnu Ramkrishna Karkare, Gopal Godse, Nathuram Godse and Narayan Dattatraya Apte – claimed that they wanted to take a photograph of Gandhi but they had no cameras with them. What they did have was a bomb that exploded harmlessly. Ten days later, as Gandhi was walking to pray, he was shot dead by Nathuram Godse in the garden of Birla House in Delhi. He fired three bullets from a Beretta into Gandhi's chest and stomach at point-blank range. There were no last words from Gandhi.

A number of conspirators were arrested and Nathuram Godse and Narayan Apte were hanged at Ambala Jail on 15 November 1949. Pahwa, Gopal Godse and Kishtaiyya were sentenced to life imprisonment. Kishtaiyya later had his sentence overturned.

King George III (1738–1820)

"Farmer George" had two narrow escapes on the same day, 15 May 1800. The first occurred as the king was reviewing the Grenadier Guards in Hyde Park, London. The man next to him was shot in the leg, a bullet very obviously intended for George. That night he went to the Theatre Royal, Drury Lane and, as the crowd rose for the national anthem, two more bullets whizzed past his head.

The attempted assassin was James Hadfield (born 1771), a war veteran and religious maniac. He believed that the second coming of Jesus Christ would occur if the government killed him. As a consequence, he plotted with one Bannister Truelock (little more than his name is known about Truelock) to kill the king so that he (Hadfield) would be sentenced to death. He fired twice and then shouted, "God bless your royal highness. I like you very well; you are a good fellow." Hadfield was tried for high treason but acquitted on the grounds of insanity. It was usual for lunatics to be released into the care of their families, but in Hadfield's case he was sent to Bethlem Royal Hospital (the infamous Bedlam) for the rest of his life. He died there of tuberculosis on 23 January 1841 aged 69. As a result of Hadfield's actions, Parliament passed the Criminal Lunatics Act 1800 to lock up insane defendants.

James I (1566–1625)

James I of England and VI of Scotland was subject to many plots to kill him. The Gunpowder Plot is probably the most famous failed assassination attempt of all time. The plotters planned to blow up the House of Lords during the state opening of Parliament in 1604. After Parliament had been blown up there would then be an insurrection that would return a Catholic monarch to the country. The plotters, led by Robert Catesby, included Thomas Winter, Robert Winter, Christopher Wright, Thomas Percy, John Wright, Ambrose Rokewood, Robert Keyes, Sir Everard Digby, Thomas Bates, Catesby's servant and Guy Fawkes, who was put in charge of the explosives. In May 1604 Percy rented a house opposite Parliament. The plan was to dig a tunnel under the Lords to plant their explosives. Catesby's house in Lambeth was used to store the gunpowder.

The opening of Parliament was delayed until 1605 because London had been hit by the plague. The conspirators moved their gunpowder to Percy's house and then discovered that a cellar under the Lords was available for rent. They took a lease on the cellar and filled it with 1,800 pounds (816.5 kilograms) of gunpowder in 36 barrels. The opening of Parliament was postponed again and again, so the plotters left London for their homes around the country so as not to arouse suspicion by being seen together.

The conspirators needed money and materiel so they asked Francis Tresham, who had recently inherited a large property, to join them. It was not a wise decision. On Saturday 26 October 1605, Lord Monteagle received an anonymous letter warning him not to attend the opening of Parliament, probably written by Tresham. It said:

My lord out of the love i beare to some of youere frends i have a care of youer preseruasion therefor i would advise youe as youe tender youre life to devise some excuse to shift of youre attendance at this parliament for god and man hath concurred to punishe the wickedness of this time and think not slightly of this advertisement but retire youre self into youre contri where youe may expect the event in safti for thoughe there be no appearance of any stir yet i saye they shall receive a terrible blowe this parliament and yet they shall not see who hurts them this councel is not to be condemned because it may do youe good and can do youe no harme for the dangere is passed as soon as youe have burnt the letter and i hope god will give youe the grace to maketh good use of it to whose holy protection i commend youe.

Monteagle passed the letter on to the Secretary of State, Robert Cecil, 1st Earl of Salisbury. At midnight on Wednesday 5 November 1605, Guy Fawkes was discovered guarding a pile of faggots, not far from the barrels of gunpowder. Far from denying his purpose, he admitted it and was taken to the Tower of London where, on the king's authority, he was tortured. The conspirators fled but were caught and tried on 27 January 1606 at Westminster Hall, before a crowd who paid ten shillings to watch. All pleaded not guilty apart from Sir Everard Digby, who claimed that James had gone back on his word on Catholic toleration. All were found guilty.

Four of the plotters were executed in St Paul's Churchyard on 30 January. The following day Fawkes, Winter and a number of others implicated in the conspiracy were taken to Old Palace Yard in Westminster, in front of the scene of the intended crime, where they were hung, drawn and quartered.

Airey Neave (1916–1979)

After Eton and Oxford, Airey Middleton Sheffield Neave joined the army at the beginning of the Second World War. He was wounded and captured in May 1940 and in May 1941 was sent to Colditz. He tried to escape on 28 August 1941 and failed, but on 5 January 1942 he succeeded. After the war he joined MI9 (his underling was Michael Bentine, the British comedian). In July 1953 he was elected Conservative MP for the Abingdon division of Berkshire in a by-election and in 1975 he was Margaret Thatcher's campaign manager during her successful leadership campaign. She appointed him shadow Northern Ireland Secretary.

At 2.58pm on 30 March 1979, as he was driving out of the Palace of Westminster car park, a bomb exploded. Both his legs were blown off and an hour later Neave died in hospital. The Irish National Liberation Army claimed responsibility for the assassination. Nobody has ever been charged with his murder.

Olof Palme (1927–1986)

Olof Palme joined Sweden's Social Democratic Party, becoming head of its youth section in 1955 when he was 28. On 1 October 1969 he became prime minister but lost power in October 1976 when he tried to raise taxes to pay for welfare benefits. He was returned to office in 1982.

Four years later, on 28 February 1986, he and his wife, Lisbet, went to the cinema. After the film they left the cinema and were walking home. (Palme did not have any bodyguards and freely walked the streets day and night.) That night, at 11.21pm, as he and his wife walked down Sveavägen in Stockholm, a gunman shot Palme in the back outside a pen shop. The prime minister was taken to hospital but was pronounced dead at 12.06am on 1 March 1986. Mrs Palme was also shot but recovered.

In December 1988, an alcoholic petty crook called Christer Pettersson (born at Solna, near Stockholm on 23 April 1947, died in the Karolinska University Hospital, Stockholm, 29 September 2004 of brain haemorrhaging and organ failure) was arrested for the murder and picked out of a line-up by Mrs Palme. He was sentenced to life imprisonment but released in 1989 after his conviction was deemed unsafe. Despite his acquittal, Pettersson once confessed to shooting Palme. "Sure as hell it was me who shot [him], but they can never nail me for it. The weapon is gone," he told Swedish writer Gert Fylking in 2001. He later retracted the statement and said he was not involved in the killing. The gun used in the murder was never found and officially the assassination remains unsolved.

Park Chung Hee (1917–1979)

General Park Chung Hee led a bloodless coup to install himself as the president of South Korea on 16 May 1961. For the most part, the people welcomed him and he transformed his country from a backward land into a powerful industrialized state. However, he made himself unpopular by making alliances with Japan, the country that had once colonized his own. Park claimed that the Republic of Korea needed help from Japan as well as the United States.

Park escaped an assassination attempt by North Korean soldiers on 21 January 1968 and another on 15

August 1974, when Mun Segwang (born in Japan 1951), a North Korean agent, shot at him as he finished a speech. Park was unhurt but his wife, Yuk Young-soo, was hit in the head by a stray bullet and died that day. Mun was executed four months later.

On 26 October 1979, Park was shot dead during an argument with Kim Jaeguy (born 6 March 1926), the head of his own security service. Kim claimed that Park was preventing democracy in the country. On 24 May 1980 Kim was executed.

Spencer Perceval (1762–1812)

The only British prime minister to be assassinated, Spencer Perceval assumed office on 4 October 1809 after the Duke of Portland suffered a stroke. Educated at Trinity College, Cambridge, he married the elder sister of his sister-in-law against family wishes and fathered 12 children. He was called to the Bar but sought a life in politics, becoming an MP on 9 May 1796. It was a year before he made his maiden speech.

On 26 March 1807 the Duke of Portland appointed him Chancellor of the Exchequer. He moved into 10 Downing Street two years later. On 11 May 1812, Perceval was shot dead in the lobby of the House of Commons by John Bellingham (born at St Neots, Huntingdonshire 1770), a mentally unbalanced salesman. On 16 May Perceval was buried in Lord Egmont's family vault at St Luke's, Charlton, near to his birthplace. Bellingham was tried and condemned to death, his plea of insanity rejected. On 18 May he was hanged.

Yitzhak Rabin (1922–1995)

The fifth prime minister of Israel, Rabin had been active in the Palmach, the underground army of Jewish settlers, in the 1940s. He became Chief of Staff of the Israeli defence forces and was regarded as a hero for his part in the 1967 Arab-Israeli War.

On 3 June 1974 he became prime minister of Israel, succeeding Golda Meir. He resigned in June 1977 after a financial scandal involving his wife. Fifteen years later he returned to office and began to work towards a peace settlement between the Arabs and Jews, for which he shared the Nobel Peace Prize with Yasser Arafat and Shimon Peres. On 4 November 1995, as Rabin was leaving a rally in Tel Aviv in support of the peace plan, he was shot with a Beretta semi-automatic pistol by Yigal Amir (born in Herzliya 23 May 1970), a right-wing Orthodox Jewish extremist. Rabin was taken to Ichilov Hospital, but he died while on the operating table of a punctured lung and massive blood loss.

The square where he was shot, Kikar Malchei Yisrael, was renamed Kikar Rabin. Amir was sentenced to life imprisonment. In prison he married Larisa Trembovler, who abandoned her husband for the convicted killer.

Anwar al Sadat (1918–1981)

Muhammad Anwar Al Sadat became the president of Egypt on 17 October 1970, replacing Colonel Nasser. He replaced many of his political opponents on taking power in an action dubbed the "Corrective Revolution" by the state-owned media. He worked to find a settlement between the Arabs and Jews for which he was awarded a Nobel Peace Prize in 1979, shared with Israel's Menachem Begin. However, some Arabs believed that Sadat had sold out and a fatwa was placed on him by Omar Abdel-Rahman (born 3 May 1938), an Egyptian Muslim leader who would later be convicted for his part in the 26 February 1993 World Trade Center bombing.

On 6 October 1981 Sadat was in Cairo watching a military parade when members of Islamic Jihad opened fire on him and threw grenades to finish off the job. His loyal troops returned fire. Seven others were killed, including the Cuban ambassador. Sadat was rushed to hospital but died there. The head of the assassins was Lieutenant Khalid Ahmed Showky el-Islambouli. He was arrested, tried, convicted and, on 15 April 1982, executed. Iran named a street after Islambouli. Four American presidents – Reagan, Carter, Ford and Nixon – attended

Sadat's funeral but only one Arab leader, President Gaafar Nimeiry of Sudan, was present.

King Umberto I of Italy (1844–1900)

In 1878 Umberto went on a tour of his kingdom, accompanied by his prime minister Benedetto Cairoli. During a parade in Naples on 17 November the king was attacked by the anarchist Giovanni Passannante. Pulling his sabre, Umberto fought off his assailant but in the mêlée Cairoli was stabbed in the thigh. Passannante was sentenced to death but Umberto showed mercy and the sentence was commuted to penal servitude for life.

On 22 April 1897 Pietro Umberto Acciarito (1871–1943), an ironsmith and anarchist, tried to stab the Italian king as he watched a horse race in Naples in honour of his 29th wedding anniversary. Acciarito was sent to prison for life.

Three years later, on 29 July 1900, the king was assassinated by Gaetano Bresci (born in Coiano, Prato, Tuscany 11 November 1869), another anarchist, as he handed out prizes at a sports event in Monza, 10 miles (16 kilometres) north of Milan. Bresci blamed the monarch for the deaths of several hundred people during a demonstration in Milan on 6 May 1898. On 29 August, Bresci was sentenced to a life of hard labour on Santo Stefano, a prison island. On 22 May 1901 he was found hanged in his cell, his body being thrown into the sea by prison guards soon after. Although suicide was given as the official explanation for his death, this was disputed at the time and it seems more likely that his guards killed him.

Hendrik Verwoerd (1901–1966)

Born in Weesp, Holland, Hendrik Frensch Verwoerd was offered a chance to study at Oxford, but refused because of his and his family's deep distrust of the British. In 1927 he became professor of sociology at Stellenbosch University, South Africa. He developed an interest in racial segregation and campaigned for South Africa to become a republic. When he was appointed editor of the *Die Transvaler* newspaper he ran articles criticizing miscegenation and the Jews, and promoted Hitlerian policies.

During the Second World War his animosity towards Britain increased, and when King George VI and Queen Elizabeth visited South Africa his newspaper ignored their visit, save to report on the "congestion" caused by "visitors from overseas". He joined the cabinet in 1950 and became prime minister of South Africa on 2 September 1958. It was under his rule that apartheid was implemented in the country. It was also while Verwoerd was leader that South Africa became one of the most brutal regimes in the world. Verwoerd banned the African National Congress and imprisoned its leader Nelson Mandela.

On 21 March 1960, police opened fire on protesters, an event that became known as the Sharpeville Massacre. A month later, on 16 April 1960, David Pratt (born 1908), a farmer and father of three, shot Verwoerd twice in the face while he was opening the Rand Easter Show at Milner Park, Johannesburg. One bullet entered Verwoerd's right cheek, the other his right ear, but amazingly these were not lasting injuries.

Pratt was declared insane and sent to a mental institution in Bloemfontein, where he hanged himself in October 1961.

On 31 May 1961, South Africa became a republic after a vote by the whites – no coloured people were allowed a say. On 6 September 1966 Verwoerd was stabbed four times as he took his seat in the House of Assembly. The assassin was Dimitri Tsafendas (born in Maputo, Mozambique 14 January 1918). Verwoerd was taken to Groote Schuur Hospital but was pronounced dead on arrival. Tsafendas, a paranoid schizophrenic, escaped the death penalty by claiming that there was a large tapeworm inside him that was slowly eating away at his insides and the worm spoke to him and told him what to do. Tsafendas was sent to Weskoppies, a psychiatric hospital, where he stayed until his death on 7 October 1999.

Pancho Villa (1878–1923)

The Mexican revolutionary was born as José Doroteo Arango Arámbula near San Juan del Río, Durango. Much of Villa's story is disputed. It is said that when he was 16 he discovered that a local rancher had raped his 12-year-old sister. He sought the man out and shot him before stealing a horse and going on the run. He changed his name to Francisco Villa to avoid detection. He became a miner but the pay and conditions were so poor he took to robbing banks. When he started sharing the proceeds of his bounty with locals, he garnered a reputation as a Robin Hood figure.

The government of General Porfirio Diaz (1830–1915), in power since 1 December 1884, was unpopular not least because of its punitive tax rates. In November 1910 the people rose up against Diaz, and Villa and his band of men helped the leader, Francisco Madero, to overthrow the government. The new order collapsed when Madero was assassinated on 18 February 1913. On that day, Pedro Lascuráin (1856–1952) became the head of state and ruled for less than 1 hour, the shortest rule on record. Lascuráin was sworn in, appointed Victoriano Huerta (1854–1916) as his successor and promptly resigned.

Villa was still in charge of his peasant army and refused to submit to Huerta. Villa ruled Chihuahua and northern Mexico. His reputation grew and he became a hero in the United States. He even appeared as himself in films in 1912, 1913 and 1914. It did not harm his sex appeal either – it was said he married 26 times. However, Villa did not rule over a pleasant land. He had opponents or those who upset him summarily shot. As word reached north of the border, the people of the United States changed their opinion of him but that just enhanced his reputation with his own people. Eventually, his fellow revolutionaries forced him into retirement and he moved to Durango.

On 20 July 1923, as he drove back from Parral, Chihuahua, he was assassinated for reasons that are still unknown. His last words were, "No permitas que esto acabe así. Cuentales que he dicho algo." ("Don't let it end like this. Tell them I said something.") In 1926 his grave was robbed and his head was stolen. It is still missing.

Sir Henry Wilson (1864–1922)

Born at Currygrane, Ballinalee, County Longford, Ireland, Henry Hughes Wilson joined the British army and won the Distinguished Service Order during the Boer War. In 1910 he became Director of Military Operations at the War Office. Four years later his career stuttered when he refused to authorize the use of troops against Ulster Unionist opponents of the Third Irish Home Rule Bill in the Curragh Mutiny. In February 1918, he was promoted to Chief of the Imperial General Staff. Seventeen months later, on 3 July 1919, he moved up to Field Marshal, was awarded £10,000 by Parliament and made a baronet. During the postwar peace conference he found himself in disagreement with the prime minister, Lloyd George. When he retired from the army in February 1922 he became MP for North Down.

On 22 June 1922 he dedicated a memorial at Liverpool Street Station, London, to those who had fallen in the First World War. After the ceremony, he and Lady Wilson caught a taxi back to their home at 36 Eaton Place in Belgravia. As Sir Henry paid the cabbie, Reginald Dunne and Joseph O'Sullivan, two members of the IRA, fatally shot him in the back four times. The two murderers then fled and were chased by PC March, who they shot in the stomach, and PC Sayer, who was shot in the leg. When finally cornered, the police saved the two men from a lynching. They were tried at the Central Criminal Court at the Old Bailey and found guilty. Dunne and O'Sullivan were hanged on 10 August 1922 at Wandsworth Prison. Michael Collins (see pages 69–75) had ordered the murder of Sir Henry. Sir Henry was buried in the crypt of St Paul's Cathedral on 26 June 1922.

Select Bibliography

Andersen, Christopher, *The Day John Died* (New York: Morrow, 2000)

Ayton, Mel, *A Racial Crime: James Earl Ray and the Murder of Dr Martin Luther King, Jr* (Las Vegas: ArcheBooks, 2005)

Balsamo, William and George Carpozi, Jr, *Crime Incorporated* (London: W. H. Allen, 1988)

Beadle, Jeremy, *Today's the Day* (London: W. H. Allen, 1979)

Bellenger, Dominic Adrian and Stella Fletcher, *The Mitre & The Crown* (Stroud: Sutton, 2005)

Black, Conrad, *Richard Milhous Nixon: The Invincible Quest* (London: Quercus, 2007)

Bradford, Sarah, *America's Queen: The Life of Jacqueline Kennedy Onassis* (London: Viking, 2000)

Bugliosi, Vincent, *Reclaiming History: The Assassination of President John F. Kennedy* (New York: W. W. Norton, 2007)

Bunson, Matthew, *The Pope Encyclopaedia* (New York: Crown Paperbacks, 1995)

Carpozi, Jr, George, *Bugsy: The Godfather of Las Vegas* (London: Everest, 1976)

Castañeda, Jorge, *Compañero: The Life and Death of Che Guevara* (London: Bloomsbury, 1998)

Coogan, Tim Pat, *Michael Collins: The Man Who Made Ireland* (London: Arrow Books, 1991)

Cook, Andrew, *To Kill Rasputin* (Stroud: Tempus, 2005)

Crozier, Brian, *De Gaulle The Statesman* (London: Eyre Methuen, 1973)

Dallek, Robert, *An Unfinished Life: John F. Kennedy, 1917–1963* (London: Penguin Books, 2003)

— *Lyndon B. Johnson: Portrait of a President* (London: Penguin Books, 2005)

David, Lester, *Ethel* (New York: Dell, 1972)

Davis, John H., *The Kennedy Clan* (London: New English Library/Sidgwick & Jackson, 1986)

De Gregorio, William A., *The Complete Book of US Presidents* (5th Ed) (New Jersey: Barricade Books, 2002)

De Jonge, Alex, *The Life and Times of Grigorii Rasputin* (London: Fontana, 1983)

Dederichs, Mario R., *Heydrich: The Face of Evil* (London: Greenhill Books, 2006)

Donovan, Robert J., *PT109* (London: Panther Books, 1963)

Dwyer, T. Ryle, *Big Fellow, Long Fellow: A Joint Biography of Collins and de Valera* (Dublin: Gill & Macmillan, 2006)

Eddowes, Michael, *Nov 22: How They Killed Kennedy* (St Helier, Jersey: Neville Spearman, 1976)

Eisenberg, D., Dan, U. and Landau, E., *Meyer Lansky: Mogul of the Mob* (London: Corgi Books, 1980)

English, Richard *Armed Struggle: A History of the IRA* (London: Macmillan, 2003)

Epstein, Edward J., *Legend: The Secret World of Lee Harvey Oswald* (London: Arrow Books, 1978)

Ferguson, Niall, *The War of the Worlds* (London: Allen Lane, 2006)

Garraty, John A. (Ed), *Dictionary of American Biography*, Supplement Seven (New York: Charles Scribner's Sons, 1981)

Garraty, John A. and Carnes, Mark C. (Eds), *Dictionary of American Biography*, Supplement Eight (New York: Charles Scribner's Sons, 1988)

— *American National Biography* (Eds) (New York: Oxford University Press, 1999)

Goldworthy, Adrian, *Cæsar* (London: Weidenfeld & Nicolson, 2006)

Goodwin, Doris Kearns, *The Fitzgeralds and the Kennedys* (New York: St Martin's Press, 1988)

Gosch, Martin and Hammer, Richard, *The Luciano Testament* (London: Pan, 1976)

Hamilton, Nigel, *JFK: Life and Death of an American President Volume One: Reckless Youth* (London: Century, 1992)

— *Bill Clinton Volume One: An American Journey* (London: Century, 2003)

Heyman, C. David, *A Woman Named Jackie* (London: William Heinemann, 1989)

— *American Legacy: The Story of John and Caroline Kennedy* (New York: Atria Books, 2007)

— *RFK: A Candid Biography* (London: William Heinemann, 1998)

Higham, Charles, *Murdering Mr Lincoln* (Beverly Hills: New Millennium Press, 2004)

— *Rose: The Life and Times of Rose Fitzgerald Kennedy* (New York: Pocket Books, 1995)

Hildreth, Peter, *Namedropper* (London: McWhirter Publishing, 1970)

Holmes, Richard and Marix Evans, Martin, *Battlefield: Decisive Conflicts in History* (Oxford: Oxford University Press, 2006)

Hutchinson, Lester, "The Birth of the Irish Free State" in *Fifty Events that Amazed the World* (London: Odhams Press, n.d.)

Infield, Glenn B., *Hitler's Secret Life* (London: Hamlyn, 1980)

Jacobson, Philip, *Murder At Manila Airport* (*Unsolved #34*, London: Orbis, 1984)

Jenkins, Gareth, *John F. Kennedy Handbook* (London: MQ Publications, 2006)

Jennings, Dean, *We Only Kill Each Other* (New York: Pocket Books 1992)

Kane, Joseph Nathan, *Facts About the Presidents* (5th Ed) (New York: H. W. Wilson, 1989)

Kantor, Seth, *The Ruby Cover-up* (New York: Zebra Books, 1992)

Katz, Leonard, *Uncle Frank: The Biography of Frank Costello* (London: W. H. Allen, 1974)

Kelley, Kitty, *Jackie Oh!* (Secaucus, New Jersey: Lyle Stuart, 1978)

Kennedy, Rose Fitzgerald, *Times to Remember* (London: Collins, 1974)

King, Greg, *The Murder of Rasputin* (London: Century, 1996)

Knappman, Edward W. (Ed), *Great American Trials* (Detroit: Visible Ink, 1994)

— *Great World Trials* (Detroit: Visible Ink, 1997)

Kubizek, August, *The Young Hitler I Knew* (London: Greenhill Books, 2006)

Lacey, Robert, *Little Man: Meyer Lansky and the Gangster Life* (Boston: Little, Brown, 1991)

Leamer, Laurence, *The Kennedy Women* (London: Bantam, 1994)

— *The Kennedy Men 1901-1963* (New York: Perennial, 2002)

Leaming, Barbara, *Jack Kennedy: The Making of a President* (London: Weidenfeld & Nicolson, 2006)

— *Mrs Kennedy: The Missing History of the Kennedy Years* (London: Orion, 2002)

Malone, Dumas (Ed), *Dictionary of American Biography* (New York: Charles Scribner's Sons, 1935)

Manchester, William, *The Death of a President November 1963* (London: Michael Joseph, 1967)

Matthew, H.C.G. and Harrison, Sir Brian (Eds), *Oxford Dictionary of National Biography* (Oxford: Oxford University Press, 2004)

McMillan, Priscilla Johnson, *Marina and Lee* (New York: Harper & Row, 1977)

McWhirter, Norris, *Ross: The Story of a Shared Life* (London: Churchill Press, 1976)

Miller, René Fülöp, *Rasputin: The Holy Devil* (New York: Putnam, 1928)

Minney, R. J., *Rasputin* (London: Cassell, 1972)

Montgomery-Massingberd, Hugh (Ed), *Burke's Royal Families of the World, Volume 1 Europe & Latin America* (London: Burke's Peerage, 1977)

— *Burke's Presidential Families of the United States of America* (2nd Ed) (London: Burke's Peerage, 1981)

Moorhouse, Roger, *Killing Hitler: The Third Reich and the Plots to Kill the Führer* (London: Vintage, 2007)

Moritz, Charles (Ed), *Current Biography Yearbook 1986* (New York: H. W. Wilson, 1987)

Morrow, Robert D., *First Hand Knowledge: How I Participated in the CIA-Mafia Murder of President Kennedy* (New York: SPI Books, 1992)

Nash, Jay Robert, *Crime Chronology: A Worldwide Record 1900-1983* (New York: Facts on File, 1984)

— *World Encyclopedia of Organized Crime* (London: Headline, 1993)

Noguchi, M. D, Thomas T. with DiMona, J., *Coroner to the Stars* (London: Corgi, 1984)

Payne, Robert, *The Life and Death of Adolf Hitler* (London: Corgi Books, 1975)

Powers, Richard Gid, *The Life of J. Edgar Hoover* (London: Arrow, 1989)

Prall, Robert H. and Mockridge, Norton, *This is Costello* (New York: Gold Medal, 1951)

Rasputin, Maria and Barham, Patte, *Rasputin* (London: Arrow, 1979)

Reeves, Richard, *President Reagan: The Triumph of Imagination* (New York: Simon & Schuster, 2005)

Reeves, Thomas C., *A Question of Character: A Life of John F. Kennedy* (London: Bloomsbury, 1991)

Reinhert, Gerard H., *Death Certificates of the Rich & Famous* (Lake Arrowhead: Perpetual Publications, 1996)

Richardson, Nigel (Ed), *Murder Casebook: The Kennedy Assassination* (London: Marshall Cavendish, 1990)

Sann, Paul, *Kill the Dutchman: The Story of Dutch Schultz* (New York: Da Capo Books, 1991)

Scheim, David E., *The Mafia Killed President Kennedy* (London: W.H. Allen, 1988)

Schlesinger, Jr, Arthur, *A Thousand Days: John F. Kennedy in the White House* (London: Andre Deutsch, 1965)

— *Robert Kennedy And His Times* (London: Andre Deutsch, 1978)

Shirer, William L., *The Rise and Fall of the Third Reich* (London: Pan, 1964)

Sifakis, Carl, *The Encyclopaedia of American Crime* (New York: Facts on File, 1982)

— *The Mafia File* (Wellingborough: Equation, 1988)

Snyder, Louis L., *Encyclopaedia of the Third Reich* (London: Robert Hale, 1976)

Sorensen, Theodore C., *Kennedy* (London: Hodder & Stoughton, 1965)

Sparrow, Judge Gerald, *The Great Assassins* (London: John Long, 1968)

Spoto, Donald, *Jacqueline Bouvier Kennedy Onassis: A Life* (New York: St Martin's Paperbacks, 2000)

Starr, Harris E. (Ed), *Dictionary of American Biography*, Supplement One (New York: Charles Scribner's Sons, 1944)

Stephen, Sir Leslie and Lee, Sir Sidney (Eds) *The Dictionary of National Biography* (London: Oxford University Press, 1917)

Summers, Anthony, *Conspiracy* (London: Fontana, 1980)

— *Official and Confidential: The Secret Life of J. Edgar Hoover* (London: Victor Gollancz, 1993)

— *The Arrogance of Power: The Secret World of Richard Nixon* (London: Victor Gollancz, 2000)

Talbot, David, *Brothers: The Hidden History of the Kennedy Years* (London: Simon & Schuster, 2007)

Taraborrelli, J. Randy, *Jackie, Ethel, Joan: Women of Camelot* (New York: Warner Books, 2000)

Taylor, Tim, *The Book of Presidents* (New York: Arno Press, 1972)

Thomas, Evan, *Robert Kennedy: His Life* (New York: Simon & Schuster, 2000)

Toland, John, *Adolf Hitler* (New York: Ballantine Books, 1976)

Vincent, Benjamin, *A Dictionary of Biography* (London: Ward Lock, 1878)

Wallechinsky, David and Wallace, Irving, *The People's Almanac* (New York: Doubleday, 1975)

— *The People's Almanac 2* (New York: William Morrow, 1978)

Wallechinsky, D., Wallace, I., and Wallace, A., *The Book of Lists* (New York: William Morrow, 1977)

Wolf, George with DiMona, Joseph, *Frank Costello: Prime Minister of the Underworld* (London: Futura, 1976)

Zeiger, Henry A., *Frank Costello* (New York: Berkley Medallion, 1974)

Ziegler, Philip, *Mountbatten: The Official Biography* (London: Collins, 1985)

Index

Acknowledgements

For their help on this book and general support I would like to thank the following: the late Jeremy Beadle; Professor Niall Ferguson kindly read the chapter on the assassination of Franz Ferdinand; the late George Carpozi, Jr; Mel Ayton was phenomenally generous with his time and expertise; Vanessa West, the curator of the Bugsy Siegel fan site (www.bugsysiegel.org), kindly checked the Siegel chapter; a similar function on the Michael Collins entry was performed by two respected educators, Dave Mclean and Mark White, although their conclusions were violently different; Iain Martin, the former deputy editor of *The Sunday Telegraph* read and commented on parts of the manuscript for which I am grateful; Stacey Wike; the pulchritudinous Stacey Upson; Liz Williams; Suzanne Kerins, who is always there when I need her; Nicola Wilson, one of my dearest friends; Mitch Symons; James Steen; Dominic Midgley; Catherine Townsend.